PRAISE for the Algebra Survival Guide

LEADING JOURNALS SAY ...

"We give the **Algebra Survival Guide** our highest Four-Star 'Awesome!' Rating. The author did a great job with this book ... and the illustrations are excellent."
— *The Washington Times*

"The **Algebra Survival Guide** is a non-threatening first-year algebra tutorial guide ... The question-and answer format is great, and the questions actually sound as if they are being asked by eighth or ninth graders ... Teachers and tutors will find that the questions are typical, and the answers are complete."
— *Mathematics Teacher*, a publication of the National Council of Teachers of Mathematics

"This book will teach algebra to anyone who unleashes its power — especially daunted parents and weary teachers."
— *Northwest Family Magazine*

"Now there is a tool available to help parents and students decipher the difficult aspects of basic algebra: the **Algebra Survival Guide**."
— *Charlotte Parent Magazine*

"The **Algebra Survival Guide** is fun to handle and stunning to to read ... It is a friendly book that de-mystifies algebra, and — believe it or not — even makes it fun."
— *Kern County Family Magazine*

"A perfect tool for those who are lost in 'Algebra Land.' I would recommend the **Survival Guide** not just for your children who are studying algebra, but also for those parents who will be teaching it shortly."
— *Crusader News*, an online educational newsletter

"Breaks down the barriers that regular algebra textbooks inadvertently put up."
— *The Albuquerque Journal*

"The **Algebra Survival Guide** offers hope to students of all ages who are having trouble grasping the abstract world of algebra."
— *The Saint John's Reporter*

"If you've got a nervous algebra student ... consider acquiring a copy of this reassuring self-teaching text ... delivered with a sense of humor, which is definitely rare in algebraic circles."
— *Home Education Magazine*

"A clear exposition of all the materials in an Algebra 1 course. Works well as a supplement/review to other math materials ... and as a stand-alone alternative to those with a distaste for any math textbook."
— *John Holt's Bookstore*, a catalog of educational products

EDUCATORS SAY ...

" The girls in my school are using the **Guide** because it helps them understand algebra and feel confident. I would definitely say that the format of the guide has helped these girls overcome their anxiety about math."
— Sarah Pearce, Directress, Milwaukee Montessori School

"Delightful self-paced book that is sure to help those with math anxiety!"
— Linda Day, Ph.D., Director of the UNM / Santa Fe Public Schools Teacher Education Program

"The **Algebra Survival Guide** is SUPERB! It is a wonderful tool that speaks to the students in a language they can understand. I've already asked my school to order copies for our library."

— Mary Gambrel, 7th grade regular and honors math teacher at Travis Middle School, Amarillo, Texas

"Everything you always wanted to know about algebra -- and MORE -- written in a style that anyone can understand. I recommend this book to teachers, students and parents."

— Eleanor Ortiz, President of the New MexicoState Board of Education, and one-time algebra teacher herself

"The **Algebra Survival Guide** is excellent! I've always been a supporter of the idea that math doesn't need to be boring and is quite practical in everyday life. The **Survival Guide** exemplifies this idea with its unconventional flavor."

— Jill Miller, tutor, Harrisburg, Pennsylvania

"I like the book so much that at parents night I copied the book's order form and gave it out to all the parents of my students."

— Linda Barkley, math teacher, Sacred Heart School, Dearborn, Michigan

PARENTS SAY ...

"Yes! I bought the **Algebra Survival Guide** to help my public schooled daughter to help with concept review for SATs, but it really helped me too! I plan to use it for my other daughter too!"

— Becky Fisher in Delaware

"Wow! After years and years of trying in public school, the **Algebra Survival Guide** has taught my math-phobic 16-year-old daughter, now homeschooled, to do algebra."

— Karen Grawe, homeschooling mother

"Your **Algebra Survival Guide** has been a godsend for someone trying to understand algebra!"

— Sue Conant, Adelanto, California

"This book is fantastic. I was going over it with my daughter last night, and for the first time in my life I understood absolute value."

— Rob Steinmetz, Ph.D., President, Learning System Sciences, a company that manufactures educational CD-ROMS

STUDENTS SAY ...

"Kids could learn math without a teacher using this book!"

— Celeste Due, soon-to-be-famous 12th grader, Santa Fe,New Mexico

" I would definitely tell friends about the **Algebra Survival Guide** because if they're having a much trouble as I've had, I know they'd benefit from it as much as I did."

— Nick Fabin, 9th grader at the Colorado Rocky Mountain School, Carbondale, Colorado

"I want to thank you because my school just loves your book! I have switched over from my old textbook to the **Algebra Survival Guide**, and now my friends are going to do it too."

— Alia Triliegi, 8th grader at Milwaukee Montessori

"The **Survival Guide** is wonderful. It is informative and easy-to-grasp. I only wish I'd had it three months ago — when the semester started!"

— Christopher McDonal, Flagstaff, Arizona

"This book helped me get over my dread of math so I could pass the GRE. Thank goodness for it!"

— Ann Marie Fitzgerald, graduate student in nursing, Albuquerque, New Mexico

Algebra Survival Guide

A Conversational Handbook
for the Thoroughly Befuddled

Written by Josh Rappaport
Illustrated by Sally Blakemore

Singing Turtle Press
Santa Fe, New Mexico

Algebra Survival Guide
A Conversational Handbook for the Thoroughly Befuddled

Published by:
Singing Turtle Press
#770, 3530 Zafarano Drive #6
Santa Fe, NM 87507

Tel: 1/505-438-3418
Fax: 1/505-438-7742
E-mail: kyle@AlgebraWizard.com

Publisher's Cataloging-in-Publication
(Provided by Quality Books, Inc.)

Rappaport, Josh.
    Algebra survival guide : a conversational
handbook for the thoroughly befuddled / written by
Josh Rappaport ; illustrated by Sally Blakemore.
-- 1st ed.
    p. cm
    Includes index.
    LCCN: 99-72866
    ISBN: 0-9659113-8-1

    1. Algebra.   I. Title.

QA152.2.R37 2000   512
                        QBI99-1133

— Attention Teachers / Administrators —
For information on volume discounts to schools, visit us at: www.AlgebraWizard.com
Or call us at the phone number above.

Note from the Author

Tutoring brings me many rewards. It gives me the joy of working with students and watching them learn. Tutoring also rewards me, interestingly enough, by offering me an in-depth look at the confusion students face. Most of my students, once over their initial anxiety (who is this guy, and will he laugh at me?), become quite willing to confess their confusion to me. In this book, I've tried to recycle this confusion to help students learn. For in the **Algebra Survival Guide** I use the very questions students have asked me about algebra, and then I offer the best answers that I've found during my years of teaching and tutoring. In doing so, I've tried to develop a self-teaching program that students can follow easily.

As I see it, the **Algebra Survival Guide** is an **Algebra I reference book — PLUS**. It's more **comprehensive** than a typical algebra reference book, and it's also (I hope) more **clear, conversational, user-friendly** and **fun**. (It also is written in accord with national standards. For details, see the note on **NCTM Standards** in the **Supplies** section.)

To help students succeed, the **Guide** includes **QuikChek practice problems** after nearly every new idea, no matter how minute the concept. This is because, from my vantage point, 95% of students' confusion in algebra stems from a simple fact: they're overwhelmed. In tutoring I've found that whenever I can break algebraic ideas and procedures into mini-steps, students experience success. This success helps students "stay in the saddle" as concepts become tougher. These **QuikChek** problems give students the chance to experience success on nearly every page.

Here are some ways that the **Algebra Survival Guide** can help your student(s).

First, students can use the **Guide** to **learn how to perform essential algebraic operations**. Example: let's say that despite teacher and textbook, a student can't figure out how to eliminate negative exponents from answers. S/he can go to the index, locate the pages on negative exponents and do the **QuikChek** problems on that topic. The **Guide**'s careful, step-by-step instructions teach students how to master difficult Algebra I operations.

Secondly, students may use the **Guide** to **deepen their understanding** of a concept. Suppose, for example, that after a lesson on the neighbor sign rule a student knows that $7 -- 2$ can be re-written as $7 + 2$, but hasn't a clue as to why. Solution: look up the neighbor-sign rule in the index and study up on it. The **explanation and cartoons** help students grasp the **why** by connecting algebraic ideas to everyday life.

Thirdly, students can use the **Guide** like a regular textbook in the sense that it's **arranged sequentially**. Starting at the beginning of the book and working through to the end, students will gain a **thorough grasp** of Algebra I concepts and operations. And keep in mind that students often have algebraic amnesia after a year of geometry, so don't toss the **Guide**. It can serve as a **refresher course** — to help students brush up on Algebra I before entering Algebra II … or before taking college entrance exams.

Finally, use the **Guide** to let students have **fun** with math. Before plunging into a new concept, encourage students to play the **"Bored" Game** to review previously learned concepts. Or use the **Guide** to engage them **creatively**. For example, you might challenge an artistic student to make cartoons -- like those in the book -- to explain a concept s/he has recently mastered. I'd be honored if you send me any creative extensions on how you use the **Guide.** (Contact me through my publisher, Singing Turtle Press. See ways to contact Singing Turtle on back of title page.)

Josh Rappaport
Santa Fe, New Mexico

ACKNOWLEDGMENTS

The **Algebra Survival Guide** was created as much through dialogue as through my own effort. In that light, I must first thank the hundreds of children I've had the pleasure to tutor over the past ten years. It's through their quest to learn that this book grew. Among the adults who played a role in creating the **Algebra Survival Guide**, I first thank my wife, Kathy, a gifted and creative teacher, who offered invaluable feedback and urged me to always keep the befuddled student foremost in mind. Second, I owe a huge debt of gratitude to Sally Blakemore, who not only created the illustrations and developed the book's overall design, but also provided humor, support and inspiration each step of the way. I also wish to thank my production staff: David Cox, Byron Grush, Janice St. Marie and Madeleine Tillin. Teachers who offered peer critiques are: Michael Carroll, Lucille Cueva, Marilyn Gardner, Debbie Gibbs, Peter Graham and Mary Hackler. Other adults who offered help in various ways are: Seymour Bortz, Martin Casdagli, Janet Dennison, MacDonnell Gordon, Barbara Holmes, Ann Lacy, Sarah Oberstein, Ann Pagliarulo, Phyllis Panzeter, Mary Schenck and Sam Shaffer. Finally, thanks to three students who offered particularly in-depth suggestions: Phillip Holmes, Katie Kelley and Laura Schenck.

· ·

TABLE OF CONTENTS

EMERGENCY FACT SHEET POSTER

Algebra Wilderness "Bored" Game

Hello and welcome!

You're trapped in a classroom. People are talking in what seems to be a foreign language.

Gibberish about exponents, variables, monomials, the Pythagorean theorem.

They expect you to "get it". And there's a test on all this stuff tomorrow! You are in danger of perishing at your very desk.

It's only a matter of time...

Thank goodness you just discovered the **Algebra Survival Guide.**

This guide, written by someone who, long ago, barely crawled out of the **Algebra Wilderness** alive, will help you find your way through this perilous territory.

But now that you have the **Guide**, how do you use it?

Just flip the page to find out!

⚠ The Guide contains five kinds of pages, along with regular QuikChek problems:

Mind Munchies pages give you "food for thought," to help you make sense of algebraic ideas.

Pitfall pages teach you misunderstandings and mistakes to avoid.

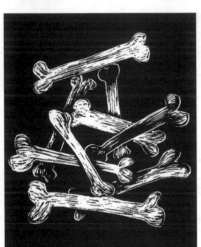

Bare Bones pages present basic information you'll want to memorize cold.

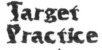

Target Practice pages let you test your understanding by working out practice problems.

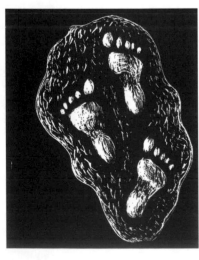

Step by Step pages show how to perform the steps for algebraic operations. These pages also illustrate those steps with an example.

QuikChek problems give you a chance to check your grasp of the concept just taught.

How is the Guide organized?

Since you never know what you may run across in the **Algebra Wilderness**, the **Algebra Survival Guide** is equipped for any emergency. First, it's organized into **12 content sections**, which provide detailed instruction on: Properties; Sets of Numbers; Positive & Negative Numbers; Order of Operations & Like Terms; Absolute Value; Exponents; Radicals; Factoring; Cancelling; Equations; the Coordinate Plane; and Word Problems.

Here are four specific ways you'll use the Guide:

1) as a quick reference guide — Whenever you're puzzled by a large topic — for example, "factoring" — just flip to that section and dig in for information. The **index** and **glossary** help you learn about specific concepts — for example, "irrational numbers" — in a flash.

2) as a memorization tool — Since you need loads of info to survive your trek through the wilderness, the kit provides info in an easy-to-learn format. Both the **Bare Bones** and **Step by Step** pages have information you can and should **memorize**. Also, the **Emergency Fact Sheet** lets you see the rules of algebra at a glance.

3) as a self-teaching program — By reading any section carefully, you'll get a thorough overview of that particular topic. In addition, working out the **QuikChek** problems (at bottom of most pages) will tell you whether or not you're on the right track. For a more comprehensive check-up, do the **Target Practice** problems at the end of each section.

4) as your survival buddy — The **Pitfall** pages show you **common mistakes** students make and **common misunderstandings** they have. Study these to avoid a perilous fall down the grade ladder.

Why is the Guide set up in a question-and-answer format?

Good question. Here are a few reasons ...

First of all, math has always evolved in this very way — through a question-and-answer process. Reading math textbooks, many people get the **wrong idea** that some brilliant person somewhere just thought up all this stuff and wrote it down. **Not at all!** People developed math in a human way — by asking questions, then looking for answers. The answers people found led to still more questions, which led to more answers, and over time, a whole branch of math, such as algebra, was woven — like a beautiful tapestry of thought.

In this book, questions are meant to be in your voice; answers, in the voice of a friendly teacher. By reading through both, you experience the question-answer process that gives birth to math. That's one reason I had for using this format, but there's another one too. Using the question-answer process helps **unleash your thinking power**. My hope is that as you read through all these questions and answers, **you'll start to hear — more clearly — your own questions about math**.

If you're even half-alert while using the **Survival Guide**, questions about math will pop into your head. I encourage you to **jot down your questions**. Try to answer them yourself, or work on them with a friend. If you get stuck, see if the book speaks to the question. If not, ask someone for help. But most of all, treasure your questions. For they give you the power to learn.

Q: What else does the Guide provide? And, just out of curiosity, can I contact the author?

A: First, the Guide has an introductory section called, **What is algebra?** This gives you a sense of what algebra covers, why you're learning it, and how you'll benefit by studying it.

At the very back is the **Supplies** section, which contains:

— a **Glossary** with quick-and-easy definitions of algebra terms,

— a **Note** on how the Guide meets national math standards,

— a handy **Order Form**,

— and an **Index** (conveniently located on the last page) to help you locate any concept in the Guide.

At the very back of the **Supplies** section you'll discover a special poster. The first three panels of the poster make up the **Emergency Fact Sheet**, which displays all the rules of Algebra I on a sheet you can post up or tuck into your notebook.

The last two panels of the poster contain the **Algebra Wilderness "Bored" Game**, which gives you a fun way to practice your lessons. The rules for playing this exciting board game are included on a special page in the **Supplies**.

And yes, you can reach me courtesy of **Singing Turtle Press** (see ways to reach my publisher on back of title page). And here's a fun challenge: find a stupendously brilliant and creative way to explain some algebraic concept, then send it my way. If I like it a lot, I'll print it in the next edition along with an acknowledgment of your name. Looking forward to hearing from you.

Josh Rappaport
your guide

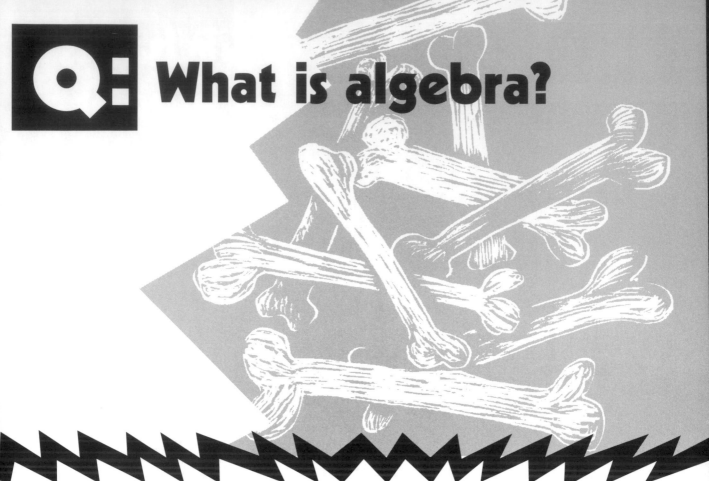

Q: What is algebra?

A: Algebra is a branch of math that performs a magic trick — it takes something that's **unknown** and - poof! - turns it into something **known**. Algebra does this by:
a) using letters (**variables**) to stand for **mystery numbers**, and
b) giving you a **process** to let you discover the value of the variables.

Simple example of an algebra problem

Joan has an <u>unknown</u> amount of money in her purse. If Joan had $5 more, she would have $100. How much money does Joan have?

Using algebra, you'd work out the solution like this:
Let the variable, **j**, stand for the amount of money **Joan** has. Since Joan would have $100 if she had five dollars more,

$$j + 5 = 100$$

Then, using rules for solving equations (**pp. 188-198**),

$$j + 5 = 100$$
$$-5 \quad\quad -5$$
$$j = 95$$

meaning: Joan has **$95** in her purse

Seems simple? Don't worry ... in a little while, you'll be challenged by problems like this: **Two trains start heading toward Amityville at the same time. One's coming down from the north at 100 mph; the other is steaming up from the south at 150 mph. If it takes the trains three hours to reach Amityville, how far apart were they when they started?**

Q: Why does algebra seem so much stranger — and harder — than any math I've done up to this point?

 Algebra is weirder because it uses **abstract ideas**.

To grasp what is meant by **abstract ideas**, it helps to learn the difference between concrete and abstract thinking. Thinking about concrete things (not to be confused with thinking about cement) means thinking about stuff you can take in through your five senses, things you can touch, taste, smell, see or hear. Thinking about abstract things means thinking about pure ideas. Here's a little chart showing how you can take something concrete and make it more and more abstract.

Concrete		Somewhat abstract		More abstract		Abstract
my dog Rover	→	dogs in general	→	living things	→	life
how Mr. X treats students	→	is Mr. X fair?	→	what is fairness?	→	justice

As you can see, concrete things are **specific**, while abstract ideas are **general**. Now, you might be wondering how this relates to math. It relates because algebra takes the idea of a number (already fairly abstract) and lifts it to an even more abstract level. You can see this in the development of your sense of what a number is. For example, the idea of ....

- **three puppies** is a **concrete** idea (learned around age 3)
- **the number three**, standing for three of anything, is a **more abstract** idea (learned around age 7)
- **a variable like x**, which can stand for any number, is a **completely abstract** idea
  (learned during adolescence through algebra)

Since a variable like **x** can stand for any number, it's hard to think about at first. But just as you made the earlier leaps toward abstract thinking, you'll make this leap too. Hang on for the ride.

Why do most schools start teaching algebra around 8th, 9th or 10th grade? Is this really the best time for people to learn it?

A: Actually the reason students start learning algebra at this time has to do with the development of their minds. And yes, it's the perfect time to learn algebra.

Jean Piaget, a famous frenchman, studied how children's thinking changes as they grow up. Piaget noticed that during early adolescence children's minds undergo a huge change.

While in early years children focus on concrete things, stuff they take in through their five senses (things like: trucks, candy, flowers, stars, dinosaurs) — in teen years, kids start to focus on abstract ideas. That's why during this time people find themselves asking the **big questions** like, "Why am I on this planet?" "What's the purpose of school? "Why is the universe here?" It's also why teen-agers tune in to music lyrics — because they're searching for meaning.

Teen-agers naturally start to develop abstract thinking. And learning algebra gives them another big push along that path. So the answer is this: **you learn algebra during early adolescence because that's when your mind is most ready to grow in this way.**

 **Q:** Other than helping me learn to think in abstract ways, why should I study algebra? What good is it in a practical sense?

 Here are a few additional reasons:

1) Studying algebra boosts your chances of going to college and succeeding in today's world. Studies show that taking algebra, and following it with geometry, dramatically boosts a student's chance of going to college. In fact, a **1990 College Board study** found that students who take **algebra and geometry** stand a much greater chance of attending college than students who don't take these courses. And, of course, to succeed in today's high-tech/information-age economy, you must have a good education.

2) Learning algebra can help you find a good-paying job. Anyone who wants to work in any field of science — computer science, astronomy, medicine, psychology, genetics, etc. — needs to know algebra. That's because all the sciences rely on algebra and on the higher maths.

3) Knowing algebra will help you survive the "big, bad world." Understanding algebraic ratios helps you become a smart comparison shopper; understanding percentages helps you make sense of the statistics thrown at you by the media. The ways to use algebra are numerous. As you work through the **Survival Guide**, consider how you might use algebra in your life.

4) Algebra teaches you to solve difficult problems. By developing your algebraic mental muscles, you strengthen your ability to tackle problems in life, for learning algebra improves your ability to think clearly.

5) Learning algebra teaches you about yourself. Since algebra is a product of the human mind, studying algebra gives you insight into how your own mind works. Learning this subject shows the logical thought patterns that are part of you just because you're human.

Q: Just out of curiosity,
when was algebra developed?
And why did anyone
bother to come up with it?

A: Simple algebra has been around since the time of the ancient Greeks, but algebra didn't become a well developed branch of math until about 1,200 years ago — during the great Islamic empire.

According to the "father of algebra," a man named Muhammed ibn Musa al-Khwarizmi, algebra was developed for purely practical purposes, to help people solve everyday problems.

In his famous book, written in the early ninth century, al-Khwarizmi says he developed algebra to help people deal with "what is easiest and most useful," and he goes on to list these areas: inheritance, lawsuits, trade, land measurements, and the digging of canals.[1]

Since al-Khwarizmi's day, people have discovered many additional uses for algebra. And today algebra is used in virtually every kind of science; it is also considered the foundation of all higher math.

In case you were wondering, the word **algebra** comes from the Arabic word **al-jabr**, which means **restoring**. This name was taken from the title of al-Khwarizmi's treatise, Al-jabr wa'l muqabalah, commonly translated as **The Book of Restoring and Balancing**.

1. L.C. Karpinski, ed. *Robert of Chester's Latin Translation of the Algebra of al-Khowarizmi* (New York: Macmillan, 1915), p. 96.

Properties

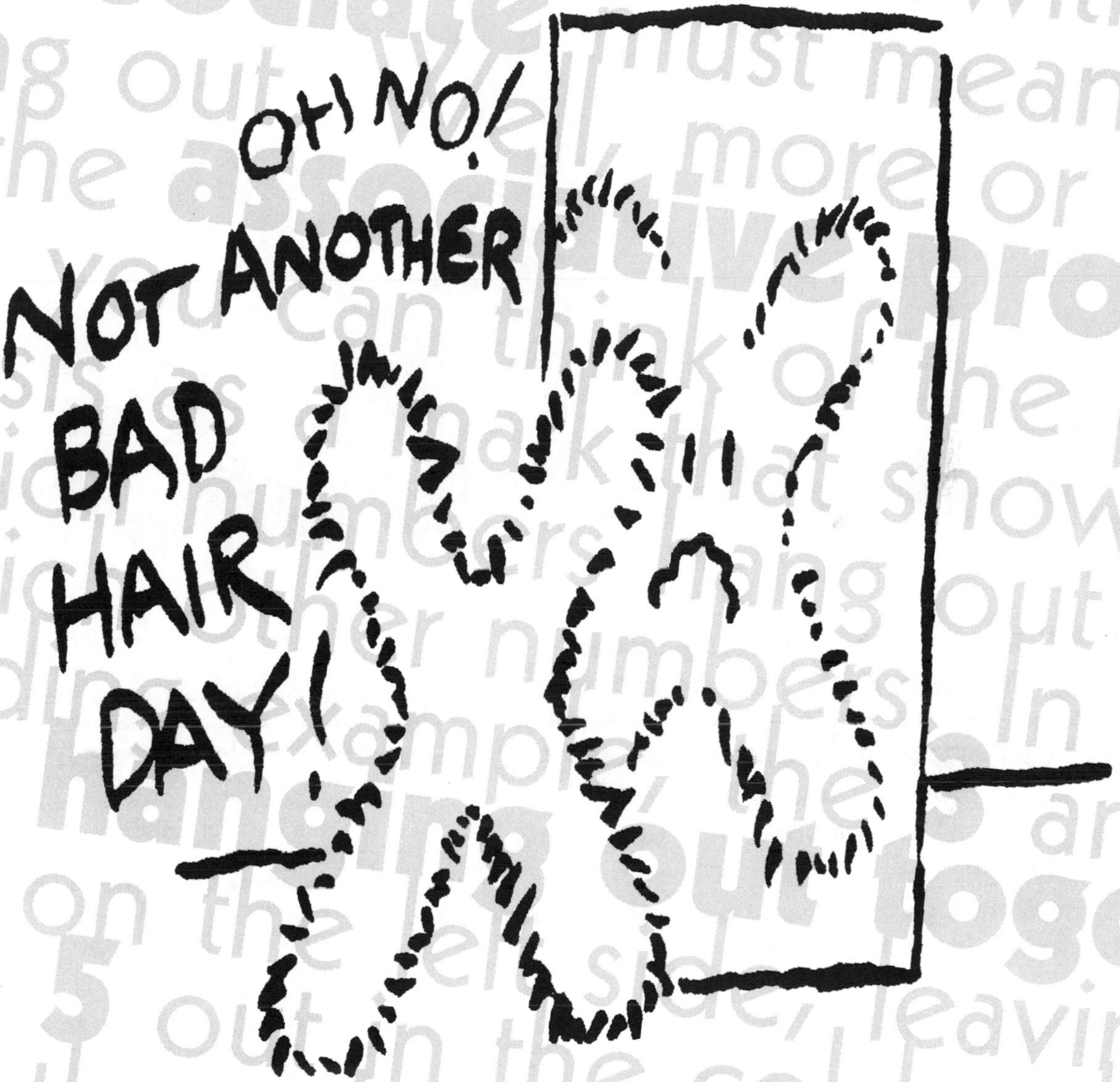

Why do I need to learn the properties when so many of them seem obvious?

A: Even though many of the properties — for example, the reflexive and symmetric properties — seem so obvious that even most two-year-olds would understand them (reflexive property: Susie is Susie), still you need to memorize these properties so you can:

a) perform algebraic operations with confidence, and
b) prove algebraic principles.

Think of it this way. If algebra is viewed as a huge mansion that you're wandering around in for a year or so, this house had better have a strong foundation. For if it doesn't, a strong gust of logic could blow it down like a house of cards. The **properties of algebra**, which you'll learn in this section, **create the secure foundation for the House of Algebra**. They're what you'll rely on as you go tiptoeing about — performing algebraic operations and trying to prove basic principles — to make sure that your footing is always one hundred percent secure.

Q: What does the reflexive property say?

 The reflexive property tells you this simple truth:

$$a = a$$

Or, in plain English: any quantity is equal to itself.

Examples of the reflexive property

$2 = 2$	$ms = ms$
$1/3 = 1/3$	$x^2 = x^2$
$.8 = .8$	$ac^2x = ac^2x$

Teachers will often give you quizzes on these different properties. So it helps to have a way to remember them. These pages will help you remember the properties by making a connection between the property's name and what it means.

So how can you remember why this is called the "reflexive property"? It's because the reflexive property deals with a **reflection**. Just as you always see yourself when you look at your reflection in the mirror (well, at least on good days!), a number or variable sees itself when it looks in the mirror of the equal sign.

Which of the following statements gives an example of the reflexive property?

a) $a = b = c$
b) $b = b$
c) If $a = a$, then $b = b$.

Answer:
only statement b

Q: What does the symmetric property say?

 The symmetric property says this:

If a = b, then b = a.

Or: if a first quantity is equal to a second quantity, then the second quantity is equal to the first quantity.

Examples of the symmetric property

If 2 = 4/2, then 4/2 = 2.

If 0.6 = 6/10, then 6/10 = 0.6.

If 0/3 = 0, then 0 = 0/3.

If x^2 = x · x, then x · x = x^2.

If a + c = 10, then 10 = a + c.

If r · m = 30, then 30 = r · m.

And how can you remember why this is called the "symmetric property"? First remember that **symmetry** is just a fancy word for **balance**. This property is called the symmetric property because it shows balance; it shows that the left and right sides of an equation are fundamentally the same. In other words, the phrase: "if **a = b**, then **b = a**" tells us that it makes no difference whether the **a** is on the left and the **b** on the right, or the **a** on the right and the **b** on the left. The two sides are balanced in the sense that they are basically the same.

Which properties, if any, are shown by the following statements?

a) If ab = xy, then xy = ab.
b) xy = xy
c) If 5 = 10/2, then 10/2 = 5.
d) q = q
e) If s = t, then t = v.

Answers:
a) symmetric
b) reflexive
c) symmetric
d) reflexive
e) none

What does the transitive property say?

 The transitive property says this:

If a = b, and b = c, then a = c.

Or: if a first quantity is equal to a second quantity, and the second quantity is equal to a third quantity, then the first quantity is equal to the third quantity.

Examples of the transitive property

If $2 \cdot 4 = 8,$
and $8 = 16 \div 2,$
then $2 \cdot 4 = 16 \div 2.$

If $x + c = a,$
and $a = m + r,$
then $x + c = m + r.$

To understand why this is called the "transitive property," think about the word "transition." From English class, you know that **transitions** are little words English teachers love you to use because they form **bridges**, or connections, between ideas — words like 'despite,' 'however,' 'consequently,' etc. When you use the algebraic transitive property, you also make a bridge, but it's a bridge between quantities rather than between ideas. And instead of using a word to make the bridge, you use a variable. Look again at the phrase: "If **a = b**, and **b = c**, then **a = c**." Which letter acts as a bridge between quantities? The letter **b**. Through **b** you show that **a** is equal to **c**. Since this property uses a mathematical bridge, or transition, it's called the "transitive property."

Which properties, if any, are shown by these statements?

a) $xy = xy$
b) If $x = y,$ and $y = z,$ then $x = z.$
c) If $a = b,$ and $b = c,$ then $b = d.$
d) If $xy = 7,$ then $7 = xy.$
e) If $4 = 8/2,$ and $8/2 = 10 - 6,$ then $4 = 10 - 6.$

Answers:
a) reflexive
b) transitive
c) none
d) symmetric
e) transitive

Q: What does the commutative property say?

 The commutative property tells you that:

$$a + b = b + a$$

and that

$$a \cdot b = b \cdot a$$

In other words, when you're adding or multiplying, the order of the terms makes no difference.

Examples of the commutative property

adding	multiplying
$5 + 3 = 3 + 5$	$5 \cdot 3 = 3 \cdot 5$
$8 = 8$	$15 = 15$

To **commute** is to go from one place to another and back again. People can commute to and from school, to and from work, and so on. This property is called the "commutative property" because in it the numbers or variables go through a commute; they go back and forth. This property assures you that just as the drive from your house to your friend's house is the same distance no matter whose house you start at, in addition and multiplication the answer comes out the same no matter which number you start with. In other words, it makes no difference whether you start with **3** or with **5** ....

**3 + 5 is the same as 5 + 3.
And 3 · 5 is the same as 5 · 3.**

Which properties, if any, are shown by these statements?

a) If $7 + 8 = 15$, then $15 = 7 + 8$.
b) $7 + 8 = 8 + 7$
c) $7 + 8 = 7 + 8$
d) If $7 + 8 = 15$, and $15 = 20 - 5$, then $7 + 8 = 20 - 5$.
e) $6 \cdot 5 = 5 \cdot 6$

Answers:
a) **symmetric**
b) **commutative**
c) **reflexive**
d) **transitive**
e) **commutative**

Q: What does the associative property say?

A: The associative property tells you that:

$$a + (b + c) = (a + b) + c$$

and also that:

$$a \cdot (b \cdot c) = (a \cdot b) \cdot c$$

Or, in English: when you're adding or multiplying, the way the terms are grouped makes no difference.

Examples of the associative property

<u>adding</u>

$$5 + (3 + 7) = (5 + 3) + 7$$
$$5 + 10 = 8 + 7$$
$$15 = 15$$

<u>multiplying</u>

$$5 \cdot (3 \cdot 7) = (5 \cdot 3) \cdot 7$$
$$5 \cdot 21 = 15 \cdot 7$$
$$105 = 105$$

If someone worries about the kind of people you "associate with," s/he worries about the people you hang out with. So to **associate** must mean to hang out. Well, more or less. In the associative property, you can think of the parenthesis as a mark that shows which numbers hang out with which other numbers. In the adding example, the **3** and **7** are hanging out together on the left side, leaving the **5** out in the cold; while on the right side of this equation, the **5** and **3** are buddies, and the **7** is left all alone. So what does this property say? Basically, it assures you that whenever you're adding or multiplying, how numbers or variables are grouped — whom they associate with — makes no difference at all.

Which properties, if any, are shown by the following statements?

a) If $6 + (2 + 8) = 16$, then $16 = 8 \cdot 2$.

b) $6 + (2 + 9) = (6 + 2) + 9$

c) $6 + 2 = 2 + 6$

d) $a \cdot (b \cdot c) = (a \cdot b) \cdot c$

e) $4 + (3 + 5) = 4 + (3 \cdot 5)$

Answers:
a) none
b) associative
c) commutative
d) associative
e) none

© Singing Turtle Press

Q: Since the commutative and associative properties work for addition and multiplication, they must also work for subtraction and division. Isn't that right?

A: **No, no, perish the thought!**

These propeties are true only for addition and multiplication, as a moment's consideration will show.

Commutative property

not true for subtraction

$$7 - 3 = 3 - 7$$
$$4 = -4$$

nope!

not true for division

$$8 \div 2 = 2 \div 8$$
$$4 = 1/4$$

nope!

Associative property

not true for subtraction

$$7 - (5 - 3) = (7 - 5) - 3$$
$$7 - 2 = 2 - 3$$
$$5 = -1$$

nope!

not true for division

$$8 \div (4 \div 2) = (8 \div 4) \div 2$$
$$8 \div 2 = 2 \div 2$$
$$4 = 1$$

nope!

Q: What does the distributive property say?

A: The distributive property tells you that

$$a(b + c) = a \cdot b + a \cdot c$$

and that

$$a(b - c) = a \cdot b - a \cdot c$$

Translation: suppose you have a parenthesis containing a bunch of terms linked by addition or subtraction signs. If any term stands outside and multiplies the parenthesis, it multiplies every term within the parenthesis.

Examples of the distributive property

$$
\begin{aligned}
3(7 + 5) &= 3 \cdot 7 + 3 \cdot 5 \\
&= 21 \quad + \quad 15 \\
&= 36
\end{aligned}
$$

$$
\begin{aligned}
3(7 - 5) &= 3 \cdot 7 - 3 \cdot 5 \\
&= 21 \quad - \quad 15 \\
&= 6
\end{aligned}
$$

$$
\begin{aligned}
3(a + 5) &= 3 \cdot a + 3 \cdot 5 \\
&= 3a \quad + \quad 15
\end{aligned}
$$

$$
\begin{aligned}
3(a - 5) &= 3 \cdot a - 3 \cdot 5 \\
&= 3a \quad - \quad 15
\end{aligned}
$$

To understand this property's name, think of what it means for someone to **distribute** a piece of paper to everyone in a class. If a student named Kyle distributes a piece of paper to his classmates, he gives a piece of paper to each student. So distributing means giving something to a number of people. In the distributive property, think of the number outside the parenthesis as like Kyle, and the terms inside parentheses as like the students. But instead of giving a piece of paper to every student, the number on the outside gives itself to every term on the inside by multiplying it. It distributes itself through multiplication. Therefore, this is the "distributive property."

Which of the properties, if any, are shown by the following statements?

a) $4(3 + 8) = 4 \cdot 3 + 4 \cdot 8$

b) $a(b + c) = c(a + b)$

c) $a(b + c) = a(b + c)$

d) $2 + (3 + 5) = (2 + 3) + 5$

e) If $b = q$, and $q = r$, then $b = r$.

Answers:

a) distributive
b) none
c) reflexive
d) associative
e) transitive

How do you actually work out the steps of the distributive property in a problem?

 Just follow the four steps below.

Multiply using the distributive property: $-3(2a - 5)$

Steps	**Example**	**Steps**	**Example**
1st) Write down any invisible positive signs.	$-3 \cdot (2a - 5)$ $= -3 (+2a - 5)$ Note: **2a** means **+ 2a**	**3rd)** Multiply term outside parenthesis with next term in parenthesis.	$(-3) \cdot (-5) = +15$
2nd) Multiply term outside parenthesis with the first term in parenthesis. Use multiplication rule (**p. 49**) to get the sign.	$(-3) \cdot (+2a) = -6a$	**4th)** Write down the answers from steps two and three in the order that you got them. Together they give you the whole answer.	$-6a + 15$

 **Work out the following products using the distributive property:**

a) $q(r + v)$

b) $5(m + r)$

c) $3(5n + 1)$

d) $7(5a - 4)$

e) $-9(3c - 5)$

Answers:

a) qr + qv d) 35a − 28

b) 5m + 5r e) − 27c + 45

c) 15n + 3

Q: What does the additive identity property say?

A: The additive identity property guarantees that

$$a + 0 = a$$

Or, even more simply: when you add zero to any term, the answer you get is just the term.

Examples of the additive identity property

$7 + 0 = 7$ $c + 0 = c$

$3/5 + 0 = 3/5$ $ac^2 + 0 = ac^2$

$-4.2 + 0 = -4.2$ $ms + 0 = ms$

It's obvious that this property is about addition, but why is it called the additive **identity** property? What does "identity" have to do with it? Well, think about what "identity" means; it means who you are. In the additive identity property, the operation gives back the identity of the original number. When you add zero to any number, you get back the very number you started with.

Which properties, if any, are shown by these statements?

a) $5 + 3 = 3 + 5$ d) $0 = 0$

b) $3 = 3 + 0$ e) $18 = 0 + 18$

c) $5 + (3 + 2) = (5 + 3) + 2$

Answers:
a) commutative
b) additive identity
c) associative
d) reflexive
e) additive identity

Q: What does the multiplicative identity property say?

 The multiplicative identity property guarantees that

$$a \cdot 1 = a$$

When you take any term and multiply it by one, the answer you get is just the term.

What **0** does in addition, **1** does in multiplication. It gives you back the **identity** of the number you started with. This is why multiplying by **1** is called the "multiplicative identity" property.

Examples of the multiplicative identity property

$7 \cdot 1 = 7$	$c \cdot 1 = c$
$3/5 \cdot 1 = 3/5$	$ac^2 \cdot 1 = ac^2$
$-4.2 \cdot 1 = -4.2$	$ms \cdot 1 = ms$

Which properties, if any, are shown by these statements?

a) $6(a + 2) = 6 \cdot a + 6 \cdot 2$

b) $6 \cdot 1 = 3 \cdot 2$

c) If $12 = 4 \cdot 3$, and $4 \cdot 3 = 14 - 2$, then $12 = 14 - 2$.

d) $1 \cdot r = r$

e) $13 + 0 = 13$

Answers:
a) distributive
b) none
c) transitive
d) multiplicative identity
e) additive identity

a) If $m = c$, then $c = m$.

b) $4 \cdot (3 \cdot 8) = (4 \cdot 3) \cdot 8$

c) $5(a + 2) = 5 \cdot a + 5 \cdot 2$

d) If $a = a$, then $a = b$.

e) If $x = y$, and $y = z$, then $x = z$.

f) $m = m$

g) $m + v = v + m$

h) If $25 = 5 \cdot 5$, and $5 \cdot 5 = 50 \div 2$, then $25 = 50 \div 2$.

j) $(6 + 5) + 9 = 6 + (5 + 9)$

k) $8(a + 3) = 8 \cdot 3 \cdot a$

l) $7 \cdot 4 = 4 \cdot 7$

m) $8(m - 3) = 8m - 24$

n) If $4 + 7 = 11$, then $11 = 4 + 7$.

p) $ab = ab$

q) If $a = x + y + z$, then $x + y + z = a$.

r) If $r = v \cdot w$, and $v \cdot w = z$, then $r = z$.

s) $pqr \cdot 1 = pqr$

t) $7 + 9 = 9 + 7$

u) $-4(-3a + 4) = 12a - 16$

v) $14 - (7 - 2) = (14 - 7) - 2$

w) $16.4 + 0 = 16.4$

Multiply using the distributive property:

x) $3(4 + 5)$

y) $5(a + 2)$

z) $7(a - 4)$

A) $9(3a - 9)$

B) $-2(6a + 5)$

C) $-3(7a - 5)$

D) $-8(-4a - 6)$

A:

a) symmetric

b) associative

c) distributive

d) none

e) transitive

f) reflexive

g) commutative

h) transitive

j) associative

k) none

l) commutative

m) distributive

n) symmetric

p) reflexive

q) symmetric

r) transitive

s) multiplicative Identity

t) commutative

u) distributive

v) none

w) additive Identity

x) 27

y) $5a + 10$

z) $7a - 28$

A) $27a - 81$

B) $-12a - 10$

C) $-21a + 15$

D) $32a + 48$

...en in decimal form. Here's the rule: The decimal for a rational number has two choices in life. Either terminate... it dies / or ends (ex. 3/8 = .375 such x.) ... babbles the same ... forever and ever (ex. 43/99 = .4343... such x.) This is called repeating. The ... decimal ... tional form of any ... of these ... doesn't terminate ... it do? ... expect an irrational number to do? Just what you'd crazy. It ... goes on and on endlessly, in either no pattern at all, or in a pattern strange that it's

Q: Why do I need to learn about these different sets of numbers? Aren't all numbers just numbers?

A: Up till now, you've probably viewed all numbers as "just numbers." But beginning with algebra, you start to look at numbers in more sophisticated ways. The names for the sets of numbers, which you'll learn in this section, will become your new vocabulary for talking about numbers with greater understanding.

Think about it ... Way back when you were in third or fourth grade, you probably paid little attention to the various groups of kids in junior high or high school. But when you got to junior high or high school, you noticed that various people dressed and acted in different ways. And eventually you "learned the ropes"; you realized that some kids were viewed as "jocks," others as "brains," still others as "preppies," "skaters," etc.

In the same way, you probably viewed all numbers as "just numbers" in early math because you didn't need to know any better. But when you study algebra, you find out that **not all numbers are alike**. Just like people, they can be viewed by the groups they belong to, and numbers from different groups behave differently. Distinguishing types of numbers may seem hard, but with a little practice you'll be able to spot the difference between an irrational number and an integer as quickly as you can pick out a "skater" from a "preppie."

What are the natural numbers?

 The natural numbers make up the set of all counting numbers.

$$\{1, \ 2, \ 3, \ 4, \ 5 \ ... \ \infty\}$$

Examples of natural numbers

23   1   42,789

The smallest group of numbers are called the **natural numbers**. These are also the simplest numbers because they're **the numbers you'd use to count actual things**, like baseball cards in a collection, or calories in a candy bar.

In every society, people have used these simple numbers to count. Since these numbers come naturally to people all around the globe, they're called the "natural numbers."

By the way, that little symbol, ∞, which looks like an **8** taking a nap, means infinity. So when you see $\{5 \ ... \ \infty\}$, it means all the numbers from **5** to positive infinity. In the same way, $-\infty$ means negative infinity. So $\{-\infty \ ... \ -5\}$ means all the numbers from negative infinity to -5.

Which of the following are natural numbers?

a) -7
b) 0
c) 28
d) 6.2
e) 3/4

Answer:
only choice c

What are the whole numbers?

The whole numbers make up the set of natural numbers, plus 0.

$$\{0, 1, 2, 3, 4, 5 ... \infty\}$$

Examples of whole numbers

0   1   27   894,609

If the natural numbers are the numbers you count with, the **whole numbers are those same counting numbers, plus the number zero.** One way to remember that this set is called the "whole numbers" is to think about the shape of the number zero. Just like a donut, the number zero has a hole in the middle. The words "hole" and "whole" sound exactly the same, so you can remember that **the whole numbers include the number with the hole in the center — zero.**

Which of the following are whole numbers?
a) 13
b) 0
c) − 3
d) 2/3
e) 6,127

Answer:
choices a, b and e

What are the integers?

The integers are made up of the whole numbers and the negatives of all the natural numbers.

$$\{-\infty \ldots -5, -4, -3, -2, -1, 0, 1, 2, 3, 4, 5 \ldots \infty\}$$

Examples of integers

− 236   0   489

To get the set of **integers, just take the set of whole numbers and add to it the negatives of the natural numbers**. The negatives of the natural numbers are the natural numbers with negative signs in front. For example, the negative of **3** is **− 3**; the negative of **5** is **− 5**, etc. To remember that this set is called the integers, look at the spelling of "integer." Notice that if you take away the "t," you'd have the three letters **neg** all in a row. This can remind you that the integers contain the **negatives** of the natural numbers, as well as the natural numbers and zero.

Which of the following are integers?
a) 5.2
b) 5
c) − 2
d) 2/5
e) 0

Answer:
choices b, c and e

What are the rational numbers?

A: The rational numbers make up the set of all numbers that can be written as a fraction of integers. In other words, any time you see an integer divided by another integer, you're looking at a rational number.

Examples of rational numbers

$2/5$ $-3/8$ $7,000$ (since $7,000 = 7,000/1$)

4 (since $4 = 4/1$) $.673$ (since $.673 = 673/1,000$)

0 (since $0 = 0/3$) $-.7$ (since $-.7 = -7/10$)

"Rational" is just a highfaluting word for reasonable. So why would anyone say that a set of numbers is rational, or reasonable? We'll try to understand this, strangely enough, by thinking about laws and citizens. As you know, the real world has laws, and citizens who are rational (reasonable) obey those laws, as long as the laws make sense.

Similarly, the world of numbers has a major law, and all "rational" numbers are expected to follow it. This law states that to be upstanding citizens of the world of math, numbers must be capable of being written in terms of integers — those neat and clean, model-citizen numbers that everyone can grasp. So basically mathematicians came up with the following definition of **rational numbers: all numbers that can be written as one integer divided by another integer are "rational numbers."** As for those numbers that can't be written as an integer over an integer … ? Well, for the longest time these weren't even considered numbers! More on that next …

Note: There's one big exception to this definition: an integer divided by zero is NOT a rational number. (See pitfall page: **30**.)

Which of the following are rational numbers?

a) 2/7
b) − 12
c) 0/5
d) .137
e) − .64

Answers:
all are rational numbers

Q: What are the irrational numbers?

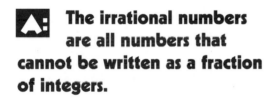

A: The irrational numbers are all numbers that cannot be written as a fraction of integers.

Examples of irrational numbers

$$\sqrt{2} \qquad \sqrt{11} \qquad \pi$$

The problem with laws - sigh - is that there are always some who will break them. So too in the world of numbers. For centuries, the only known numbers were rational numbers, but eventually some numbers were discovered which just wouldn't obey the law for rational numbers. These are the **outlaw**, or "irrational numbers."

The first — and most famous — outlaw number was the square root of two, written: $\sqrt{2}$ When the ancient Greeks first stumbled upon this little fellow, they tried and tried to write its value as a fraction of integers, but the stubborn bugger refused. And to this day, $\sqrt{2}$ has never been written as a fraction of integers.

Eventually more and more **outlaw numbers** were discovered (the other infamous one is the number π, pronounced: "pie"). Finally mathematicians had to accept that these numbers were here to stay, but they tried to keep them in their place by giving them a nasty label. They called them the **"irrational numbers,"** meaning that since they, the mathematicians, couldn't make sense of them, these numbers must not make very much sense. That's a little like running around the house shouting: "Where are my stupid shoes?!" when it's you who foolishly forgot where you left them.

In any case, the outlaw irrational numbers remain with us today. And in truth we should be thankful they're here, for they make the world of numbers all the more bizarre and interesting.

try our zany lesson plans

Now I understand the basic difference between rational and irrational numbers. But is there any way to tell whether a number is rational or irrational just by looking at it?

Yes. The way to tell is to look at the number when it's written in decimal form. Here's the rule:

The decimal form of a rational number has only two choices in life: it can either terminate, meaning it dies or ends suddenly (ex. **3/8 = .375**), or it babbles the same thing forever and ever (ex. **43/99 = .434343 ...**). This is called "repeating."

On the other hand, the decimal form of an irrational number does neither of these things. So if it doesn't terminate and it doesn't repeat, what does it do? Just what you'd expect an irrational number to do ... it acts kind of crazy. It goes on and on endlessly in either no pattern at all, or in a pattern so strange that it's not even a repeating pattern.

Difference between rational and irrational numbers

a) Rational number: **7/8 = .875** (The decimal terminates.)

b) Rational number: **4/11 = .363636 ...** (The decimal repeats in a regular pattern.)

c) Irrational number: **√3 = 1.732058 ...** (This decimal goes on and on in a pattern no human being has ever made sense of.)

Which of the following are irrational numbers?

a) **.272727 ...**

b) **6.01364 ...**

c) **.378**

d) **.564198 ...**

e) **.2094**

Answer:
choices b and d only

28

Q: What are the real numbers?

A: The real numbers make up the set of all the rational numbers and all the irrational numbers.

In short, the set of real numbers includes every type of number you can possibly think of.

Examples of real numbers

$$\pi \quad \sqrt{5} \quad 4^7 \quad \sqrt[3]{11} \quad .7272\ldots$$

$$-1/5 \quad \quad 0 \quad -.0067 \quad 1$$

Finally, with the set of **real numbers, you have the largest set of numbers you'll use in beginning algebra**. As you can imagine, this is a huge set of numbers. To grasp its awesome size, think of a number line like the one below, shooting out toward positive infinity on the right and toward negative infinity on the left, with various integer lengths marked off. Now imagine taking a superfine needle and placing its point anywhere at all on this infinitely long number line. No matter where you set down the needle's point, there's a real number that corresponds to the point you've marked.

Are there other types of numbers beyond the real numbers? Yes, but don't worry about them now since you won't work with them till advanced algebra. Instead, pat yourself on the back. For in addition to distinguishing "brains" from "jocks," now you should also be able to distinguish the major groups of numbers.

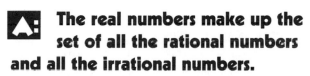

One last question ...
there's no difference between zero divided by a number and a number divided by zero. Right?

$$0/3 \overset{?}{=} 3/0$$

▲: Wrong. There's a huge difference!

Zero divided by a number equals **zero**. But a number divided by zero is **undefined**, which means that it is no actual number. That is:

$$0/3 = 0$$
but
$$3/0 = \textbf{undefined}$$

You have two choices: either try to follow a short, brain-twisting proof of this idea, or just kick back and accept it. But note the warning above.

Beware: this little proof may make you dizzy if you study it for more than ten minutes.

First, remember that division is just the opposite of multiplication. In other words, when you say that $8 \div 2 = 4$, it's the same as saying that $4 \times 2 = 8$. To put this in general terms, saying that $c \div b = a$ is basically the same thing as saying that $a \times b = c$. So far, so good?

Now let's use this idea to see if dividing by zero could make sense. So, if you try to say that $8 \div 0$ is <u>not</u> undefined ... in other words, if you try to say that $8 \div 0 = \textbf{some number}$, you'd be forced into saying that **some number** $\times \, 0 = 8$. And why don't you try this. Think of some number which you can multiply by **0** so that you wind up with **8** as an answer. If you can find such a number, you must be the newest, undiscovered math genius of this century. But if you're a mere mortal, like the rest of us, you can't find any such number. Since this operation is impossible, $8 \div 0$ must not be a real number. That means that $8 \div 0$ must be considered undefined. And that means that not only **8/0** — but all fractions like **8/0**, in which you have a number divided by zero — must be undefined.

On the other hand, what allows us to confidently say that $0 \div 8 = 0$? Well, if we reverse things here, this would mean that $0 \times 8 = 0$. And we all know that that's true. So $0 \div 8$ does equal zero. And all fractions like **0/8** — in which you have zero divided by a number — must also equal zero.

Note: most teachers will ask you to write "undefined" or "no answer" for answers that come out like **3/0**.

Q: To which sets of numbers, if any, do the following numbers belong?

a) 4/9

b) − 3

c) .395

d) 1, 000, 000

e) √2

f) 0/4

g) − 3/11

h) .4747 ...

j) − .568

k) − .6193708 ...

l) √− 2

m) − 7, 000

n) 642.5

p) 4, 076

q) 81/37

r) 17/0

s) .636363 ...

t) 78.999 ...

u) 4.00008

v) 9/2

w) √7/5

a) reals, rationals

b) reals, rationals, integers

c) reals, rationals

d) reals, rationals, integers, whole numbers, natural numbers

e) reals, irrationals

f) reals, rationals, integers, whole numbers

g) reals, rationals

h) reals, rationals

j) reals, rationals

k) reals, irrationals

l) no sets (undefined)

m) reals, rationals, integers

n) reals, rationals

p) reals, rationals, integers, whole numbers, natural numbers

q) reals, rationals

r) no sets (undefined)

s) reals, rationals

t) reals, rationals

u) reals, rationals

v) reals, rationals

w) reals, irrationals

Positive & Negative Numbers

Why do I need to learn all these rules for working with positive and negative numbers? I never had to learn rules like these before.

A: In the math you've done before algebra, problems were set up so that answers would always come out positive. But now that you're older and smarter, you get a new challenge. Beginning with algebra, it's just as likely that problems will have negative answers as that they'll have positive answers. The rules for signed numbers teach you how to perform basic operations with positive and negative numbers so you can tell if your answers will be positive or negative.

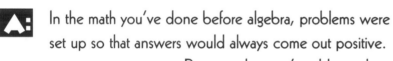

In this section, you'll learn how to combine positive and negative numbers through the **same-sign rule**, the **mixed-sign rule** and the **neighbor-sign rule**. You'll also learn rules for doing **multiplication** and **division** with positive and negative numbers.

 **First of all,
what exactly
is a negative number?
And is there any way
to relate negative numbers
to my everyday life?**

A: Negative numbers are numbers with negative signs, which means they have a value less than zero. "But wait," you say, "how can any number have a value less than zero? Isn't zero the lowest value possible?"

To get a grip on this idea, consider the meaning of a debt — an amount of money you owe someone. Suppose you have seven dollars in your pocket; it's as if your financial status is **+7**. But now suppose you've spent your seven dollars. You have nothing left, but at least you don't owe anyone any money; now you can view your financial status as **0**. Finally imagine that you borrow seven dollars from someone; at this point, your financial status is **−7**. In other words, negative seven is seven less (or here, worse) than **0**.

The same idea pops up with temperature readings. A temperature of positive **10** degrees means **10** degrees above **0**. But a temperature of negative **10** degrees means **10** degrees below **0**. In other words, freezing! Here too, you see that in real life you do have a concept of negative numbers, numbers with values less than zero.

Q: What does the same-sign rule say?

$$+\,a + c = \,?$$

$$-\,a - c = \,?$$

A: The same-sign rule says:

When you're combining numbers with the same sign, keep the sign and add the numbers.

$$+\,a + c = +\left(a + c\right) \qquad -\,a - c = -\left(a + c\right)$$

Examples of the same-sign rule

$$+\ 3 + 8$$
$$= +\left(3 + 8\right)$$
$$= +\ 11$$

$$-\ 3 - 8$$
$$= -\left(3 + 8\right)$$
$$= -\ 11$$

$$+\ 5 + 7 + 11$$
$$= +\left(5 + 7 + 11\right)$$
$$= +\ 23$$

$$-\ 5 - 7 - 11$$
$$= -\left(5 + 7 + 11\right)$$
$$= -\ 23$$

Q: This sounds simple enough, but how do I actually work out the steps for the same-sign rule?

 A: Follow the four steps below.

Simplify: **A)** $+ 4 + 7,$ **B)** $- 4 - 7,$ **C)** $- 3 - 2 - 5$

Steps	Example A $+ 4 + 7$	Example B $- 4 - 7$	Example C $- 3 - 2 - 5$
1st) Ask yourself: is the sign of the numbers positive or negative?	sign is positive	sign is negative	sign is negative
2nd) Whichever sign the numbers have, put down that sign followed by a set of parentheses.	$+ (\quad)$	$- (\quad)$	$- (\qquad)$
3rd) Inside the parentheses, put down the numbers and stick plus signs between them.	$+ (4 + 7)$	$- (4 + 7)$	$- (3 + 2 + 5)$
4th) Add the numbers, then take away the parentheses. Behold your answer.	$+ 11$	$- 11$	$- 10$

Simplify using the same-sign rule:

a) $+ 5 + 9$
b) $- 6 - 7$
c) $+ 2 + 4 + 7$
d) $- 9 - 8 - 1$
e) $- 1 - 1 - 1 - 1 - 1$

Answers:
a) $+ 14$
b) $- 13$
c) $+ 13$
d) $- 18$
e) $- 5$

Q: What's an easy way to grasp what the same-sign rule means for positive numbers and for negative numbers?

A: When working out the same-sign rule with **positive** numbers, imagine that you **receive** money from different people.
When working it out with **negative** numbers, imagine that you **owe** money to different people.

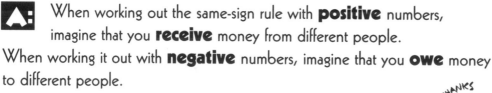

With positive numbers

Take the problem:
+ 3 + 8

Think of this as your receiving **$3** from one person and **$8** from another person. Altogether you receive **$11**, so the answer is **+ 11**.

(**Getting money** is a **positive** thing, right?)

With negative numbers

Take the problem:
− 3 − 8

Think of this as your owing **$3** to one person and also owing **$8** to another person. Altogether you owe **$11**, so the answer is **− 11**.

(**Owing money** is a pain, right? So it's a **negative** thing.)

Q: What does the mixed-sign rule say?

$$+ \, a - c = \,?$$

$$- \, a + c = \,?$$

A: The mixed-sign rule tells you how to combine numbers with different signs. It says:

Ignoring the signs, see which number is larger. Take the sign in front of that larger number and place it before a set of parentheses. Then, inside parentheses, subtract the smaller number from the larger one.

Examples of the mixed-sign rule

$$+ \, 3 - 8$$
$$= - \left(8 - 3\right)$$
$$= - 5$$

$$- \, 3 + 8$$
$$= + \left(8 - 3\right)$$
$$= + 5$$

$$+ \, 8 - 3$$
$$= + \left(8 - 3\right)$$
$$= + 5$$

$$- \, 8 + 3$$
$$= - \left(8 - 3\right)$$
$$= - 5$$

Many people get confused by this rule, wrongly thinking that in a problem like $+3 - 8$, you compare the $+3$ with the -8 to decide which of the two is larger. No, no! Danger, danger! You ignore the signs. You simply compare the pure, or absolute values of the numbers. You just compare **3** with **8**. Since **8** is larger than **3**, you take the sign in front of the **8**, and you plunk that down as the sign of the answer. Then, inside parentheses, you subtract the smaller number from the larger one. Behold, your answer appears, as if by magic.

Q: O.K., I sort of get it, but I know I'd understand the mixed-sign rule better if I could see its steps laid out one by one. What would these steps look like?

The four steps are shown below.

Simplify: A) + 2 − 7, B) − 2 + 7

<u>Steps</u>	<u>Example A</u>	<u>Example B</u>
1st) Ignoring signs, ask yourself which of the two numbers is larger.	+ 2 − 7 **7** is larger than **2**	− 2 + 7 **7** is larger than **2**
2nd) Whichever number is larger, take a look at the sign in front of it. Take that sign and put it down in front of a set of parentheses.	− ( )	+ ( )
3rd) Inside parentheses, first put down the larger number, then subtract the smaller number from it.	− (7 − 2)	+ (7 − 2)
4th) Do the subtraction and take away the parentheses. Behold your answer.	− 5	+ 5

Simplify using the mixed-sign rule:

a) + 4 − 11
b) − 3 + 9
c) + 13 − 5
d) − 17 + 6
e) − 30 + 40

Answers:
a) − 7
b) + 6
c) + 8
d) − 11
e) + 10

Q: What's an easy way to make sense of what I'm doing when I use the mixed-sign rule?

 Think of the mixed-sign rule as a tug-of-war.

From life, you know that there are positive and negative forces in the world. You can think of the mixed-sign rule as a tug-of-war between the positive forces and the negative forces.

To see an example, look at the problem: $-3 + 8 = +5$. Imagine an actual tug-of-war. Consider the "-3" as three people pulling for the negative team; consider the "$+8$" as eight people pulling for the positive team. If all people are equally strong, it's obvious that the positive team will win because it has five more people pulling than the negative team has. And that's why the answer to this problem is $+5$. It's **positive** because the positive team wins; it's **5** because the positive team has five more people than the negative team.

Apply this thinking whenever you use the mixed-sign rule. It always works.

To get the answer's sign, put down the sign of the team that wins the tug-of-war.

To get the answer's numerical value, see how many more people are on the winning team than are on the losing team, and put that number down after the sign.

Now I understand the same-sign rule and the mixed-sign rule. But what do I do when I have a problem with a whole bunch of positive signs and negative signs, a problem like this:

$$- 4 + 7 - 9 + 10 + 2 - 8$$

A: Follow these steps:

1st) **Gr**oup positives with positives and negatives with negatives.
2nd) Use the **S**ame-sign rule.
3rd) Use the **M**ixed-sign rule. You can remember these steps because they use the letters **Gr-S-M**, found in the phrase: "**Gr**eat **S**trawberry **M**ousse."

Simplify:

$$- 4 + 7 - 9 + 10 + 2 - 8$$

Steps

1st) **Gr**oup positives with positives; group negatives with negatives.

2nd) Use **S**ame-sign rule (**pp. 36-38**) on the positive group and on the negative group.

3rd) Use the **M**ixed-sign rule (**pp. 39-41**).

Example

$$- 4 + 7 - 9 + 10 + 2 - 8$$
$$= + 7 + 10 + 2 \qquad - 4 - 9 - 8$$

$$+ 7 + 10 + 2 \qquad - 4 - 9 - 8$$
$$= + (7 + 10 + 2) \qquad - (4 + 9 + 8)$$
$$= + 19 \qquad - 21$$

$$+ 19 \qquad - 21$$
$$= - (21 - 19)$$
$$= - 2$$

Simplify:

a) $- 3 + 6 - 9 + 4$
b) $+ 2 - 11 - 4 + 15$
c) $- 1 + 3 - 3 + 1 - 5$
d) $- 6 + 7 - 9 - 14 + 26 - 32$
e) $- 67 + 38 - 29 + 14 + 12 - 41 + 85$

Answers:
a) $- 2$
b) $+ 2$
c) $- 5$
d) $- 28$
e) $+ 12$

Q:
When do I use the neighbor-sign rule?
Why is it called the neighbor-sign rule?
And what is actually
happening when I use this rule?

A:
The neighbor-sign rule is the rule to use when two signs stand next to each other with no numbers in between.

In textbooks, it appears either with parentheses, like this: $a - (+ c)$, or without parentheses, like this: $a - + c$

This rule gets its name because the signs are so close, you could view them as **next-door neighbors** in Algebraville.

How does the rule work? In short, **the two signs merge to become one sign**. To make sense of this rule, it helps to give meaning to the signs. Here's how ...

First sign
If the first sign is " + ", it means:
    You **get** something.

If the first sign is " − ", it means:
    You **lose** something.

Second sign
If the second sign is " + ", it means:
    What you get or lose is **something good**.

If the second sign is " − ", it means:
    What you get or lose is **something bad**.

On the next page you'll see how to put these ideas together using mini-stories.

Tell the meaning of these signs:

a) first sign is negative
b) second sign is positive
c) second sign is negative
d) first sign is positive

Answers:
a) you lose something
b) what you get or lose is good
c) what you get or lose is bad
d) you get something

Q: How do I put these ideas together so that I can actually use the neighbor-sign rule?

A: There are four patterns for the neighbor-sign rule. Using the ideas on the last page, you can think of these patterns as mini-stories.

A " + " sign followed by a " + " sign means:
"You **get** something **good**."
Since that's a **positive** development,

+ + **turns into** +

Example

$$a + (+ c)$$
$$= a + c$$

A " − " sign followed by a " + " sign means:
"You **lose** something that was **good**."
Since that's a **negative** development,

− + **turns into** −

Example

$$a - (+ c)$$
$$= a - c$$

A " + " sign followed by a " − " sign means:
"You **get** something **bad**."
Since that's a **negative** development,

+ − **turns into** −

Example

$$a + (- c)$$
$$= a - c$$

A " − " sign followed by a " − " sign means:
"You **lose** something that was **bad**." In other words,
you lose something you're happy to be rid of. Since that's a **positive** development,

− − **turns into** +

Example

$$a - (- c)$$
$$= a + c$$

Q: Doesn't sound too hard, but again, what are the actual steps for working out the neighbor-sign rule?

 A: **Just follow the four steps below.**

Simplify: A) 9 + − 5, B) 10 − − 3

Steps	**Example A**	**Example B**
1st) Notice the two neighboring signs.	9 + − 5 Neighboring signs are: + −	10 − − 3 Neighboring signs are: − −
2nd) Using the patterns described above, ask what sign will these two signs become?	+ − **turns into** −	− − **turns into** +
3rd) Change the two signs into one sign.	9 + − 5 becomes 9 − 5	10 − − 3 becomes 10 + 3
4th) Then work out your answer.	9 − 5 = 4	10 + 3 = 13

Simplify using the neighbor-sign rule:
a) $13 - (-4)$
b) $17 + (-8)$
c) $2 - (+6)$
d) $3 + (+9)$
e) $5 + (-11)$

Answers:
a) + 17
b) 9 +
c) − 4
d) 12 +
e) − 6

Q: Let me see if I have this straight. When I use the neighbor-sign rule, the two signs turn into one sign, and that sign is the sign of the answer. Right?

A: No, no, erase that little thought from your mental blackboard. Many people **wrongly** think that the sign which the two signs turn into must be the sign of the answer. But actually the sign the two signs turn into has **no bearing** on the sign of the answer. The answer can either have this sign, or it can have the opposite sign. Look below to see examples illustrating this idea.

The sign the two signs turn into just happens to be the sign of the answer.

$$8 + - 11$$
$$= 8 - 11$$
$$= - 3$$

Here the two signs turn into a **negative** sign, and the final answer happens to be **negative**.

The sign the two signs turn into is not the sign of the answer.

$$8 + - 3$$
$$= 8 - 3$$
$$= + 5$$

Here the two signs turn into a **negative** sign, but the final answer is **positive**.

So again, the lesson you need to etch into your mind is this:
The sign the two signs turn into is not necessarily the sign of the answer.

Q: Often I can't tell whether I'm dealing with the neighbor-sign rule, or with the same- or mixed-sign rule. Is there any way to spot the neighbor-sign rule at a glance?

A: Yes. Just look at the order of signs and numbers. Remember: the neighbor-sign rule gets its name because the two signs are next-door neighbors. That means **there's no number standing between the two signs**. For example, in: **3 − − 8**, **no number** stands between the two negative signs. But with the same- and mixed-sign rules, a number **always** stands between the two signs.

As you can see to the right ...

Same-sign rule

$$+\, 3 + 8$$

Here the **3** stands between the two " + " signs.

Mixed-sign rule

$$+\, 3 - 8$$

Here the **3** stands between the " + " and " − " signs.

Tell which rule you need to use in these problems:

a) 6 + − 3   e) − 11 + 7
b) + 6 + 3   f) 11 − − 7
c)   + 6 − 3   g) − 7 − 11
d) 3 − + 6   h) − 7 + 11

Answers:
a) neighbor   e) mixed
b) same   f) neighbor
c) mixed   g) same
d) neighbor   h) mixed

 **Suppose I'm given a problem in which I have to use all three rules: same, mixed, and neighbor. In what order should I use the rules to find the answer to this kind of problem:**

$$- 3 + + 7 + 4 - 6 - + 9$$

A: You follow the same order you learned above (**p. 42**), only you add the neighbor-sign rule as the rule you use first. So the order is: **N**eighbor, **Gr**oup, **S**ame, **M**ixed. Recall this order with the letters: **N-Gr-S-M.** "**N**ate's **Gr**eat **S**trawberry **M**ousse"

Follow the steps to the right.

Simplify:

$$- 3 + + 7 + 4 - 6 - + 9$$

Steps	**Example**
1st) Use **N**eighbor-sign rule (**pp. 43-45**).	$- 3 + + 7 + 4 - 6 - + 9$ $= - 3 \ + 7 + 4 - 6 \ - 9$
2nd) Group positives; group negatives (**p. 42**).	$= + 7 + 4 \qquad - 3 - 6 - 9$
3rd) Use **S**ame-sign rule (**pp. 36-38**).	$= + (7 + 4) \qquad - (3 + 6 + 9)$ $= + 11 \qquad\qquad - 18$
4th) Use **M**ixed-sign rule (**pp. 39-41**).	$= - (18 - 11)$ $= - 7$

Simplify:

a) $- 2 - - 3 + - 4 - 10$
b) $16 + + 5 - 7 - - 8$
c) $21 - + 3 + + 2 - - 7$
d) $2 - + 31 + - 6 - 4 + 9$
e) $- 7 - - 3 - + 9 + - 8$

Answers:
a) $- 13$
b) $+ 22$
c) $+ 27$
d) $- 30$
e) $- 21$

Q: What does the multiplication rule say?

$$(+) \cdot (+) = \textbf{?}$$

$$(+) \cdot (-) = \textbf{?}$$

$$(-) \cdot (-) = \textbf{?}$$

$$(-) \cdot (+) = \textbf{?}$$

 A: The multiplication rule says this:

When you multiply two numbers with the same sign, the answer is positive. When you multiply two numbers with different signs, the answer is negative.

Multiplication rule

$$(+) \cdot (+) = +$$

ex.: $(+8) \cdot (+3) = + (8 \cdot 3)$
$= + 24$

$$(+) \cdot (-) = -$$

ex.: $(+8) \cdot (-3) = - (8 \cdot 3)$
$= - 24$

$$(-) \cdot (-) = +$$

ex.: $(-8) \cdot (-3) = + (8 \cdot 3)$
$= + 24$

$$(-) \cdot (+) = -$$

ex.: $(-8) \cdot (+3) = - (8 \cdot 3)$
$= - 24$

Solve using the multiplication rule:

a) $(+4) \cdot (-3)$
b) $(-7) \cdot (-9)$
c) $(+16) \cdot (+11)$
d) $(-8) \cdot (+13)$
e) $(-17) \cdot (-5)$

Answers:
a) $- 12$
b) $+ 63$
c) $+ 176$
d) $- 104$
e) $+ 85$

49

Now I undertand how to use the rule when I'm multiplying two numbers. But what do I do when I multiply more than two numbers and those numbers have a mixture of positive and negative signs? In other words, how would I find the answer to a problem like this:

$$(+7) \cdot (-3) \cdot (-5) \cdot (+2)$$

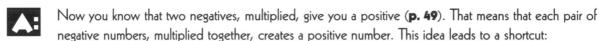

Now you know that two negatives, multiplied, give you a positive (**p. 49**). That means that each pair of negative numbers, multiplied together, creates a positive number. This idea leads to a shortcut:

- **If the number of negative signs is even (a multiple of 2), the answer will be positive.**
- **But if the number of negative signs is odd, the answer will be negative.**

Examples of the rule for multiplying a string of numbers

$(-3) \cdot (+2) \cdot (+5) = -30$	$(-3) \cdot (-2) \cdot (+5) = +30$	$(-3) \cdot (-2) \cdot (-5) = -30$
Here there's **one** negative number. That's an **odd** number of negatives, so the answer is **negative**.	Here there are **two** negative numbers. That's an **even** number of negatives, so the answer is **positive**.	Here there are **three** negative numbers. That's an **odd** number of negatives, so the answer is **negative**.

Solve:

a) $(-5) \cdot (+2) \cdot (-4)$

b) $(-1) \cdot (-1) \cdot (-1) \cdot (-1)$

c) $(-1) \cdot (+2) \cdot (+3) \cdot (+4)$

d) $(-3) \cdot (-2) \cdot (+4)$

e) $(+8) \cdot (-2) \cdot (+3)$

Answers:
a) + 40
b) + 1
c) − 24
d) + 24
e) − 48

Q: What does the division rule say?

$$+/+ = ?$$

$$+/- = ?$$

$$-/- = ?$$

$$-/+ = ?$$

A: The division rule mimics the multiplication rule. It says this: **When you divide two numbers with the same sign, the answer is positive. When you divide two numbers with different signs, the answer is negative.**

Division rule

$$+/+ = +$$

ex.: $+24/+3 = +24/3$
$= +8$

$$+/- = -$$

ex.: $+24/-3 = -24/3$
$= -8$

$$-/- = +$$

ex.: $-24/-3 = +24/3$
$= +8$

$$-/+ = -$$

ex.: $-24/+3 = -24/3$
$= -8$

Simplify:

a) $+15/-3$ d) $-36/9$
b) $-8/-20$ e) $7/-28$
c) $+63/+7$

Answers:
a) -5 d) -4
b) $+2/5$ e) $-1/4$
c) $+9$

Q: Since terms like

$$\frac{+a}{-c}, \quad \frac{-a}{+c} \quad \text{and} \quad -\frac{a}{c}$$

look different, they must have different values, true?

A: No, false. They are all equal.

Since the division rule says that both a negative divided by a positive and a positive divided by a negative will come out negative,

$$\frac{+a}{-c}, \quad \frac{-a}{+c} \quad \text{and} \quad -\frac{a}{c}$$

are just three ways of writing the same quantity.

In terms of actual numbers, this means that fractions like

$$\frac{+3}{-5}, \quad \frac{-3}{+5} \quad \text{and} \quad -\frac{3}{5}$$

are all equal.

Note: the simplest form, which teachers usually will ask you to use to write such fractions, is with the negative sign out front, like this:

$$-\frac{a}{c} \quad \text{or} \quad -\frac{3}{5}$$

Simplify using the rules for positive and negative numbers:

a) $-3-11$
b) $+3+5+6+9$
c) $-4+11$
d) $-2+6-7+9$
e) $9-+2$
f) $8+-3-10+6-+2$
g) $(-3) \cdot (+5)$
h) $(-2) \cdot (+6) \cdot (-4)$
j) $+5/-20$
k) $-11+19-31+46$
l) $(+4) \cdot (-2) \cdot (+1) \cdot (+3)$
m) $-1-9-6-7-3$

n) $+6+17$
p) $(-8) \cdot (-11)$
q) $8--16$
r) $-60/-6$
s) $+2-38$
t) $-2--3-+7-3--4$
u) $12++46$
v) $+16+14+21+29$
w) $15/25$
x) $-9++20-17+-19-11$
y) $-23-48$
z) $(+6) \cdot (-31)$

A) $+31-82+67-100$
B) $(-3) \cdot (+6) \cdot (10) \cdot (-4)$
C) $-46+57$
D) $17+-27$
E) $-38-47$
F) $(+12) \cdot (+9)$
G) $+170-130$
H) $+206+483$
J) $-31+-14--6+-9-14$
K) $-240+360-180-290$
L) $-63/9$
M) $(+1) \cdot (-2) \cdot (+3) \cdot (-4) \cdot (+5)$

a) -14
b) $+23$
c) $+7$
d) $+6$
e) $+7$
f) -1
g) -15
h) $+48$
j) $-1/4$
k) $+23$
l) -24
m) -26

n) $+23$
p) $+88$
q) $+24$
r) $+10$
s) -36
t) -5
u) $+58$
v) $+80$
w) $+3/5$
x) -36
y) -71
z) -186

A) -84
B) $+720$
C) $+11$
D) -10
E) -85
F) $+108$
G) $+40$
H) $+689$
J) -62
K) -350
L) -7
M) $+120$

Order of Operations & Like Terms

you need this ... operations? T... way. If you were a member of an organization that uses codes and secret messages, you'd need to be sure that if you sent someone a message, she or he could decode it properly. It

What is the order of operations, and why do I need to learn it?

A: The order of operations is the order that tells you what to do first, then second, then third, etc. when you're simplifying an algebraic expression. In other words, if you ever find yourself scratching your head, wondering what you're supposed to do next — multiplication? subtraction? exponents? parentheses? — go back to the trusty old order of operations and you'll find your answer.

Why do you need this order of operations? Think of it this way. If you were a member of an organization that uses codes and secret messages, you'd need to be sure that if you sent someone a message, she or he could decode it properly. It would be pretty awful to send someone the message: "Meet me at 10 Oak Street at 4 p.m. with 2 of your buddies," only to have it read as "Meet me at 4 Oak Street at 2 p.m. with 10 of your buddies." Mathematical expressions are a little like secret messages. When someone in math writes out a statement like: $10 + 4 \cdot 2$, s/he needs to make sure that this is decoded accurately. A person who doesn't know the order of operations wouldn't know whether to read $10 + 4 \cdot 2$ as $14 \cdot 2$ or as $10 + 8$. Only one of these choices is correct. Do you know which one? If not, don't worry; you'll soon find out.

In any case, the point is that you learn the order of operations so you know how to send and receive mathematical messages accurately.

What are the steps in the order of operations?

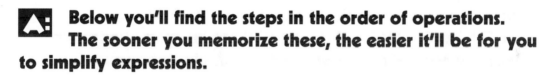 **Below you'll find the steps in the order of operations. The sooner you memorize these, the easier it'll be for you to simplify expressions.**

1st) Work out operations in **parentheses** or other enclosure marks (brackets, absolute value signs, etc.), working from the innermost enclosure marks to the outermost ones.

2nd) Raise terms to **exponents**.

3rd) Perform all **multiplication** and **division** operations, doing whichever operation comes first as you work from left to right.

4th) Use the **neighbor-sign rule**.

5th) Group positive numbers with positives and negatives with negatives.

6th) Use the **same-sign rule**.

7th) Use the **mixed-sign rule** to get your answer.

> **Note:** If you don't yet know how to raise numbers to exponents, just look at the first page of the Exponents section (**p. 86**), and you'll find out how.

Q: That's great, but how am I supposed to memorize all these steps? Is there any trick for remembering the order of operations?

A: Yes, there's a memory trick. And if you've read through the section on Positive and Negative Numbers, you already know the last half of the trick. But now you get the whole sentence:

Please **E**at **M**ore **D**essert — **N**ate's **Gr**eat **S**trawberry **M**ousse.

P stands for **P**arentheses.

E stands for **E**xponents.

M stands for **M**ultiplication.

D stands for **D**ivision.

N stands for **N**eighbor-sign rule.

Gr stands for **Gr**ouping.

S stands for **S**ame-sign rule.

M stands for **M**ixed-sign rule.

For those of you who've never had the pleasure, mousse is a light, airy dessert. Some people describe mousse as "pudding with wings."

Q: What exactly does it mean that one operation comes before another in the order of operations? And could I see some examples showing how the order of operations actually works?

A: The fact that one operation is listed before another operation simply means that you do the first operation before the second operation.

For example, the fact that **P** comes before **E** in the list means that you always work out terms inside parentheses before raising terms to their exponents. Here are some examples showing how you use the order of operations in actual problems.

Parentheses before exponents		**Exponents before multiplication**		**Multiplication before mixed-sign rule**	
<u>right</u>	<u>wrong</u>	<u>right</u>	<u>wrong</u>	<u>right</u>	<u>wrong</u>
$(2 + 3)^2$	$(2 + 3)^2$	$4 \cdot 3^2$	$4 \cdot 3^2$	$-3 \cdot 4 + 2 \cdot 8$	$-3 \cdot 4 + 2 \cdot 8$
$= (5)^2$	$= 2^2 + 3^2$	$= 4 \cdot 9$	$= 12^2$	$= -12 + 16$	$= -3 \cdot (4 + 2) \cdot 8$
$= 25$		$= 36$		$= +(16 - 12)$	
				$= +4$	

Tell which operation comes before which other one, then simplify:

a) $(7 + 1) \cdot (8 \div 2)$

b) $(20 - 15)^2$

c) $+ 4^2 - 25$

d) $- 15/3 - 11$

e) $- 3 + 4 - 6 + 7$

Answers:

a) parentheses before multiplication: 32

b) parentheses before exponents: 25

c) exponents before mixed-sign rule: − 9

d) division before same-sign rule: − 16

e) grouping before same-sign rule: 2

Q: One question about parentheses ...
I've heard that the word "parentheses" means more than just standard parentheses. What exactly is included in the concept of parentheses?

A: Right. When you hear "parentheses," remember that it means **all marks that enclose a quantity to set it off from other quantities.** So the term parentheses includes not only normal parentheses: ( ), but also these marks: [ ] , { } , and even absolute value marks, | |.

Often you'll see enclosure marks inside enclosure marks, like boxes inside boxes. When you see this, **compute whatever is within the innermost enclosure marks first, then work your way out.** For example, suppose you have this expression:

$$5 \cdot \left\{ 2 + 3 \cdot \left[12 - \left(16 \div 2 \right) \right] \right\}$$

First see which enclosure mark is innermost. Obviously that's parentheses: ( ). So you'd compute the quantity in parentheses first. Then you'd work out the quantity in the next innermost marks, angular brackets: [ ]. Finally you'd work out the quantity inside the remaining enclosure marks, curved brackets: { }.

After working out that quantity, multiply it by the **5** to the left of the curved brackets to get your answer.

Don't simplify. Just tell which enclosure marks you'd work out first, second and third in the following problems:

a) $\left(18 + \left[\left\{ 12 - 2 \right\} \div 5 \right] \right)$

b) $\left[14 \div \left\{ 8 + \left(3 \cdot 2 \right) \right\} \right]$

c) $\left\{ 26 - \left| \left(4 \cdot 3 \right) - 8 \right| \right\}$

Answers:
a) 1st { }, 2nd [ ], 3rd ( )
b) 1st ( ), 2nd { }, 3rd [ ]
c) 1st ( ), 2nd | |, 3rd { }

Q: Now I get the basic idea for working with enclosure marks. But what would these steps look like in an actual problem?

A: Below you'll see just such an example.   Simplify: $4 \cdot \left[18 - \left\{(12 \div 2) + 4\right\}\right]$

<u>Steps</u>	<u>Think it out</u>	<u>Work it out</u>
1st) Identify the innermost enclosure marks, compute the value and plug it in.	Innermost is $(12 \div 2)$ $12 \div 2 = 6$	$4 \cdot \left[18 - \left\{(12 \div 2) + 4\right\}\right]$ $= 4 \cdot \left[18 - \left\{6 + 4\right\}\right]$
2nd) Identify next innermost enclosure marks, compute the value, plug it in.	Next is $\left\{6 + 4\right\}$ $6 + 4 = 10$	$4 \cdot \left[18 - \left\{6 + 4\right\}\right]$ $= 4 \cdot \left[18 - 10\right]$
3rd) Identify final enclosure marks, compute the value, plug it in. Then work out your answer.	Final is $\left[18 - 10\right]$ $18 - 10 = 8$	$4 \cdot \left[18 - 10\right]$ $= 4 \cdot 8$ $= 32$

Now you try. Simplify using the inner-to-outer order for enclosure marks:

a) $3 \cdot \left\{24 - \left[2 + (5 \cdot 2)\right]\right\}$

b) $6\left[4\left\{2 + (3 \cdot 1)\right\} + 2(8 - 3)\right]$

c) $7\left[(2 + 3) \cdot (2 - 3)\right]$

Answers:
a) 36
b) 180
c) − 35

61

How do I actually perform all the steps in the order of operations?

A: The following problem — **and yes, it's a doozy!** — shows how to use all the steps in the order of operations. Keep in mind that few problems would require you to use **all** these steps.

Simplify using the order of operations: $+ \, 2[8 - 4] - (+3) + 5^2 - 20 \div 2$

<u>Steps</u>	<u>Example</u>	<u>Steps</u>	<u>Example</u>
Parentheses	$+ \, 2[8 - 4] - (+3) + 5^2 - 20 \div 2$	**Neighbor-sign rule**	$= \quad + \, 8 - 3 + 25 - 10$
	$= \quad + \, 2[4] - (+3) + 5^2 - 20 \div 2$	**Grouping**	$= \quad + \, 8 + 25 \quad - 3 - 10$
Exponents	$= \quad + \, 2[4] - (+3) + 25 - 20 \div 2$	**Same-sign rule**	$= \quad + (8 + 25) \quad - (3 + 10)$
Multiplication	$= \quad + \, 8 - (+3) + 25 - 20 \div 2$		$= \quad + \, 33 \qquad\quad - 13$
Division	$= \quad + \, 8 - (+3) + 25 - 10$	**Mixed-sign rule**	$= \quad + (33 - 13)$
			$= \quad + \, 20$

Now try using the order of operations yourself:

a) $8^2 - (-10) + 25 \div 5$

b) $3[4^2 - (5 + 2)]$

c) $8 - (-3) + (-4) - 3(10 - 7)$

d) $(-2) \cdot (-3) + 6\{(12 \div 6) + 2\}$

e) $7 + 2[(10 - 8)(5 - 2) - 4] - 3^2$

Answers:
a) 79
b) 27
c) − 2
d) 30
e) 2

Q: Since "M" comes before "D" in the sentence, that must mean I always do multiplication before division. Right?

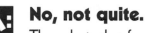

A: **No, not quite.**

The rule is that for multiplication and division, you do whichever operation comes first as you read the problem from left to right. If multiplication comes first, you multiply first. But if division comes first, you divide first.

Examples of multiplication and division in the order of operations

$$20 \times 4 \div 2$$
$$= 80 \div 2$$
$$= 40$$

Here you do multiplication before division because the times sign comes first as you read from left to right.

$$20 \div 4 \times 2$$
$$= 5 \times 2$$
$$= 10$$

But here you do division before multiplication because the division sign comes first as you read from left to right.

Try these yourself to see if the order of signs makes a difference:

a) $8 \div 2 \times 4$
b) $2 \times 4 \div 8$
c) $6 \times 5 \div 10$
d) $10 \div 5 \times 6$

Answers:
a) 16
b) 1
c) 3
d) 12

... your problems solved

Q: If I see terms like $2 \cdot 3^2$ and $(2 \cdot 3)^2$, I would work these out in exactly the same way. I mean, those silly parentheses don't really affect how I'd work it out, right?

A: Aaaaaagh! No! The "silly" parentheses make all the difference in the world.

Since exponents are worked out before multiplication,

$$2 \cdot 3^2$$
$$= 2 \cdot 9$$
$$= 18$$

Since parentheses are worked out before exponents,

$$(2 \cdot 3)^2$$
$$= 6^2$$
$$= 36$$

Moral of the story: $2 \cdot 3^2 \neq (2 \cdot 3)^2$

Other Examples

$2x^2 \neq (2x)^2$

Why?

$2x^2 = 2x^2$

But

$(2x)^2 = (2x) \cdot (2x) = 4x^2$

$4a^3 \neq (4a)^3$

Why?

$4a^3 = 4a^3$

But

$(4a)^3 = (4a) \cdot (4a) \cdot (4a) = 64a^3$

So $(2x)^2 \neq 2x^2$ and $(4a)^3 \neq 4a^3$.

So remember: when you have a quantity in parentheses raised to an exponent, the parentheses make a huge difference!

Q: There's no difference in order of operations between a term like -3^2 and one like $\left(-3\right)^2$. Isn't that true?

A: Actually, there's a big difference between these two terms.

Since you work out exponents before multiplying, the following is true:

$$-3^2$$
$$= -\left(3^2\right)$$
$$= -\left(9\right)$$
$$= -9$$

Note that putting the negative sign before the **9** in the last step is the same thing as multiplying by **−1**.

But here the parentheses around the -3 mean that this -3 is treated as one unit. So all you need to do here is work out the exponent, as follows:

$$\left(-3\right)^2$$
$$= \left(-3\right) \cdot \left(-3\right)$$
$$= +9$$

Moral of the story: $-3^2 \neq \left(-3\right)^2$

A similar example with a variable

$$-a^2$$
$$= -\left(a^2\right)$$
$$= -a^2$$

but

$$\left(-a\right)^2$$
$$= \left(-a\right) \cdot \left(-a\right)$$
$$= +a^2$$

Moral of this story: $-a^2 \neq \left(-a\right)^2$

So keep this in mind: when you have a term raised to an exponent, a negative sign inside parentheses has a different effect than a negative sign outside parentheses.

What are people talking about when they talk about "like terms"?

"Like terms" is math-talk for terms that represent the same kinds of things. Since like terms stand for the same kinds of things, you're allowed to add them to each other and subtract them from each other. This is virtually impossible to understand without examples, so here are a few:

Like terms	Why are these like terms?	Unlike terms	Why are these unlike terms?
2, – 4, 3, 0, 1/7	All are number terms.	3, y	First is a number term; second is a **y** term.
2a, – 3a, a/2	All are **a** terms.	4, 2a	First is a number term; second is an **a** term.
ac, ca, – 3ac	All are terms with **a** and **c**.	2a, 2c	First is an **a** term; second is a **c** term.
acm, mca, 4mca	All are terms with **a**, **c** and **m**.	4acm, 3ac	First is a term with **a**, **c** and **m**; second is a term with just **a** and **c**.
a²m, ma², aam	All are terms with two **a**'s and one **m**.	a²m, am²	First has two **a**'s and one **m**; second has two **m**'s and one **a**.

Q: What are the guidelines that tell me whether or not I'm working with like terms?

 Look below. These three simple guidelines will let you know at a glance.

a) All numbers are like terms.

Examples

$2, -7, 1/3, -.62$, and **478**

are all like terms

b) All terms with the same combination of variables are like terms, whether or not the variables are in the same order.

Examples

ax^2 and x^2a are like terms

ac and **ca** are like terms

c) A variable term standing alone and the same term with a number in front are like terms.

Examples

ac and **2ac** are like terms;

4xma and **axm** are like terms

Note: whenever a variable term has no number before it, be aware that there's actually an invisible **1** before it.

That is, **ac** means **1ac**; x^2y means $1x^2y$, etc.

Tell whether or not these terms are like terms:

a) $-3, .49, 4/11$
b) xy, 7xy, 300yx
c) 12mrp, 6pr, 9mr
d) $p^2q^2, q^2p^2, 7qp$
e) fgh, ghf, hgf

Answers:
a) like terms
b) like terms
c) not like terms
d) not like terms
e) like terms

Q: Does a number in front of a variable or string of variables affect whether or not I have like terms?

A: No. The number simply tells you how many of that term you have.

<u>Example</u>

7ac and **ac** are like terms.

ac means **1ac**, while **7ac** means **7ac**'s

When you do simple addition and subtraction with such terms, this becomes more clear.

$$7ac + ac = 8ac$$
$$7ac - ac = 6ac$$

Add or subtract the like terms:
a) 9b + b
b) 13xyz − xyz
c) pq + pq
d) y + y + y + y
e) qrs − qrs

Answers:
a) 10b
b) 12xyz
c) 2pq
d) 4y
e) 0 (meaning " zero")

Q: Terms like ac and ca don't seem like they should be considered like terms because they look different. What guarantees that these really are the same kinds of things?

A: If you think about it, the commutative property (p. 12) guarantees that ac and ca are in fact like terms.

Since the commutative property holds true for multiplication,

$$a \times c = c \times a$$

which means that:

$$ac = ca$$

This means that two strings of variables can be like terms even if the order of letters is switched around.

More examples of bizarre-looking like terms

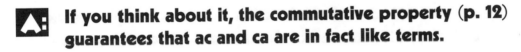

ax^2m and mx^2a

xna and $7axn$

$5mrv$ and $7rvm$

Q: What's an easy way to understand why like terms may be combined through addition and subtraction?

A: If you stretch your mind and think of like terms as things you can touch or hold, the rules for combining them start to make sense.

Most sane people would agree that: **2 cats** + **3 cats** = **5 cats** . Why? Because cats are cats. They're the same kind of thing; therefore they can be combined, or grouped together.

Most sane people also would agree that: **2 cats** + **3 dogs** = **2 cats** + **3 dogs** . Here we don't get a single answer on the right side because cats and dogs are different kinds of things, and therefore they can't be combined.

Now if we just let the letter **c** stands for cat, and the letter **d** stands for dog, we could write the same ideas algebraically, like this:

2c + 3c = 5c   but   **2c + 3d = 2c + 3d**

Like terms are just like cats or dogs; they are the same kind of thing, and that is why they can be combined.

Tip: be creative — try to think of variables as real things. For example, in a problem like: **4x + 2x** , you might imagine that **4x** stands for **four eggs**. Then the problem would read: **four eggs** + **two eggs** . Obviously in real life this would equal **six eggs**, so the answer in algebra is **6x**.

(Hmmm ... what real thing could you say "xyz" stands for? Be as creative as you dare.)

Q: Now I understand why like terms can be combined. But does that mean they can be combined using the same-sign rule, the mixed-sign rule and the neighbor-sign rule?

A: Yes, like terms can be combined using all three of these rules.

Below you'll find examples demonstrating this idea.

Same-sign rule	Mixed-sign rule	Neighbor-sign rule

Same-sign rule

$- 3a - 5a$
$= - (3a + 5a)$
$= - 8a$

$+ 3a + 5a$
$= + (3a + 5a)$
$= + 8a$

Mixed-sign rule

$+ 3pq - 8pq$
$= - (8pq - 3pq)$
$= - 5pq$

$- 3pq + 8pq$
$= + (8pq - 3pq)$
$= + 5pq$

Neighbor-sign rule

$9v + + 5v$
$= 9v + 5v$
$= 14v$

$9v + - 5v$
$= 9v - 5v$
$= 4v$

$9v - - 5v$
$= 9v + 5v$
$= 14v$

$9v - + 5v$
$= 9v - 5v$
$= 4v$

Simplify:

a) $- 3ab - 4ab$

b) $8x^2 - - 2x^2$

c) $- 7xyz + 10xyz$

d) $13a^2b + - 4a^2b$

e) $+ pv - 10pv$

f) $+ 6rs + 11rs$

Answers:

a) $- 7ab$ d) $9a^2b$
b) $10x^2$ e) $- 9pv$
c) $3xyz$ f) $17rs$

Q: O.K., now I understand how to combine like terms with the same-, mixed- and neighbor-sign rules. But what do I do when I have various kinds of like terms in the same problem? In other words, how would I simplify something like this:

$$6v - + 2xy - - 8v + 4xy$$

A: You would use **N**ate's **Gr**eat **S**trawberry **M**ousse once again, as shown to the right.

Simplify:

$$6v - + 2xy - - 8v + 4xy$$

Steps	**Example**
1st) Use the **N**eighbor-sign rule (**pp. 43-45**).	$6v - + 2xy - - 8v + 4xy$ $= 6v - 2xy + 8v + 4xy$
2nd) **Gr**oup like terms (**p. 42**).	$= 6v + 8v \qquad - 2xy + 4xy$
3rd) Use **S**ame-sign rule (**pp. 36-38**).	$= + \left(6v + 8v\right) \quad - 2xy + 4xy$ $= + 14v \qquad - 2xy + 4xy$
4th) Use **M**ixed-sign rule (**pp. 39-41**).	$= + 14v \qquad + \left(4xy - 2xy\right)$ $= + 14v + 2xy$

Try simplifying these expressions:

a) $8a + + 9c - + 2a - 5c$

b) $2 - - 3x + 7 - 4x$

c) $- 5rs - + z - 8z + - 6rs + 4z$

d) $- 1 - x + - 1 + x - - 1$

e) $y + - z - + z - - y$

Answers:
a) $6a + 4c$
b) $9 - x$
c) $- 11rs - 5z$
d) $- 1$
e) $2y - 2z$

72

There's still one situation that confuses me. It's when I have a positive or a negative sign in front of a bunch of terms inside an enclosure mark, like a parenthesis. How do I simplify expressions like:

$$+ \left(a - 7 \right)$$

and

$$- \left(a - 7 \right)$$

Good question, for this is a point that befuddles even the clearest thinkers. The easiest way to simplify these tricky little expressions is to squeeze a tiny **1** between the sign and the parenthesis, and then to multiply using the distributive property. Here are the steps:

Simplify: A) $+ \left(a - 7 \right)$, B) $- \left(a - 7 \right)$

Steps	Example A	Example B
1st) Stick a **1** between the sign and the left bracket of the parenthesis.	$+ \left(a - 7 \right)$ **becomes** $+ 1\left(a - 7 \right)$	$- \left(a - 7 \right)$ **becomes** $- 1\left(a - 7 \right)$
2nd) Multiply using the distributive property (**pp. 15-16**) to get your answer.	$+ 1\left(a - 7 \right)$ $= + a - 7$	$- 1\left(a - 7 \right)$ $= - a + 7$

What puzzles people the most is that in **Example B**, the second term of the answer becomes positive. Here's why: when you use the distributive property, you actually multiply the $- 1$ before the parenthesis with the negative term in the parenthesis. And a negative times a negative is a positive (**p. 49**), so in this case the second term is positive.

Now try these:

a) $+ \left(x - 9 \right)$
b) $- \left(x - 9 \right)$
c) $+ \left(x + y - z \right)$
d) $- \left(x + y - z \right)$
e) $+ \left(17 - m \right)$

Answers:
a) x − 9
b) − x + 9
c) x + y − z
d) − x − y + z
e) 17 − m

What about situations in which a set of parentheses comes in the midst of a larger problem. How would I simplify problems like these:

$$9 + (a - 7)$$

$$9 - (a - 7)$$

Just remember the order of operations. It tells you to do multiplication before using the same- or mixed-sign rule.
Here are the steps:

Simplify: A) $9 + (a - 7)$, **B)** $9 - (a - 7)$

<u>Steps</u>	<u>Example A</u>	<u>Example B</u>
1st) Stick in the invisible **1** and multiply using the distributive property (**pp. 15-16**).	$9 + (a - 7)$ $= 9 + 1(a - 7)$ $= 9 + a - 7$	$9 - (a - 7)$ $= 9 - 1(a - 7)$ $= 9 - a + 7$
2nd) Group like terms, then combine terms using the same- or mixed-sign rule (**pp. 36-41**).	$= +9 - 7 + a$ $= +(9 - 7) + a$ $= +2 + a$	$= +9 + 7 - a$ $= +(9 + 7) - a$ $= +16 - a$

Now try these problems:

a) $11 + (c + 4)$
b) $11 - (c + 4)$
c) $13 - (d - 9)$
d) $13 - (d + 9)$
e) $14 - (x + 2)$

Answers:
a) $15 + c$
b) $7 - c$
c) $22 - d$
d) $4 - d$
e) $12 - x$

So if I can combine like terms using the same-, mixed-, and neighbor-sign rules, that means I can also combine like terms using the multiplication and division rules. What I'm saying is:

$$(2a) \cdot (3a) = 6a$$

and

$$8a/4a = 2a$$

Right?

 No, not in the least! The multiplication and division rules don't work for like terms. Here's why:

Multiplication rule

As you'll see in the Exponents section, a variable times itself does not equal the variable; instead, it equals that variable squared. To give an example,

$$a \cdot a \neq a$$

Instead,

$$a \cdot a = a^2$$

Since that's true,

$$(2a) \cdot (3a) \neq 6a$$

Instead,

$$(2a) \cdot (3a) = 6a^2$$

If you want more details on this, turn to **p. 86**.

Division rule

As you'll see in the Cancelling section, when a variable stands over itself in a fraction, it cancels itself out, and by doing so, it turns into **1**. As an example,

$$a/a \neq a$$

Instead,

$$a/a = 1$$

Since that's true,

$$8a/4a \neq 2a$$

Instead,

$$8\cancel{a}/4\cancel{a} = 8/4 = 2$$

If you want more details on this, turn to **pp. 168-171**.

try our "challenge" problem

Q:

Simplify using the order of operations:

a) $5 \cdot 4^2$

b) $3xyz - -9xyz$

c) $2\left[6 + \left\{(4 + 2) \div (3 - 1)\right\}\right]$

d) $-3a + +4b - -12a + -6b$

e) $5(7 - 3) \cdot (8 - 6)$

f) $-(a - 3 - 6y + b)$

g) $-3x^2 - 7x^2 - 4x^2 - 2x^2$

h) $5^2 - 2^2 + (-3)^2$

j) $40 \div 8 \cdot 2$

k) $16 - 12 \div 4$

l) $-9pq + 12pq$

m) $+rs + rs + 2rs + 3rs$

n) $+6uv^2 - 11uv^2$

p) $(2 + 1) \cdot (2 + 5) + -4$

q) $-x + 4p - 7x - (+6p)$

r) $6 - (x - 2)$

s) $7\left\{(3 + 2) \cdot 4\right\}$

t) $3\left[2 + \left\{(18 \div 2) \div 3\right\} \div 3\right]$

u) $9vr - (-3vr) - (+5vr)$

v) $2^2 \div 2 + 6^2 \cdot 1 - (3 + 6)^2$

w) $6 \cdot 9 \div 27$

Answer true or false:

x) $4b + 2b = 6b$

y) $-(b - 3) = -b - 3$

z) $-5^2 = (-5)^2$

A) $4a^2b$ and $3a^2b$ are like terms.

B) $10x/2x = 5x$

C) $4 + 2 \cdot 3 = 18$

D) $3x^2 = (3x)^2$

E) a^2b and b^2a are like terms.

F) $4x \cdot 2x = 8x$

G) $4 + 2 \cdot 3 = 10$

A:

a) 80

b) 12xyz

c) 18

d) 9a − 2b

e) 40

f) − a + 3 + 6y − b

g) − 16x²

h) 30

j) 10

k) 13

l) 3pq

m) 7rs

n) − 5uv²

p) 17

q) − 8x − 2p

r) 8 − x

s) 140

t) 9

u) 7vr

v) − 43

w) 2

x) true

y) false

z) false

A) true

B) false

C) false

D) false

E) false

F) false

G) true

When you're working with absolute value, you always need to work in absolute value fenceposts before doing anything else. Otherwise the **V.I.P** absolute value will get very irritated. And you'll lose points on your tests as well. Even when all you have is a sign in front of absolute value fenceposts, you still have to work out the absolute value before applying the sign. Here are two examples that you can try if you think you have begun to grasp the idea of absolute value

What's the symbol for absolute value? What is absolute value? And why is the absolute value of a number always positive?

The symbol for absolute value, | |, looks a little like two fenceposts that trap a number or a term. |3| is read as **"the absolute value of three"**; |x| is read as **"the absolute value of x,"** etc.

When you take the absolute value of a number, you're just figuring out the distance between that number and zero. In other words, the absolute value of **3** is the distance between **3** and **0**. The absolute value of − **10** is the distance between − **10** and **0**.

Illustrations of the idea of absolute value

The number **3** is three units is also three away from **0**, so

$$|3| = 3$$

The number − **3** is three units away from **0**, so

$$|-3| = 3$$

So what's this business about absolute value always being positive? Well, this has to do with the fact that **there's no such thing as negative distance**. Common sense says that if the drive to your friend's house is **3** miles, the drive back is also **3** miles, not − **3** miles. In other words, it makes no difference in which direction you travel; **distance is always positive**. Since the absolute value of any number is just its distance from zero, the absolute value of every number — even of negative numbers — is always **positive**.

Determine the value:

a) | 6 | d) | − 3/4 |

b) | − 6 | e) | − 500 |

c) | 3/4 |

Answers:
a) 6
b) 6
c) 3/4
d) 3/4
e) 500

Q: Now I see that the basic idea of absolute value isn't hard to grasp. But suppose I need to do some operations inside absolute value fenceposts. How do I do that? In other words, how would I work out an expression like this:

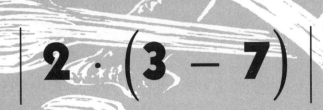

$$\left| 2 \cdot (3 - 7) \right|$$

A: Since absolute value is considered an enclosure mark, just as parentheses are, you would work out everything inside absolute value fenceposts **before** taking the absolute value of that quantity.

Examples of the order of operations for absolute value

$$\left| 2 \cdot (3 - 7) \right|$$
$$= \left| 2 \cdot (-4) \right|$$
$$= \left| -8 \right|$$
$$= 8$$

$$\left| 3 + -4 - +10 \right|$$
$$= \left| 3 - 4 - 10 \right|$$
$$= \left| 3 - 14 \right|$$
$$= \left| -11 \right|$$
$$= 11$$

$$\left| -15/-3 \right|$$
$$= \left| 15/3 \right|$$
$$= \left| 5 \right|$$
$$= 5$$

Notice that you take the absolute value only at the very end, after you've completely simplified the terms inside fenceposts. Remember the steps this way: **First)** Simplify inside fenceposts. **Then and only then)** Take absolute value.

Now try these:

a) $\left| 3 + 2 - 7 \right|$

b) $\left| (+3) \cdot (-6) \right|$

c) $\left| 4(2 - 9) \right|$

d) $\left| 63/7 \right|$

e) $\left| 7 - (3 \cdot 2) - 5 \right|$

Answers:
a) 2
b) 18
c) 28
d) 9
e) 4

Q: O.K. Now I see how to work out absolute value when I have a bunch of terms inside fenceposts. But what do I do when an absolute value term shows up in the midst of a larger problem?

A: You've heard of a **V**ery **I**mportant **P**erson, a **V.I.P.** That's someone who commands a lot of attention. Well, absolute value symbols are sort of a **V.I.P.** (**V**ery **I**mportant kind of **P**arenthesis) in algebra. They take a high priority. Since absolute value fenceposts are enclosure marks, they demand your attention ahead of the same-sign rule, the mixed-sign rule, the neighbor-sign rule, mulitplication, division or exponents. Below you'll see examples showing how you work out absolute value before the same- mixed- or neighbor-sign rules.

Absolute value before same-sign rule	**Absolute value before mixed-sign rule**	**Absolute value before neighbor-sign rule**
$+\,4 + \left\lvert\, 5 + 11\,\right\rvert$	$-\,4 + \left\lvert\, 3 - 8\,\right\rvert$	$-\,3 - \left\lvert\, -\,8\,\right\rvert$
$=\,+\,4 + \left\lvert\, 16\,\right\rvert$	$=\,-\,4 + \left\lvert\, -\,5\,\right\rvert$	$=\,-\,3 - \left(+\,8\right)$
$=\,+\,4 + 16$	$=\,-\,4 + 5$	$=\,-\,3 - 8$
$=\,+\left(4 + 16\right)$	$=\,+\left(5 - 4\right)$	$=\,-\,11$
$=\,+\,20$	$=\,+\,1$	

Now try these:

a) $+\,2 + \left\lvert\, 3 - 9\,\right\rvert$ d) $\left\lvert\, 4 - 13\,\right\rvert - 6$

b) $-\,6 + \left\lvert\, 2 \cdot 5\,\right\rvert$ e) $\left\lvert\,(5) \cdot (-\,4)\,\right\rvert - 40$

c) $-\,11 - \left\lvert\, 8 \div 4\,\right\rvert$ f) $\left\lvert\, 3 \cdot 7\,\right\rvert + 3$

Answers:
a) 8   b) 4   c) $-$ 13
d) 3   e) $-$ 20   f) 24

by visiting **www.AlgebraWizard.com**

Q: I'd also like to see examples that show how I'd work out absolute value before doing multiplication, division and exponents. What would the steps for these problems look like?

 A: See the three examples below.

Absolute value before multiplication	Absolute value before division	Absolute value before exponents
$4 \cdot \lvert 5 - 11 \rvert$	$\lvert 8 - 24 \rvert / 8$	$\left(\lvert 2 - 9 \rvert \right)^{2}$
$= 4 \cdot \lvert -6 \rvert$	$= \lvert -16 \rvert / 8$	$= \left(\lvert -7 \rvert \right)^{2}$
$= 4 \cdot 6$	$= 16/8$	$= (7)^{2}$
$= 24$	$= 2$	$= 49$

Now give these a try:

a) $6 \cdot \lvert 3 - 15 \rvert$ d) $\left(\lvert -2 \rvert \right)^{3}$

b) $\left(\lvert -4 \rvert \right)^{2}$ e) $-3 \cdot \lvert 6 \cdot 3 \rvert$

c) $\lvert 2 - 11 \rvert / -3$ f) $4 / \lvert 2 \cdot 6 \rvert$

Answers:
a) 72
b) 16
c) −3
d) 8
e) −54
f) 1/3

When I see what looks like the neighbor-sign rule with absolute value, I can just go ahead and use the neighbor-sign rule.

In other words, if I see:

$$8 - |-3|$$

I can use the old neighbor-sign rule to change the signs to:

$$8 + |3|$$

since the neighbor-sign rule says two negative signs become one positive sign. This is o.k., isn't it?

 NO! NO! NO! This breaks every rule in the absolute value book! Let's think this out again.

When you're working with absolute value, you always need to work out what's within absolute value fenceposts before doing anything else. Otherwise the **V.I.P** absolute value will get very irritated. And you'll lose points off on your tests as well.

Here's how to work out this problem:

$$8 - |-3|$$
$$= 8 - (3)$$
$$= 8 - 3$$
$$= 5$$

Even when all you have is a sign in front of absolute value fenceposts, you still have to **work out the absolute value before applying the sign.** Here are two examples:

$$+ |-7| \qquad\qquad - |-7|$$
$$= + (7) \qquad\qquad = - (7)$$
$$= + 7 \qquad\qquad = - 7$$

Now try these:

a) $9 - |-4|$

b) $11 + |+5|$

c) $6 - |+13|$

d) $- |-9|$

e) $+ |-7|$

f) $- |+17|$

Simplify these expressions using the rules for working with absolute value.

a) $\left| -9/10 \right|$

b) $6 - \left| 4 - 11 \right|$

c) $-5 - \left| 3 + 8 \right|$

d) $4/\left| 20 - 4 \right|$

e) $\left(\left| -5 \right| \right)^2$

f) $-19 + \left| 13 - 2 \right|$

g) $\left| 21/7 + 6 \cdot 2 \right|$

h) $-\left| -1 \right|$

j) $6 - \left| +15 \right|$

k) $3 \cdot \left| 2 - 12 \right|$

l) $14 + \left| 16 \right|$

m) $\left| 24 - 9 \right| \div 3$

n) $8 - \left| 12 - 3 \right|$

p) $13 - \left| +5 \right|$

q) $-\left| -17 \right| + 24$

r) $\left| -.0001 \right|$

s) $+\left| -10 \right|$

t) $8 - \left(\left| -2 \right| \right)^2$

u) $\left| (-2) \cdot \left\{ (11 + 7) \div 9 \right\} \right|$

v) $8 \cdot \left| -6 \right|$

a) 9/10

b) -1

c) -16

d) 1/4

e) 25

f) -8

g) 15

h) -1

j) -9

k) 30

l) 30

m) 5

n) -1

p) 8

q) 7

r) .0001

s) 10

t) 4

u) 4

v) 48

Exponents

$$\frac{x^3}{y^2 z^{-4}}$$

WHAT'S THE BIG IDEA?

Q: What is an exponent? What is a base? And what does an exponent, combined with a base, tell me?

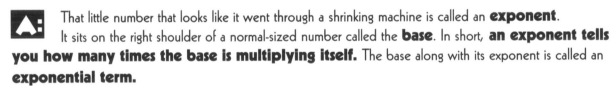

A: That little number that looks like it went through a shrinking machine is called an **exponent**. It sits on the right shoulder of a normal-sized number called the **base**. In short, **an exponent tells you how many times the base is multiplying itself.** The base along with its exponent is called an **exponential term.**

Definitions

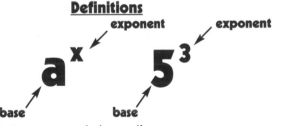

exponent

exponent

$$a^x \qquad 5^3$$

base

base

a^x means **a** is multiplying itself **x** times.

5^3 means **5** is multiplying itself **3** times.

Examples of exponential terms

$$a^2 = a \cdot a$$

$$a^5 = a \cdot a \cdot a \cdot a \cdot a$$

$$3^2 = 3 \cdot 3 = 9$$

$$3^5 = 3 \cdot 3 \cdot 3 \cdot 3 \cdot 3 = 243$$

$$(ac)^5 = (ac) \cdot (ac) \cdot (ac) \cdot (ac) \cdot (ac)$$

Try working out the value of these exponential terms:

a) 5^2

b) v^3

c) 10^3

d) $(mn)^4$

e) $(2x)^2$

Answers:
a) 25
b) $v \cdot v \cdot v$
c) 1,000
d) $(mn) \cdot (mn) \cdot (mn) \cdot (mn)$
e) $(2x) \cdot (2x)$

Why is an exponent sometimes called a "power"?

Exponents are called powers because they have amazing power to boost or shrink the value of numbers.

Remember the mushroom in *Alice in Wonderland*? When Alice took a bite out of one side of the mushroom, she became much larger; when she nibbled from the other side, she became much smaller. Exponents are a lot like the mushroom; used one way, they can make a number much larger — used another way, they can make a number much smaller.

Some examples of the power of exponents

Take a number like **100**. When you raise **100** to the second power (100^2), the value of this term suddenly shoots up to **10,000**.

On the other hand, when you raise **100** to the negative second power (100^{-2}), its value suddenly shrinks to **1/10,000**, a teensy-tiny fraction.

In this section you'll learn why exponents have such tremendous power. You'll also learn some fundamental rules for working with exponents. First you'll learn the **same-base product rule** and the **same-base quotient rule**, as well as the meaning of a^1 and of a^0. After that you'll discover the strange meaning of a **negative exponent**. Finally you'll learn the **exponent-to-exponent rule**, the **product-to-exponent rule** and the **quotient-to-exponent rule**. All along your trek through the world of exponents, you'll learn how to perform **algebraic operations** with exponents, so that by the time you finish this section, you'll be an exceptional exponent expert.

Q:

What would be the value of something raised to the first power? In other words, what would be the value of

$$a^1$$

A:

Anything raised to the first power is simply itself.

In other words, $a^1 = a$

From another viewpoint, a^1 can be thought of as **a** — one time. And in general, anything to the first power is just itself. In other words, you could say something ridiculous, like: **shoelace^1 = shoelace**, and it would still be true! (See note to the right.)

More examples of terms to the first power

$$3^1 = 3$$

$$(-5)^1 = -5$$

$$(3/4)^1 = 3/4$$

$$(\sqrt{2})^1 = \sqrt{2}$$

$$(ac)^1 = ac$$

$$(7ac)^1 = 7ac$$

From time to time, this guidebook will offer examples of algebraic rules that use goofy ideas, like crocodile, elephant, donut, etc. Textbooks don't use ideas like these, so why does this guidebook do so? Two reasons. First, many people can better survive the trek through the barren, abstract algebraic desert if they can visualize something, even if it's something ridiculous like an elephant being raised to the second power. Secondly, these examples help you see the general pattern for algebraic rules and principles. When you read goofy examples, bear in mind that the rule being discussed applies **to any algebraic term whatsoever!** In other words, if the rule works for something as ridiculous as an elephant, it will certainly work for anything you'll run across in algebra.

Simplify these terms:

a) x^1

b) 11^1

d) $(-.032)^1$

e) $(6x/y)^1$

c) ^{1}

Q: What does the same-base product rule say?

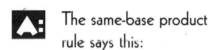

$$a^x \cdot a^n = \,?$$

A: The same-base product rule says this:

$$a^x \cdot a^n = a^{x+n}$$

Or in plain English: **when you're multiplying exponential terms whose bases are the same, keep that base and add the exponents.**

Examples of the same-base product rule

$$m^r \cdot m^u = m^{r+u}$$

$$7^r \cdot 7^u = 7^{r+u}$$

$$m^5 \cdot m^3 = m^{5+3} = m^8$$

$$7^5 \cdot 7^3 = 7^{5+3} = 7^8$$

Goofy example

$$\text{turnip}^2 \cdot \text{turnip}^5 = \text{turnip}^{2+5} = \text{turnip}^7$$

Now try simplifying these expressions:

a) $x^3 \cdot x^4$

b) $3^5 \cdot 3^7$

c) $w^z \cdot w^y \cdot w^x$

d) $5^2 \cdot 5^3 \cdot 5^4$

e) $\text{muffin}^6 \cdot \text{muffin}^8$

Answers:
a) x^7
b) 3^{12}
c) w^{z+y+x}
d) 5^9
e) muffin^{14}

© Singing Turtle Press

89

Q: Why does $a^x \cdot a^n = a^{x+n}$?

A: Good question. It's always best to understand the "why" of things in math. So let's try to understand the same-base product rule by showing that:

$$a^3 \cdot a^2 = a^{3+2} = a^5$$

Let's begin with the expression: $a^3 \cdot a^2$. Now ... the very definition of an exponent (**p. 86**) tells you that:

$$a^3 \cdot a^2 = \left(a \cdot a \cdot a\right) \cdot \left(a \cdot a\right)$$

Since all terms are multiplying one another, you can remove parentheses: $\left(a \cdot a \cdot a\right) \cdot \left(a \cdot a\right) = a \cdot a \cdot a \cdot a \cdot a$

Again the definition of an exponent tells you that:

$$a \cdot a \cdot a \cdot a \cdot a = a^5$$

Since all these terms are equal to each other, you can use the transitive property (**p. 11**) to say that what you start with is equal to what you end up with, or: $a^3 \cdot a^2 = a^5$. This is what you wanted to show, so the job is done.

So what does this say? It tells you that any problem of the form

$$a^x \cdot a^n = a^{x+n}$$ is basically an **addition** problem. In it, you're **adding** numbers of terms that are being multiplied.

In this example, **3** a's multiplied together times **2** a's multiplied together gives you **5** a's multiplied together, in the same way that

$$3 + 2 = 5$$

What does the same-base quotient rule say?

$$\frac{a^x}{a^n} = ?$$

 The same-base quotient rule tells you this:

$$\frac{a^x}{a^n} = a^{x-n}$$

Or, put more simply: **when you're dividing exponential terms whose bases are the same, keep that base and subtract the exponents.**

Examples of the same-base quotient rule

$$\frac{m^r}{m^u} = m^{r-u} \qquad \frac{m^5}{m^3} = m^{5-3} = m^2$$

$$\frac{7^r}{7^u} = 7^{r-u} \qquad \frac{7^5}{7^3} = 7^{5-3} = 7^2$$

Silly example

$$\frac{kumquat^9}{kumquat^4} = kumquat^{9-4} = kumquat^5$$

Now try to simplify these terms:

a) $\dfrac{3^{11}}{3^6}$ c) $\dfrac{p^{20}}{p^1}$

b) $\dfrac{w^r}{w^v}$ d) $\dfrac{flea^{13}}{flea^9}$

Answers:
a) 3^5 c) p^{19}
b) w^{r-v} d) $flea^4$

Why does

$$\frac{a^x}{a^n} = a^{x-n}?$$

 Let's try to understand the same-base quotient rule by showing that:

$$\frac{a^5}{a^3} = a^{5-3} = a^2$$

Let's start out with: $\frac{a^5}{a^3}$

By the definition of an exponent (**p. 86**), you know that:

$$\frac{a^5}{a^3} = \frac{a \cdot a \cdot a \cdot a \cdot a}{a \cdot a \cdot a}$$

And from the rules of cancelling (**pp. 168-171**), you can cancel three **a**'s on the top of the fraction with three **a**'s on the bottom, to get:

$$\frac{\cancel{a} \cdot \cancel{a} \cdot \cancel{a} \cdot a \cdot a}{\cancel{a} \cdot \cancel{a} \cdot \cancel{a}} = \frac{a \cdot a}{1}$$

But $\frac{a \cdot a}{1} = a \cdot a$, and $a \cdot a = a^2$, by the definition of an exponent. So again you use the transitive property (**p. 11**) to show that what you start with is equal to what you wind up with. That is: $\frac{a^5}{a^3} = a^2$

In short, any problem like

$$\frac{a^x}{a^n}$$ is basically a

subtraction problem. In it, you're **subtracting** the number of terms in the denominator from the number of terms in the numerator.

In this example, **5 a**'s multiplied together divided by **3 a**'s multiplied together gives you **2 a**'s multiplied together, just as sure as

5 − 3 = 2

at www.AlgebraWizard.com

Now I see that the same-base product and quotient rules work when the bases are the same. But don't they also work when the bases are different?

In other words, if I see something like $a^2 \cdot c^3$,

I can just simplify it as: $(ac)^5$

And if I see $\dfrac{a^5}{c^3}$, **I can simplify it as:** $\left(\dfrac{a}{c}\right)^2$

Uh ... can't I?

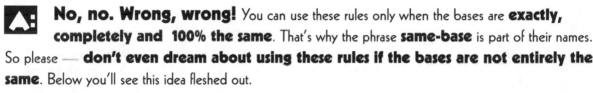

No, no. Wrong, wrong! You can use these rules only when the bases are **exactly, completely and 100% the same**. That's why the phrase **same-base** is part of their names. So please — **don't even dream about using these rules if the bases are not entirely the same**. Below you'll see this idea fleshed out.

Same-base product rule

A term like $a^2 \cdot a^3$ can be simplified as a^5 only because both terms being multiplied have exactly the same base, **a**. But a term like $a^2 \cdot c^3$ cannot be simplified because the two terms have different bases: the first has a base of **a**; the second a base of **c**. So this expression must be left as is.

Same-base quotient rule

A term like $\dfrac{a^5}{a^3}$ can be simplified as a^2 because both bases are **a**'s. But a term like $\dfrac{a^5}{c^3}$ cannot be simplified because the terms have different bases: the numerator has a base of **a**; the denominator, a base of **c**. So this expression also must be left as is.

Tell whether or not these terms can be simplified. If they can, go ahead and simplify them.

a) $3^x \cdot x^3$ c) $\dfrac{b^y}{7^y}$ e) $\dfrac{m^5}{m^4}$

b) $a^4 \cdot a^4$ d) $r^y \cdot r^r$ f) $(2m)^7 \cdot (2n)^8$

Answers:
a) can't   d) can, r^{y+r}
b) can, a^8 e) can, m^1
c) can't   f) can't

Q: What is the value of a^0? And why does a^0 have this value?

A: Any term raised to the zero power equals **1**, not **0**, as you might expect. Or, to put this in math-talk: no matter what value **a** might have,

$$a^0 = 1$$

Examples

$$3^0 = 1$$

$$(.6)^0 = 1$$

$$(-4)^0 = 1$$

$$(x/y)^0 = 1$$

$$\pi^0 = 1$$

Why do terms raised to the zero power equal **1**? Let's try to understand this idea by examining a little fraction: a^5/a^5

If you have faith in the same-base quotient rule (**p. 91**), you'd probably have to agree that: $a^5/a^5 = a^{5-5}$, and by simple subtraction, you know that: $a^{5-5} = a^0$. Then, using the transitive property (**p. 11**), you can see that: $a^5/a^5 = a^0$

But why not look at a^5/a^5 in a different way — as a fraction whose numerator and denominator are the same. From elementary math you know that whenever a fraction's numerator and denominator are the same, that fraction equals **1**. So that means: $a^5/a^5 = 1$

Now look at your two findings. First you saw that: $a^5/a^5 = a^0$

And then you saw that: $a^5/a^5 = 1$. And if you just use the transitive property one more time, it tells you that: $a^0 = 1$

Since **a** stands for any number or term, this tells you that any term raised to the zero power always equals **1**.

Note: there's one exception to this rule. $0^0 \neq 1$. Instead, 0^0 is "undefined" because it involves dividing by zero, which as you saw earlier (**p. 30**) was an algebraic "no-no."

Q: When I have a term raised to the zero power showing up in my answer, I may as well ignore it because it will always disappear from the final answer. Right?

A: No, not always. Terms to the zero power do disappear from final answers when they are multiplying or dividing other terms. This is because any term to the zero power equals **1**, and multiplying or dividing any term by **1** just gives you back the term you started with. But when terms to the zero power are being added to or subtracted from other terms, they do not disappear; they affect the final answer. Below are some illustrations of this idea.

zero power term disappears from final answer

multiplication

$$x^2 c^3 a^0$$
$$= x^2 c^3 \cdot 1$$
$$= x^2 c^3$$

division

$$\frac{x^2}{a^0}$$
$$= \frac{x^2}{1}$$
$$= x^2$$

zero power term affects final answer

addition

$$4 + x^0$$
$$= 4 + 1$$
$$= 5$$

subtraction

$$4 - x^0$$
$$= 4 - 1$$
$$= 3$$

Tell what the final answer would be:

a) $x^6 y^0 z^9$

b) $x^6 + x^0$

c) $\dfrac{a^2 b^4 c^0}{m^4 n^3}$

d) $8 - z^0$

e) $v^0 + e^0 + w^0$

f) $4a^0 b^0 c^0 d^0$

Answers:

a) $x^6 z^9$

b) $x^6 + 1$

c) $\dfrac{a^2 b^4}{m^4 n^3}$

d) 7

e) 3

f) 4

Q: Since 3^0 and $(-3)^0$ both equal 1, that means that terms like -3^0 also equal 1. Right?

 Sorry, but no. But if you just think back to the order of operations, you'll quickly see why this is not the case.

With both 3^0 and $(-3)^0$ you have only one operation to work out, and that is to raise the term to the exponent. Since any term raised to the zero power equals **1**, both of these terms equal **1**.

But when you look at -3^0, you really should think of it as: $-\left(3^0\right)$. When you view the term this way, you can see that you have two operations to do:

1st) working out the **exponent**, and

2nd) multiplying by -1. Since **E** comes before **M**, you first work out the **exponent**, then **multiply** by -1, as shown to the right:

$$-\left(3^0\right)$$
$$= -(1)$$
$$= -1$$

Try stating the value of these terms:

a) -4^0 d) $7 + 4^0$

b) $(-4)^0$ e) $7 - 4^0$

c) 4^0

Answers:
a) -1 d) 8
b) 1   e) 6
c) 1

Q: My teacher always asks me to write my answers in "descending order." What is descending order, and how do I use it to write my answers?

A: To understand descending order, think about what it means to walk down, or to descend, a short flight of stairs.

You start out, say, three steps above the floor, and you descend the stairs one at a time till you reach the bottom. Now imagine that instead of real stairs, you're walking down a stairway of exponents. You start out at the highest exponent, then drop to the next highest one, and so on, until finally you reach the smallest exponent. When you arrange a bunch of terms this way, making the exponents descend across the page from left to right, you're arranging them in descending order.

Below you'll see the difference between scrambled terms and terms in descending order.

Terms scrambled	Same terms in descending order
$-2a^2 + 8a^5 - 7 - 4a^3 + 3a + 6a^4$ $\rightarrow$	$+8a^5 + 6a^4 - 4a^3 - 2a^2 + 3a - 7$
$-3m + 6m^4 - 9 + 8m^7$ $\rightarrow$	$+8m^7 + 6m^4 - 3m - 9$

Note: — A variable with no exponent shown has an invisible exponent of **1**. (ex.: **a** means a^1, **m** means m^1)
— Number terms always go last.

Try arranging these terms in descending order:

a) $-5 + 3x$
b) $+4y - y^2 - 11$
c) $17 - 3z^4 + 12z - 2z^3$
d) $-n^3 + 6n^5 - 2 + 3n^2 + 8n^4$

Answers:
a) $+3x - 5$
b) $-y^2 + 4y - 11$
c) $-3z^4 - 2z^3 + 12z + 17$
d) $+6n^5 + 8n^4 - n^3 + 3n^2 - 2$

Q: What is the value of a negative exponent?

$$a^{-x} = \,?$$

A: The value of a negative exponent is this:

$$a^{-x} = \frac{1}{a^x}$$

Or in simple English: whenever you have a term raised to a negative exponent, you can restate the value of that term by:
a) pushing it across the fraction bar, and
b) making its exponent positive.

Examples of negative exponents

$$m^{-r} = \frac{1}{m^r} \qquad 6^{-r} = \frac{1}{6^r}$$

$$m^{-3} = \frac{1}{m^3} \qquad 6^{-3} = \frac{1}{6^3} = \frac{1}{216}$$

Silly example

$$\text{frog}^{-4} = \frac{1}{\text{frog}^4}$$

Try simplifying these terms:

a) v^{-5} c) fish^{-7}

b) x^{-a} d) 3^{-2}

Answers:
a) $\dfrac{1}{v^5}$ c) $\dfrac{1}{\text{fish}^7}$

b) $\dfrac{1}{x^a}$ d) $\dfrac{1}{3^2} = \dfrac{1}{9}$

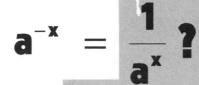

Why does

$$a^{-x} = \frac{1}{a^x} ?$$

A: Let's try to understand this rule by showing that: $a^{-3} = \dfrac{1}{a^3}$

Let's start out with the term: a^2/a^5. Once again, if you have faith in the same-base quotient rule (**p. 91**), it would be hard to deny that: $a^2/a^5 = a^{2-5}$. And using simple subtraction, $a^{2-5} = a^{-3}$. So using the transitive property (**p. 11**), you can see that: $a^2/a^5 = a^{-3}$

But now let's look at a^2/a^5 in a different way, as $a \cdot a/a \cdot a \cdot a \cdot a \cdot a$. Using the rules for cancelling (**pp. 168-171**), you cancel the two **a**'s on the top with two of the **a**'s on the bottom, to give you: $\cancel{a} \cdot \cancel{a}/\cancel{a} \cdot \cancel{a} \cdot a \cdot a \cdot a = 1/a \cdot a \cdot a$. And using the definition of an exponent (**p. 86**), you can say that: $1/a \cdot a \cdot a = 1/a^3$. Since all these terms are equal to each other, you can use the transitive property again to say that: $a^2/a^5 = 1/a^3$

Now just look at the two main findings here. First you saw that: $a^2/a^5 = a^{-3}$. And then you saw that: $a^2/a^5 = 1/a^3$. Since all these terms are equal to each other, you can use the

transitive property once more to say that: $a^{-3} = \dfrac{1}{a^3}$. And in general, any

term to a negative exponent is the same as **1** over that term to a positive exponent.

By the way, if your brains feel like they're turning into spaghetti, it just means you're making a courageous effort to figure this stuff out.

What is the value of $\dfrac{1}{a^{-x}}$?

A: The term's value is this: $\dfrac{1}{a^{-x}} = a^x$

Examples

$$\frac{1}{m^{-r}} = m^r \qquad \frac{1}{6^{-r}} = 6^r$$

$$\frac{1}{m^{-3}} = m^3 \qquad \frac{1}{6^{-3}} = 6^3 = 216$$

Silly example

$$\frac{1}{hen^{-5}} = hen^5$$

In other words: **1** over any term raised to a negative exponent is the same as that term raised to a positive exponent.

The reason this is true is quite simple. As we saw on the last page, $a^{-x} = \dfrac{1}{a^x}$. If we just substitute $\dfrac{1}{a^x}$ for a^{-x},

you see that: $\dfrac{1}{a^{-x}} = \dfrac{1}{\dfrac{1}{a^x}}$. And from basic arithmetic,

when you divide a term by a fraction, you just multiply the term by the flip (or, reciprocal) of the fraction. So...

$$\frac{1}{a^{-x}} = \frac{1}{\dfrac{1}{a^x}} = 1 \cdot \frac{a^x}{1} = a^x$$

Try simplifying these terms:

a) $\dfrac{1}{w^{-3}}$

c) $\dfrac{1}{2^{-3}}$

b) $\dfrac{1}{tadpole^{-7}}$

d) $\dfrac{1}{c^{-d}}$

Answers: a) w^3 c) $2^3 = 8$ b) tadpole⁷ d) c^d

Q: Is there a larger lesson to be learned from the fact that

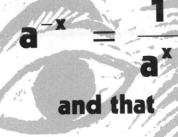

$$a^{-x} = \frac{1}{a^x}$$

and that

$$\frac{1}{a^{-x}} = a^x \;?$$

A: Actually there is a big lesson, and it is this:
Whenever you push an exponential term across the fraction bar, the exponent's sign changes. If the exponent's sign was positive, it becomes negative; if its sign was negative, it becomes positive. Below are illustrations of this idea.

exponent's sign changes from negative to positive

$$\frac{5a^{-3}}{7} = \frac{5}{7a^3}$$

$$\frac{1}{2c^{-4}} = \frac{c^4}{2}$$

$$\frac{\text{popsicle}^{-2}}{\text{lollipop}^{-5}} = \frac{\text{lollipop}^5}{\text{popsicle}^2}$$

exponent's sign changes from positive to negative

$$\frac{8x^4}{11} = \frac{8}{11x^{-4}}$$

$$\frac{1}{6w^3} = \frac{w^{-3}}{6}$$

$$\frac{\text{popsicle}^8}{\text{lollipop}^3} = \frac{\text{lollipop}^{-3}}{\text{popsicle}^{-8}}$$

My teacher asks me to write my answers without negative exponents. Can I use the idea from the previous page to make exponents positive in my answer?

Yes, just move your terms so that the exponents become positive.
Follow the two steps below.

Make the exponents positive: A) $\dfrac{4\,a^{-2}}{c^{3}}$, B) $\dfrac{4a^{2}}{c^{-3}}$, C) $\dfrac{4a^{-2}}{c^{-3}}$

<u>Steps</u>	<u>Example A</u>	<u>Example B</u>	<u>Example C</u>
1st) Original problem.	$\dfrac{4a^{-2}}{c^{3}}$	$\dfrac{4a^{2}}{c^{-3}}$	$\dfrac{4a^{-2}}{c^{-3}}$
2nd) Move the term with the negative exponent across the fraction bar and make its sign positive.	$= \dfrac{4}{a^{2}c^{3}}$	$= 4a^{2}c^{3}$	$= \dfrac{4c^{3}}{a^{2}}$

Try rewriting these terms so that they have only positive exponents:

a) $4a^{-2}b^{-3}$

b) $8^{-2}x^{-3}y^{-4}$

c) $\dfrac{6}{a^{-2}m^{-4}}$

d) $\dfrac{x^{-3}}{a^{-4}}$

e) $\dfrac{a^{-1}b^{-2}c^{-3}}{d^{-3}e^{-2}f^{-1}}$

Answers:

a) $\dfrac{4}{a^{2}b^{3}}$

b) $\dfrac{1}{8^{2}x^{3}y^{4}}$

c) $6a^{2}m^{4}$

d) $\dfrac{a^{4}}{x^{3}}$

e) $\dfrac{d^{3}e^{2}f}{a\,b^{2}c^{3}}$

102

 Now I know how to get rid of negative exponents in simple problems. But how do I get rid of negative exponents when the same variable stands on both sides of the fraction bar? In other words, how would I simplify problems like these:

$$\frac{c^3}{c^5}, \quad \frac{a^5}{a^{-3}} \quad \text{or} \quad \frac{n^{-3}}{n^{-5}}$$

 It's easy if you remember this simple rule-of-thumb.

When it comes time to move exponential terms across the fraction bar, always move the term that has the smaller exponent.

Follow the steps to the right.

Steps	**Example A**	**Example B**	**Example C**
1st) For each term, notice which of the exponents is smaller.	$\dfrac{c^3}{c^5}$ $(3 < 5)$	$\dfrac{a^5}{a^{-3}}$ $(-3 < 5)$	$\dfrac{n^{-3}}{n^{-5}}$ $(-5 < -3)$
2nd) Move the term with the smaller exponent across the fraction bar and change its sign.	$= \dfrac{1}{c^5 c^{-3}}$	$= \dfrac{a^5 \cdot a^3}{1}$	$= \dfrac{n^{-3} \cdot n^5}{1}$
3rd) Simplify by using the same-base product rule (**p. 89**).	$= \dfrac{1}{c^{5+-3}} = \dfrac{1}{c^2}$	$= a^{5+3}$ $= a^8$	$= n^{-3+5}$ $= n^2$

Try these:

a) $\dfrac{v^3}{v^{11}}$ c) $\dfrac{m^{-1}}{m^{-3}}$

b) $\dfrac{y^{-5}}{y^8}$ d) $\dfrac{5^{-13}}{5^{-20}}$

Answers:

a) $\dfrac{1}{v^8}$ c) m^2

b) $\dfrac{1}{y^{13}}$ d) 5^7

Q: Now I see how to get rid of negative exponents. But I also need to know what to do when I have more than one term in the numerator or in the denominator. In other words, how would I simplify an expression like this:

$$\frac{x^{-4} x^{10} x^0}{x^{13} x^{-2}}$$

A: Just follow the three steps illustrated to the right.

Simplify:

Steps

1st) Use the same-base product rule (**p. 89**) on the terms in the numerator and on the terms in the denominator.

2nd) Move the term with the smaller exponent.

3rd) Use the same-base product rule again.

Example

$$\frac{x^{-4} x^{10} x^0}{x^{13} x^{-2}}$$

$$= \frac{x^{-4+10+0}}{x^{13+-2}}$$

$$= \frac{x^6}{x^{11}}$$

$$= \frac{1}{x^{-6} \cdot x^{11}}$$

$$= \frac{1}{x^5}$$

Now try simplifying these terms in the same way:

a) $\dfrac{a^{-5} a^9}{a^{11} a^0 a^{-2}}$

c) $\dfrac{n^2 n^3 n^4}{n^{-4} n^{-3} n^{-2}}$

b) $\dfrac{4^{10} \cdot 4^{-6}}{4^{-20} \cdot 4^5}$

d) $\dfrac{r^{18} r^{18}}{r^{-2} r^{-2}}$

Answers:

a) $\dfrac{1}{a^5}$ c) n^{18}

b) 4^{19} d) r^{40}

O.K., that wasn't too hard. But I can think of an even tougher problem — one in which altogether different bases stand on opposite sides of the fraction bar. How would I simplify a scary-looking thing like this:

$$\frac{a^{-4}c^3a^2c^{-12}}{c^7a^0c^{-5}a^{-10}}$$

Don't get too scared, because this is not so hard as it looks. Just follow the four steps to the right.

Simplify:

$$\frac{a^{-4}c^3a^2c^{-12}}{c^7a^0c^{-5}a^{-10}}$$

<u>**Steps**</u>

1st) Group terms with the same bases.

<u>**Example**</u>

$$\frac{a^{-4}c^3a^2c^{-12}}{c^7a^0c^{-5}a^{-10}}$$

$$= \frac{a^{-4}a^2 \quad c^3c^{-12}}{a^0a^{-10} \cdot c^7c^{-5}}$$

2nd) Use same-base product rule (**p. 89**).

$$= \frac{a^{-2} \cdot c^{-9}}{a^{-10} \cdot c^2}$$

<u>**Steps**</u>

3rd) Move terms with the smaller exponents.

<u>**Example**</u>

$$= \frac{a^{-2}a^{10}}{c^9c^2}$$

4th) Use same-base product rule.

$$= \frac{a^8}{c^{11}}$$

Now give these a shot:

a) $\dfrac{x^3w^{-4}}{w^{-8}x^7}$

b) $\dfrac{u^{-4}v^6}{v^{-14}u^3v^{17}}$

c) $\dfrac{a^0n^2n^{-6}a^{-14}}{n^{-3}a^4a^{-5}n^{-9}}$

d) $\dfrac{x^{-3}x^2r^{-10}x}{x^8r^{-2}r^{-3}r^9}$

Answers:

a) $\dfrac{w^4}{x^4}$

b) $\dfrac{v^3}{u^7}$

c) $\dfrac{a^8}{n^{13}}$

d) $\dfrac{1}{x^8r^{14}}$

What does the exponent-to-exponent rule say?

$$\left(a^x\right)^n = ?$$

A: The exponent-to-exponent rule says this:

$$\left(a^x\right)^n = a^{x \cdot n}$$

Or: **when an exponential term itself gets raised to an exponent, keep the base and multiply the exponents.**

Examples of the exponent-to-exponent rule

$$\left(m^r\right)^u = m^{r \cdot u} \qquad \left(m^3\right)^{-5} = m^{3 \cdot -5} = m^{-15}$$

$$\left(5^r\right)^u = 5^{r \cdot u} \qquad \left(5^3\right)^5 = 5^{3 \cdot 5} = 5^{15}$$

Silly example

$$\left(porcupine^3\right)^4 = porcupine^{3 \cdot 4} = porcupine^{12}$$

Now try simplifying these using the exponent-to-exponent rule:

a) $\left(2^3\right)^5$ d) $\left(gumball^2\right)^5$

b) $\left(x^y\right)^u$ e) $\left(3^3\right)^{-3}$

c) $\left(a^{-5}\right)^4$

Answers:

a) 2^{15} d) $gumball^{10}$

b) $x^{y \cdot u}$ e) 3^{-9}

c) a^{-20}

Q: Why does $\left(a^x\right)^n = a^{x \cdot n}$?

 A: Let's try to understand this rule by showing that:

$$\left(a^2\right)^3 = a^{2 \cdot 3} = a^6$$

Let's begin with: $\left(a^2\right)^3$

Now from the defintion of an exponent (**p. 86**), you know that

$\left(a^2\right)^3$ means that a^2 is multiplying itself three times. Or, in

math language: $\left(a^2\right)^3 = \left(a^2\right) \cdot \left(a^2\right) \cdot \left(a^2\right)$

By the same-base product rule (**p. 89**):

$\left(a^2\right) \cdot \left(a^2\right) \cdot \left(a^2\right) = a^{2+2+2}$

Adding up these exponents, you see that: $a^{2+2+2} = a^6$

And using the transitive property (**p. 11**), you note that what you

start with is equal to what you end with, or: $\left(a^2\right)^3 = a^6$

In short, any problem of the

form: $\left(a^x\right)^n$, in which you have

an exponential term raised to

an exponent, is essentially a

multiplication problem. In

this kind of problem, you're just

multiplying one exponent by

the other exponent.

In this example, a^2 is

multiplying itself **3** times, then

each of those a^2's can be

viewed as **a** multiplying itself **2**

times. All in all, **a** ends up

multipliying itself **6** times, just as

$3 \cdot 2 = 6$

107

What do I do first when I have to use both the exponent-to-exponent rule and the same-base product rule in the same problem? In other words, what steps would I use to simplify terms like these:

$$a^4\left(a^2\right)^3 a^0 a^{-3} \qquad \text{or} \qquad \frac{a^{-4}\left(a^3\right)^{-2}}{\left(a^1\right)^4 a^{-10}}$$

Work out the exponent-to-exponent rule first.

Then simplify just as you've done before. Just follow the three steps to the right.

Simplify:

A) $a^4\left(a^2\right)^3 a^0 a^{-3}$,

B) $\dfrac{a^{-4}\left(a^3\right)^{-2}}{\left(a^1\right)^4 a^{-10}}$

Steps	Example A	Example B
1st) Use exponent-to-exponent rule **(p. 106)**.	$a^4\left(a^2\right)^3 a^0 a^{-3}$ $= a^4 a^6 a^0 a^{-3}$	$\dfrac{a^{-4}\left(a^3\right)^{-2}}{\left(a^1\right)^4 a^{-10}}$ $= \dfrac{a^{-4} a^{-6}}{a^4 a^{-10}}$
2nd) Use same-base product rule **(p. 89)**.	$= a^{4+6+0+-3}$	$= \dfrac{a^{-10}}{a^{-6}}$
3rd) Simplify.	$= a^7$	$= \dfrac{1}{a^4}$

Now try these for yourself:

a) $\dfrac{x^{-3}\left(x^2\right)^{-4}}{\left(x^3\right)^4 x^{-5}}$

b) $m^{-7}\left(m^{-2}\right)^4 m^0$

c) $\dfrac{\left(c^4\right)^{-5} c^{-3}}{c^7\left(c^3\right)^4}$

d) $n^8\left(n^{-1}\right)^1\left(n^3\right)^2$

Answers:

a) $\dfrac{1}{x^{18}}$

b) $\dfrac{1}{m^{15}}$

c) $\dfrac{1}{c^{42}}$

d) n^{13}

Q: What does the product-to-exponent rule say?

$$\left(a \cdot c\right)^x = \,?$$

A: The product-to-exponent rule says this:

$$\left(a \cdot c\right)^x = a^x \cdot c^x$$

Or, in simple language: **when a product gets raised to an exponent, each term in the product gets raised to that exponent.**

Examples of the product-to-exponent rule

$$\left(m \cdot v\right)^r = m^r \cdot v^r \qquad \left(5 \cdot 7\right)^r = 5^r \cdot 7^r$$

$$\left(m \cdot v\right)^{-3} = m^{-3} \cdot v^{-3} \qquad \left(5 \cdot 7\right)^3 = 5^3 \cdot 7^3$$

Silly example

$$\left(dog \cdot cat\right)^7 = \left(dog\right)^7 \cdot \left(cat\right)^7$$

Now try to simplify these using the product-to-exponent rule:

a) $\left(m \cdot n\right)^5$ d) $\left(eye \cdot ear\right)^{-9}$

b) $\left(2 \cdot 3\right)^{-x}$ e) $\left(p \cdot q\right)^z$

c) $\left(2 \cdot 4 \cdot 5\right)^3$

Answers:
a) $m^5 \cdot n^5$
b) $2^{-x} \cdot 3^{-x}$
c) $2^3 \cdot 4^3 \cdot 5^3$
d) $\left(eye\right)^{-9} \cdot \left(ear\right)^{-9}$
e) $p^z \cdot q^z$

Suppose I have a problem in which I need to use both the product-to-exponent rule along with the same-base product rule.

What steps would I use to simplify expressions like these:

$$\left(wx\right)^{3} w^{-4} x^{7}$$

or

$$\frac{\left(wx\right)^{4} x^{-7}}{w^{3}\left(wx\right)^{-2}}$$

Work out the product-to-exponent rule before the same-base product rule. Follow the steps to the right.

Simplify:

A) $\left(wx\right)^{3} w^{-4} x^{7}$,

B) $\dfrac{\left(wx\right)^{4} x^{-7}}{w^{3}\left(wx\right)^{-2}}$

Steps	**Example A**	**Example B**
1st) Use the product-to-exponent rule (**p. 109**).	$\left(wx\right)^{3} w^{-4} x^{7}$ $= w^{3}x^{3}w^{-4}x^{7}$	$\dfrac{\left(wx\right)^{4} x^{-7}}{w^{3}\left(wx\right)^{-2}}$ $= \dfrac{w^{4}x^{4}x^{-7}}{w^{3}w^{-2}x^{-2}}$
2nd) Use the same-base product rule (**p. 89**).	$= w^{-1}x^{10}$	$= \dfrac{w^{4}x^{-3}}{wx^{-2}}$
3rd) Simplify.	$= \dfrac{x^{10}}{w}$	$= \dfrac{w^{3}}{x}$

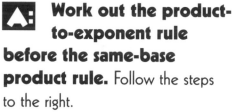

Now try simplifying these:

a) $a^{3}\left(ac\right)^{-6}c^{7}$

b) $\dfrac{\left(xz\right)^{-3} x}{z^{4}}$

c) $\dfrac{\left(mn\right)^{4} n^{3}}{\left(mn\right)^{7} m^{4}}$

d) $\left(rs\right)^{-8} r^{0}s^{6}$

Answers:

a) $\dfrac{c}{a^{3}}$

b) $\dfrac{1}{x^{7}z_{2}}$

c) $\dfrac{1}{m^{7}}$

d) $\dfrac{1}{r^{8}s^{2}}$

What does the quotient-to-exponent rule say?

$$\left(\frac{a}{c}\right)^x = \; ?$$

 The quotient-to-exponent rule says this:

$$\left(\frac{a}{c}\right)^x = \frac{a^x}{c^x}$$

Or, in simple language: **when a quotient gets raised to an exponent, both the numerator and the denominator get raised to that exponent.**

Examples of the quotient-to-exponent rule

$$\left(\frac{m}{v}\right)^r = \frac{m^r}{v^r} \qquad \left(\frac{m}{v}\right)^3 = \frac{m^3}{v^3}$$

$$\left(\frac{5}{7}\right)^r = \frac{5^r}{7^r} \qquad \left(\frac{5}{7}\right)^{-3} = \frac{5^{-3}}{7^{-3}}$$

Silly example

$$\left(\frac{dog}{cat}\right)^7 = \frac{(dog)^7}{(cat)^7}$$

Try to simplify these expressions using the quotient-to-exponent rule:

a) $\left(\dfrac{c}{e}\right)^{-7}$ c) $\left(\dfrac{3}{4}\right)^5$

b) $\left(\dfrac{w}{v}\right)^z$ d) $\left(\dfrac{tic}{tac}\right)^9$

Answers:

a) $\dfrac{c^{-7}}{e^{-7}}$ c) $\dfrac{3^5}{4^5}$

b) $\dfrac{w^z}{v^z}$ d) $\dfrac{tic^9}{tac^9}$

Q: Suppose I have a problem in which I need to use the **quotient-to-exponent rule** along with the **same-base product rule**. What steps would I use to simplify an expression like this:

$$\left(\frac{w}{x}\right)^{-3} \cdot \frac{w^4 x^{-2}}{x^7 w^{-5}}$$

A: Yikes, this problem looks scary. But if you remember to **work out the quotient-to-exponent rule first,** you'll do fine. Just follow the steps at right.

Simplify:

$$\left(\frac{w}{x}\right)^{-3} \cdot \frac{w^4 x^{-2}}{x^7 w^{-5}}$$

Steps	**Example**
1st) Use quotient-to-exponent rule **(p. 111)**.	$\left(\dfrac{w}{x}\right)^{-3} \cdot \dfrac{w^4 x^{-2}}{x^7 w^{-5}}$ $= \dfrac{w^{-3}}{x^{-3}} \cdot \dfrac{w^4 x^{-2}}{x^7 w^{-5}}$
2nd) Combine numerators and denominators.	$= \dfrac{w^{-3} w^4 x^{-2}}{x^{-3} x^7 w^{-5}}$

Steps	**Example**
3rd) Use same-base product rule **(p. 89)**.	$= \dfrac{w^1 x^{-2}}{w^{-5} x^4}$
4th) Simplify.	$= \dfrac{w^6}{x^6}$

Now try these:

a) $\left(\dfrac{a}{c}\right)^4 \cdot \dfrac{c^3}{a^5}$

c) $\dfrac{m^{-3}n^6}{m^4 n^{-7}} \cdot \left(\dfrac{m}{n}\right)^{-2}$

b) $\left(\dfrac{x}{y}\right)^{-3} \cdot \dfrac{xy^2}{yx^3}$

d) $\left(\dfrac{a}{b}\right)^{-2} \cdot \left(\dfrac{b}{a}\right)^{-3}$

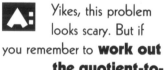

Answers:
a) $\dfrac{1}{ac}$
c) $\dfrac{n^{15}}{m^9}$
b) $\dfrac{y^4}{x^5}$
d) $\dfrac{e}{b}$

Use the exponent rules to simplify the expressions below.

State the value: **Simplify and write without negative exponents:**

a) 2^5

b) $(-2)^2$

c) 7^1

d) 8^0

e) $(-8)^0$

f) -8^0

g) $5 + 3^0$

h) $5 \cdot 3^0$

j) $5 - 3^0$

k) $\dfrac{5}{3^0}$

l) $a^4 \cdot a^7$

m) $a^{-6} \cdot a^{14}$

n) $\dfrac{m^{11}}{m^3}$

p) $a^2 a^0 b^4 b^0$

q) m^{-5}

r) $\dfrac{1}{y^{-7}}$

s) $8x^{-2}y^{-3}$

t) $\dfrac{r^{-2}t^{-4}}{a^{-7}b^{-5}}$

u) $\dfrac{a^4}{a^7}$

v) $\dfrac{y^8}{y^{-4}}$

w) $\dfrac{x^{-2}}{x^{-9}}$

x) $\dfrac{a^{-2}a^5a^0}{a^7a^{-4}}$

y) $\dfrac{x^{-6}y^8z^2x^{10}}{y^4x^{11}y^0z^{-6}}$

z) $\left(y^2\right)^{-3}$

A) $\left(5^x\right)^y$

B) $b^3\left(b^2\right)^4 b^0 b^{-7}$

C) $\dfrac{\left(c^4\right)^{-2}c^3}{c^0c^{-10}}$

D) $(pq)^{-6}$

E) $(mr)^{-2}m^{-9}r^8$

F) $\dfrac{(wy)^{-5}w^{-7}}{y^{10}(wy)^3}$

G) $\left(\dfrac{x}{y}\right)^7$

H) $\left(\dfrac{2}{a}\right)^2$

J) $\left(\dfrac{p}{q}\right)^{-4}$

A:

a) 32

b) 4

c) 7

d) 1

e) 1

f) -1

g) 6

h) 5

j) 4

k) 5

l) a^{11}

m) a^8

n) m^8

p) a^2b^4

q) $\dfrac{1}{m^5}$

r) y^7

s) $\dfrac{8}{x^2y^3}$

t) $\dfrac{a^7b^5}{r^2t^4}$

u) $\dfrac{1}{a^3}$

v) y^{12}

w) x^7

x) 1

y) $\dfrac{y^4z^8}{x^7}$

z) $\dfrac{1}{y^6}$

A) $5^{x \cdot y}$

B) b^4

C) c^5

D) $\dfrac{1}{p^6q^6}$

E) $\dfrac{r^6}{m^{11}}$

F) $\dfrac{1}{w^{15}y^{18}}$

G) $\dfrac{x^7}{y^7}$

H) $\dfrac{4}{a^2}$

J) $\dfrac{q^4}{p^4}$

The rule for adding and subtracting radicals is simple. As long as what's under the radical sign is exactly the same, you can treat radicals as if they were "like terms." In other words, two radicals are like terms if they have exactly the same "stuff" underneath the radical,

 **What is the symbol for a square root? What is a square root? And how can I put the idea of a square root into simple language?**

The symbol for a square root looks like this: $\sqrt{}$

You might think of it as a division sign that had a check mark glued to the front of it.

Since $\sqrt{}$ means "square root," $\sqrt{5}$ is read "square root of **5**"; $\sqrt{a}$ is read "square root of **a**," etc. As to the symbol's meaning, the square root of **a** is that special number which, when multiplied by itself, equals **a**. In math, we write the idea like this: $\sqrt{a} \cdot \sqrt{a} = a$, and we call this the **definition of a square root**.

Examples of square roots

The square root of **9** is that special number, which, when multiplied by itself, equals **9**. We know that $3 \cdot 3 = 9$, so **3** is the square root of **9**. In math, this is written: $\sqrt{9} = 3$

The square root of **64** is that special number which, when multiplied by itself, equals **64**. We know that $8 \cdot 8 = 64$, so **8** is the square root of **64**. This is written: $\sqrt{64} = 8$

In the **Exponents** section (**p. 86**), you learned that a^2 is read: "**a** to the second power," and that it means $a \cdot a$. Now you learn a nifty nickname for terms like a^2. Instead of saying "**a** to the second power," you can use the shortcut of saying "**a** squared." This works for numbers too. If you want to talk about a number times itself, like $7 \cdot 7$, you can just say "**7** squared," which is written: 7^2. This way of talking comes in handy when working with square roots, so you'll see it in this and in upcoming sections.

Find the square roots:

a) $\sqrt{4}$ d) $\sqrt{100}$
b) $\sqrt{36}$
c) $\sqrt{81}$ e) $\sqrt{49}$

Answers: a) 2   d) 10   b) 6   e) 7   c) 9

get HELP now!

Q: Why should I learn how to work with square roots? How will I ever use them?

A: Square roots, also known as **radicals**, have a wide range of uses both in math and in the "real world."

Take math first. Since the Pythagorean theorem (**pp. 206-210**) is based on the idea of square roots, you'll use roots to calculate the lengths of the sides of right triangles. When you study the **Coordinate Plane**, you'll reach into your square root toolbag to find the distance between any two points in the universe (**pp. 241-242**). In the next section, **Factoring**, you'll also use square roots to factor, or take apart, mathematical expressions.

How about the use of square roots in the real world? For starters, home builders use roots and the 4,000-year-old Pythagorean theorem to figure out the sizes of their kitchens and living rooms. Architects use roots to determine dimensions in the buildings, bridges and roads they design. Engineers use roots to figure out how much stress bridges can bear. Beyond that, square roots are used in the sciences of chemistry, physics, computer science, astronomy, atomic physics and statistics, to name just a few.

In this section, you'll learn about **square roots**. In addition to learning the basic meaning of a **square root**, you'll learn the meaning of a **perfect square**. After that, you'll find out how to **add and subtract similar radical terms**. You'll also find out how to multiply and divide roots using a variety of rules, including the **radical product rule** and the **radical quotient rule.** All along the way you'll find out how to do various **operations** with square roots. Last but not least, you'll learn how to **rationalize denominators** of fractions.

117

I hear people using two terms, square root and radical, to talk about what seems to be the same thing. Is there a difference between these two terms? And what exactly is meant by the term "radical"?

A: Good question. Yes, in higher math there is a distinction between the term **square root** and the term **radical**. But in Algebra I you don't have to worry about this difference, for at this point, the two terms mean the same thing. As to the word **radical**, be aware that it has three shades of meaning. Here they are:

1) Radical means the mere **idea** of a square root, as in the sentence: "This week we're going to study radicals." Translation: This week we're going to study square roots.

2) Radical also means the actual **symbol** for a root, i.e.: $\sqrt{\ }$
So if a teacher points to a term like $\sqrt{5}$ and asks: "Which term is under (or inside) the radical?" s/he is asking you what is inside the radical sign. In this case, the answer would be the number **5**.

3) Mathematicians use the word **radical** to mean **both the symbol and the number or term under it**. For example, if you write down $\sqrt{25}$ as the answer to a problem, a teacher might ask you to "simplify the radical." S/he would be asking you to simplify the entire term $\sqrt{25}$ to **5**.

Info tidbit: We use the word **radical** because it comes from the Latin word **radix**, meaning **root**. The idea seems to be this: just as a root is the **foundation of a tree**, a radical is the **foundation of a number**. For example, since **5 · 5 = 25**, you can imagine that the number **25** depends on the number **5** for its existence just as an apple tree depends on a root for its existence.

Q: I think I understand the basic idea of a square root. But what would be the value of a square root times itself? In other words, what would be the value of this expression:

$$\sqrt{a} \cdot \sqrt{a}$$

A: The value of this expression is so obvious, it's easy to miss — like trying to see your nose. In any case, here it is:

$$\sqrt{a} \cdot \sqrt{a} = a$$

In other words, **a square root times itself equals the very number it's the square root of.** Since this idea comes from the defintion of a square root (**p. 116**), it's true for any number or term. You could even say something ridiculous, like:

$$\sqrt{\text{elephant}} \cdot \sqrt{\text{elephant}} = \text{elephant},$$

and it would be true! To your right are more examples of this concept.

Examples

$$\sqrt{9} \cdot \sqrt{9} = 9$$

$$\sqrt{7x} \cdot \sqrt{7x} = 7x$$

$$\sqrt{ax^2} \cdot \sqrt{ax^2} = ax^2$$

$$\sqrt{7xyz^2} \cdot \sqrt{7xyz^2} = 7xyz^2$$

Silly example

$$\sqrt{\text{chocolate}} \cdot \sqrt{\text{chocolate}} = \text{chocolate}$$

Note: in Algebra I, the square root of a negative number, e.g. $\sqrt{-5}$, is considered "undefined." That means it gives you no real answer.

Now try these:

a) $\sqrt{y} \cdot \sqrt{y}$
b) $\sqrt{7} \cdot \sqrt{7}$
c) $\sqrt{200ab} \cdot \sqrt{200ab}$

d) $\sqrt{\text{pizza}} \cdot \sqrt{\text{pizza}}$
e) $\sqrt{45x^2y} \cdot \sqrt{45x^2y}$

Answers:
a) y   d) pizza
b) 7   e) 45x²y
c) 200ab

Q: O.K. Now I understand the value of terms like: $\sqrt{a} \cdot \sqrt{a}$ But what would be the value of a weird-looking term like this:

$$\left(\sqrt{a}\right)^2$$

A: Don't let the weird look of this term toss you out of the saddle. Remember from the **Exponents** section **(p. 86)** that a term to the second power means that the term is just multiplying itself. In other words: $\left(\sqrt{a}\right)^2 = \sqrt{a} \cdot \sqrt{a}$

On the previous page you saw that: $\left(\sqrt{a}\right) \cdot \left(\sqrt{a}\right) = a$

And the transitive property **(p. 11)** says that when all terms are equal to each other, the term you start with equals the term you end up with. So the point is this:

$$\left(\sqrt{a}\right)^2 = a$$

Examples

$$\left(\sqrt{9}\right)^2 = 9$$

$$\left(\sqrt{7x}\right)^2 = 7x$$

$$\left(\sqrt{ax^2}\right)^2 = ax^2$$

$$\left(\sqrt{17pqr}\right)^2 = 17pqr$$

Silly example

$$\left(\sqrt{hotdog}\right)^2 = hotdog$$

Try these:

a) $\left(\sqrt{j}\right)^2$

b) $\left(\sqrt{pq}\right)^2$

c) $\left(\sqrt{300}\right)^2$

d) $\left(\sqrt{hamburger}\right)^2$

e) $\left(\sqrt{11r^2}\right)^2$

Answers:
a) j
b) pq
c) 300
d) hamburger
e) $11r^2$

 **O.K., now I get the basic idea of a square root (and I'm getting hungry, too!). But why do they call it a "square" root? What do squares have to do with it?**

A: **It's called a "square" root because you can understand its length by thinking about a square.** Here's how: pick a number, any number. Then find a square whose area is equal to that number. Next measure the length of a side of this square. The length of that side, it turns out, is the square root of the number you started with. Presto, nothing up the sleeve. And ... now that you may be more confused than ever, here's an example to help you out.

Example

You know from geometry that the area of a square is just the length of one of its sides times itself. For example, if a side of a square is **4 inches**, the area of this square would be:

$$(\textbf{4 inches}) \cdot (\textbf{4 inches}) \text{ or } \textbf{16 square inches}.$$

But if you think about it, **4** is the square root of **16**. In other words, the length of the side is the square root of the area of the square.

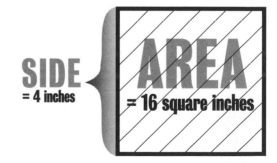
SIDE = 4 inches
AREA = 16 square inches

Length of side	=	square root of area of the square
4 inches	=	$\sqrt{16 \text{ square inches}}$

Why do I sometimes see two answers — one positive, the other negative — for the square root of a number? For example, I've heard that the square root of 9 is both +3 and −3. Why in the world would this be?

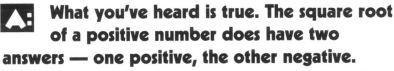

What you've heard is true. The square root of a positive number does have two answers — one positive, the other negative.

But why does the square root of nine equal negative three as well as positive three? Well, just think about it. The multiplication rule (**p. 49**) tells you that $(-3) \cdot (-3) = +9$. Therefore −**3** must be a square root of **9** because it fits the definition of a square root (**p. 116**). To show both the positive and negative value of $\sqrt{9}$, you write: $\sqrt{9} = \pm 3$. This means that the square root of **9** is both +**3** and −**3**.

In Algebra I, teachers rarely ask you to write both answers. Teachers usually want only the positive answer. Check with your instructor to find out her/his preference.

Give both values for these square roots:

a) $\sqrt{4}$ d) $\sqrt{81}$
b) $\sqrt{25}$ e) $\sqrt{100}$
c) $\sqrt{49}$

Answers:
a) ± 2 d) ± 9
b) ± 5 e) ± 10
c) ± 7

Now I thoroughly understand what a square root is. But what is a perfect square?

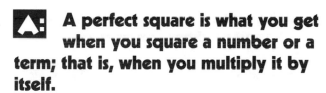 **A perfect square is what you get when you square a number or a term; that is, when you multiply it by itself.**

Examples

9 is the perfect square of **3** because **3 · 3 = 9**

a² is the perfect square of **a** because **a · a = a²**

9a² is the perfect square of **3a** because

$$(3a) \cdot (3a) = 9a^2$$

Some perfect squares to memorize

#	→	perfect square	#	→	perfect square
1	→	1	9	→	81
2	→	4	10	→	100
3	→	9	11	→	121
4	→	16	12	→	144
5	→	25	13	→	169
6	→	36	14	→	196
7	→	49	15	→	225
8	→	64	16	→	256

 **Find the perfect squares of these terms:**

a) 17   d) 9t

b) 20   e) 100

c) y

Answers:

a) 289   d) 81t²

b) 400   e) 10,000

c) y²

What is the rule for adding and subtracting radicals?

 **A:** The rule for adding and subtracting radicals is simple. As long as what's under the radical sign is exactly the same, you can treat radicals as if they were "like terms" (**p. 66**).

In other words, terms like **2√7** and **5√7** are like terms because they both show a **7** under the radical. Since such terms are like terms, you can combine them using the same-, mixed- and neighbor-sign rules (**pp. 36-45**).

Combining radicals using the same-, mixed- and neighbor-sign rules

Same-sign rule

$$- 4\sqrt{5} - 7\sqrt{5}$$
$$= -\left(4\sqrt{5} + 7\sqrt{5}\right)$$
$$= -11\sqrt{5}$$

Mixed-sign rule

$$+ 4\sqrt{5} - 7\sqrt{5}$$
$$= -\left(7\sqrt{5} - 4\sqrt{5}\right)$$
$$= -3\sqrt{5}$$

Neighbor-sign rule

$$4\sqrt{5} - - 7\sqrt{5}$$
$$= 4\sqrt{5} + 7\sqrt{5}$$
$$= 11\sqrt{5}$$

Now try these:

a) $+ 5\sqrt{7} + 3\sqrt{7}$
b) $- 2\sqrt{9} + 13\sqrt{9}$
c) $8\sqrt{5} + - 6\sqrt{5}$
d) $+ 17\sqrt{2} - 21\sqrt{2}$
e) $- 6\sqrt{11} - 3\sqrt{11}$
f) $2\sqrt{14} - - 3\sqrt{14}$

Answers:
a) $+ 8\sqrt{7}$
b) $+ 11\sqrt{9}$
c) $+ 2\sqrt{5}$
d) $- 4\sqrt{2}$
e) $- 9\sqrt{11}$
f) $5\sqrt{14}$

Q: Now I see that I can combine radicals when they have the same numbers beneath them. But can I also combine radicals containing the same variables or groups of variables?

A: Yes, you may.
Again, the rule is that as long as what's under the radical sign is the same, you can combine radicals using the same-, mixed- and neighbor-sign rules.

Examples showing how radicals with variables can be combined

Same-sign rule

$$+ 3\sqrt{m} + 8\sqrt{m}$$
$$= + \left(3\sqrt{m} + 8\sqrt{m}\right)$$
$$= + 11\sqrt{m}$$

Mixed-sign rule

$$- 4\sqrt{x} + 11\sqrt{x}$$
$$= + \left(11\sqrt{x} - 4\sqrt{x}\right)$$
$$= + 7\sqrt{x}$$

Neighbor-sign rule

$$9\sqrt{vw} + \left(- 3\sqrt{vw}\right)$$
$$= 9\sqrt{vw} - 3\sqrt{vw}$$
$$= 6\sqrt{vw}$$

Now try these:

a) $- 4\sqrt{u} - 5\sqrt{u}$

b) $12\sqrt{w} + \left(+ 2\sqrt{w}\right)$

c) $- 3\sqrt{n} + 13\sqrt{n}$

d) $15\sqrt{r} - \left(- 2\sqrt{r}\right)$

e) $+ \sqrt{x} + \sqrt{x}$

f) $+ \sqrt{c} - 6\sqrt{c}$

Answers:

a) $- 9\sqrt{u}$ d) $17\sqrt{r}$

b) $14\sqrt{w}$ e) $2\sqrt{x}$

c) $+ 10\sqrt{n}$ f) $- 5\sqrt{c}$

Q: What does the radical product rule say?

$$\sqrt{a} \cdot \sqrt{c} = ?$$

A: The radical product rule says you can simplify a product of radicals in this nice easy way:

$$\sqrt{a} \cdot \sqrt{c} = \sqrt{a \cdot c}$$

Here's how you can remember this rule: **When two or more radical terms are multiplying each other, you can simplify them by making one big, happy radical sign and multiplying all the terms underneath it.**

Examples of the radical product rule

$$\sqrt{m} \cdot \sqrt{v} = \sqrt{m \cdot v}$$

$$\sqrt{2} \cdot \sqrt{5} = \sqrt{2 \cdot 5} = \sqrt{10}$$

$$\sqrt{r} \cdot \sqrt{s} \cdot \sqrt{u} = \sqrt{r \cdot s \cdot u} = \sqrt{rsu}$$

$$\sqrt{2} \cdot \sqrt{3} \cdot \sqrt{5} = \sqrt{2 \cdot 3 \cdot 5} = \sqrt{30}$$

Note: This rule is very flexible. As the examples show, you can use it on any number of terms. And it makes no difference whether those terms are numbers, variables, or a combination of numbers and variables.

Combine using the radical product rule:

a) $\sqrt{2} \cdot \sqrt{3}$

b) $\sqrt{4} \cdot \sqrt{5} \cdot \sqrt{7}$

c) $\sqrt{p} \cdot \sqrt{q}$

d) $\sqrt{6} \cdot \sqrt{v} \cdot \sqrt{w}$

e) $\sqrt{3} \cdot \sqrt{7} \cdot \sqrt{r} \cdot \sqrt{u}$

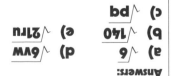

Answers:
a) $\sqrt{6}$
b) $\sqrt{140}$
c) $\sqrt{pq}$
d) $\sqrt{6vw}$
e) $\sqrt{21ru}$

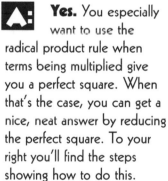

Is there any time when it's especially convenient to use the radical product rule?

A: **Yes.** You especially want to use the radical product rule when terms being multiplied give you a perfect square. When that's the case, you can get a nice, neat answer by reducing the perfect square. To your right you'll find the steps showing how to do this.

Simplify:

A) $\sqrt{2} \cdot \sqrt{8}$,

B) $\sqrt{4a} \cdot \sqrt{a}$

Steps

1st) Study the terms under the radical sign to see if, when multiplied, they would give you a perfect square.

2nd) Use the radical product rule (**p. 126**).

3rd) Reduce the radical to get your answer.

Example A

$\sqrt{2} \cdot \sqrt{8}$

($2 \cdot 8 = 16$; and **16** is a perfect square)

$\sqrt{2} \cdot \sqrt{8} = \sqrt{2 \cdot 8}$
$= \sqrt{16}$

$\sqrt{16} = 4$

Example B

$\sqrt{4a} \cdot \sqrt{a}$

($4a \cdot a = 4a^2$; and $4a^2$ is a perfect square)

$\sqrt{4a} \cdot \sqrt{a} = \sqrt{4a^2}$

$\sqrt{4a^2} = 2a$

Now try simplifying these expressions using the radical product rule:

a) $\sqrt{18} \cdot \sqrt{2}$

b) $\sqrt{32} \cdot \sqrt{2}$

c) $\sqrt{20x} \cdot \sqrt{5x}$

d) $\sqrt{8} \cdot \sqrt{18}$

e) $\sqrt{5m} \cdot \sqrt{45m}$

Answers:
a) 6   d) 12
b) 8   e) 15m
c) 10x

Q: Can I also use the radical product rule backwards? In other words, can I say this:

$$\sqrt{a \cdot c} = \sqrt{a} \cdot \sqrt{c}$$

A: Yes, thanks to the symmetric property (**p. 10**), you can flip terms around the equal sign. This rule is called the **reverse radical product rule**. It's also called **splitting the square** because you can imagine that you're taking an axe and splitting the radical apart. Notice that you can split the radical even if it contains more than two terms.

Examples of the reverse radical product rule

$$\sqrt{m \cdot v} = \sqrt{m} \cdot \sqrt{v}$$

$$\sqrt{e \cdot m \cdot v} = \sqrt{e} \cdot \sqrt{m} \cdot \sqrt{v}$$

$$\sqrt{3 \cdot m} = \sqrt{3} \cdot \sqrt{m}$$

$$\sqrt{9 \cdot r^2 \cdot u} = \sqrt{9} \cdot \sqrt{r^2} \cdot \sqrt{u}$$

$$\sqrt{25 \cdot 3} = \sqrt{25} \cdot \sqrt{3}$$

Take out your axe and split these squares:

a) $\sqrt{r \cdot s}$ d) $\sqrt{36 \cdot x^2}$

b) $\sqrt{9 \cdot 7}$ e) $\sqrt{50 \cdot y^2 \cdot z^3}$

c) $\sqrt{16 \cdot v}$

Answers:

a) $\sqrt{r} \cdot \sqrt{s}$ d) $\sqrt{36} \cdot \sqrt{x^2}$

b) $\sqrt{9} \cdot \sqrt{7}$ e) $\sqrt{50} \cdot \sqrt{y^2} \cdot \sqrt{z^3}$

c) $\sqrt{16} \cdot \sqrt{v}$

How do I use the reverse radical product rule in a problem?

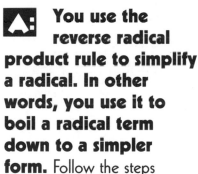 **You use the reverse radical product rule to simplify a radical. In other words, you use it to boil a radical term down to a simpler form.** Follow the steps shown to your right.

Simplify:

A) $\sqrt{75}$, B) $\sqrt{a^2c}$

Steps	Example A	Example B
1st) See if the term under the radical has a factor which is a perfect square. If it does, rewrite the term to show this perfect square.	$\sqrt{75}$ $= \sqrt{25 \cdot 3}$ (**25** is a perfect square)	$\sqrt{a^2c}$ $= \sqrt{a^2 \cdot c}$ (a^2 is a perfect square)
2nd) Take out your axe and split the radical.	$= \sqrt{25} \cdot \sqrt{3}$	$= \sqrt{a^2} \cdot \sqrt{c}$
3rd) Simplify the square root of the perfect square.	$= 5 \cdot \sqrt{3}$ $= 5\sqrt{3}$	$= a \cdot \sqrt{c}$ $= a\sqrt{c}$

Now try simplifying these terms:

a) $\sqrt{8}$
b) $\sqrt{50}$
c) $\sqrt{48}$
d) $\sqrt{100a^2}$
e) $\sqrt{c^2e^2n}$

Answers:
a) $2\sqrt{2}$ d) $10a$
b) $5\sqrt{2}$ e) $ce\sqrt{n}$
c) $4\sqrt{3}$

129

Q: Now I grasp the basic idea behind the radical product rules, but this makes me wonder about something:

$$\text{If } \sqrt{a \cdot c} = \sqrt{a} \cdot \sqrt{c},$$
$$\text{wouldn't it also be true that}$$
$$\sqrt{a + c} = \sqrt{a} + \sqrt{c},$$
$$\text{and that}$$
$$\sqrt{a - c} = \sqrt{a} - \sqrt{c} \ ?$$

A: **Not a chance. This is what you call "creative, wrong thinking."**

Neither $\sqrt{a + c}$ nor $\sqrt{a - c}$ can be simplified in any special way.

But maybe you need to see this to believe it. Let's check it by testing whether $\sqrt{16 + 9} = \sqrt{16} + \sqrt{9}$ and also whether $\sqrt{169 - 144} = \sqrt{169} - \sqrt{144}$

$$\sqrt{16 + 9} = \sqrt{16} + \sqrt{9} \qquad\qquad \sqrt{169 - 144} = \sqrt{169} - \sqrt{144}$$
$$\sqrt{25} = 4 + 3 \qquad\qquad\qquad \sqrt{25} = 13 - 12$$
$$5 = 7 \qquad\qquad\qquad\qquad\quad 5 = 1$$

$$\text{nope!} \qquad\qquad\qquad\qquad\qquad \text{nope!}$$

So remember: $\sqrt{a + c} \neq \sqrt{a} + \sqrt{c}$

and $\sqrt{a - c} \neq \sqrt{a} - \sqrt{c}$

True or false?

a) $\sqrt{e \cdot r} = \sqrt{e} \cdot \sqrt{r}$ 　　 d) $\sqrt{5mr} = \sqrt{5} \cdot \sqrt{m} \cdot \sqrt{r}$

b) $\sqrt{r + u} = \sqrt{r} \cdot \sqrt{u}$ 　　 e) $\sqrt{9 - 3} = \sqrt{9} - \sqrt{3}$

c) $\sqrt{x + y} = \sqrt{x} + \sqrt{y}$

Answers:
a) true d) true
b) false e) false
c) false

Q: What would be the value of a term like this:

$$\sqrt{a^2}$$

 A: The value of this term is so simple that it's confusing.

$$\sqrt{a^2} = a$$

See below if you want to know why this is true.

From the definition of an exponent (**p. 86**) you know that: $\sqrt{a^2} = \sqrt{a \cdot a}$ (since $a^2 = a \cdot a$). And when you take your axe to the square root, you get: $\sqrt{a \cdot a} = \sqrt{a} \cdot \sqrt{a}$. Then, by the very definition of a square root (**p. 116**), you know that: $\sqrt{a} \cdot \sqrt{a} = a$. Now, if you look at these three statements, you'll see that everything is equal to everything else, so with a grand use of the transitive property (**p. 11**), you say that the first is equal to the last. That is: $\sqrt{a^2} = a$. To the right are more examples.

Examples

$$\sqrt{5^2} = 5$$

$$\sqrt{y^2} = y$$

$$\sqrt{(5y)^2} = 5y$$

$$\sqrt{(mn)^2} = mn$$

Silly example

$$\sqrt{(popcorn)^2} = popcorn$$

Simplify these terms:

a) $\sqrt{11^2}$ d) $\sqrt{(frog)^2}$

b) $\sqrt{r^2}$ e) $\sqrt{(12x^2)^2}$

c) $\sqrt{(7c)^2}$

Answers:
a) 11 d) frog
b) r e) $12x^2$
c) 7c

 Now I understand how to multiply two radicals together, but how would I multiply terms with numbers both inside and outside radical signs? In other words, how would I work out the answer to something like this:

$$2\sqrt{3} \cdot 5\sqrt{7}$$

The rule is this: you multiply the terms **outside** the radical and keep that answer **outside the radical sign**; then you multiply the terms **inside** the radical and keep that answer **inside the radical sign**. The general form for the solution is this:

$$a\sqrt{c} \cdot x\sqrt{n} = a \cdot x\sqrt{c \cdot n}$$

This rule is called the **complex radical product rule**, "complex" meaning "complicated." To the right are examples showing how you'd use the **complex radical product rule**.

<u>Examples</u>

$$m\sqrt{v} \cdot r\sqrt{u} = mr\sqrt{vu}$$

$$m\sqrt{2} \cdot r\sqrt{5} = mr\sqrt{10}$$

$$2\sqrt{m} \cdot 5\sqrt{r} = 10\sqrt{mr}$$

$$2\sqrt{3} \cdot 5\sqrt{7} = 10\sqrt{21}$$

 **Work out these products using the complex radical product rule:**

a) $5\sqrt{2} \cdot 7\sqrt{3}$

b) $a\sqrt{6} \cdot b\sqrt{11}$

c) $8\sqrt{m} \cdot 10\sqrt{n}$

d) $x\sqrt{v} \cdot r\sqrt{u}$

e) $12\sqrt{ax} \cdot w\sqrt{13}$

Answers:

a) $35\sqrt{6}$

b) $ab\sqrt{66}$

c) $80\sqrt{mn}$

d) $xr\sqrt{vu}$

e) $12w\sqrt{13ax}$

Sometimes I see a number outside a radical multiplying a term inside a radical, and this entire expression is itself squared.

Is there any shortcut for working out this kind of term, a term like:

$$\left(5\sqrt{3}\right)^2$$

Yes, there's a shortcut, and it's this:

$$\left(5\sqrt{3}\right)^2 = 5^2 \cdot 3 = 75$$

Or, in general:

$$\left(a\sqrt{c}\right)^2 = a^2 \cdot c$$

You can remember this as the **radical product shortcut**. To the right are examples showing how you'd use this wonderful little shortcut.

Examples

$$\left(m\sqrt{v}\right)^2 = m^2 \cdot v$$

$$\left(v\sqrt{5}\right)^2 = v^2 \cdot 5 = 5v^2$$

$$\left(3\sqrt{m}\right)^2 = 3^2 \cdot m = 9m$$

$$\left(3\sqrt{7}\right)^2 = 3^2 \cdot 7 = 9 \cdot 7 = 63$$

Use the radical product shortcut to simplify these terms:

a) $\left(3\sqrt{5}\right)^2$ d) $\left(p\sqrt{q}\right)^2$

b) $\left(8\sqrt{a}\right)^2$ e) $\left(3x\sqrt{4y}\right)^2$

c) $\left(c\sqrt{7}\right)^2$

Answers:

a) 45   d) p^2q

b) 64a   e) $36x^2y$

c) $7c^2$

Q: What does the radical quotient rule say?

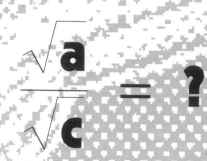

$$\frac{\sqrt{a}}{\sqrt{c}} = ?$$

A: The radical quotient rule works just like the radical product rule, except that it deals with a quotient instead of with a product. Here's what it says:

$$\frac{\sqrt{a}}{\sqrt{c}} = \sqrt{\frac{a}{c}}$$

Or in English: **if a fraction has a radical over a radical, you can combine the two separate radicals into one big, happy radical.** To the right are examples showing how you'd use the radical quotient rule.

Examples

$$\frac{\sqrt{m}}{\sqrt{v}} = \sqrt{\frac{m}{v}} \qquad \frac{\sqrt{m}}{\sqrt{3}} = \sqrt{\frac{m}{3}}$$

$$\frac{\sqrt{3}}{\sqrt{m}} = \sqrt{\frac{3}{m}} \qquad \frac{\sqrt{25}}{\sqrt{3}} = \sqrt{\frac{25}{3}}$$

Silly example

$$\frac{\sqrt{zig}}{\sqrt{zag}} = \sqrt{\frac{zig}{zag}}$$

Combine using the radical quotient rule:

a) $\dfrac{\sqrt{v}}{\sqrt{w}}$ c) $\dfrac{\sqrt{ant}}{\sqrt{fly}}$

b) $\dfrac{\sqrt{20}}{\sqrt{5}}$ d) $\dfrac{\sqrt{4a}}{\sqrt{2a}}$

Answers:

a) $\sqrt{\dfrac{v}{w}}$ c) $\sqrt{\dfrac{ant}{fly}}$

b) $\sqrt{\dfrac{20}{5}}$ d) $\sqrt{\dfrac{4a}{2a}}$

134

Q: When do I use the radical quotient rule in a problem?

A: You use the radical quotient rule when two or more terms divide to make a perfect square. Follow the steps shown to the right.

Simplify:

A) $\dfrac{\sqrt{8}}{\sqrt{2}}$, B) $\dfrac{\sqrt{a^3}}{\sqrt{a}}$

Steps

1st) Look at the terms under the radical signs to see if, when divided, they make a perfect square.

2nd) Use the radical quotient rule (**p. 134**).

3rd) Reduce radical using definition of a square root (**p. 116**).

Example A

$\dfrac{\sqrt{8}}{\sqrt{2}} \Big\} \dfrac{8}{2} = 4$

(**4** is a perfect square)

$\dfrac{\sqrt{8}}{\sqrt{2}} = \sqrt{\dfrac{8}{2}} = \sqrt{4}$

$\sqrt{4} = 2$

Example B

$\dfrac{\sqrt{a^3}}{\sqrt{a}} \Big\} \dfrac{a^3}{a} = a^2$

(a^2 is a perfect square)

$\dfrac{\sqrt{a^3}}{\sqrt{a}} = \sqrt{\dfrac{a^3}{a}} = \sqrt{a^2}$

$\sqrt{a^2} = a$

Simplify using the radical quotient rule:

a) $\dfrac{\sqrt{50}}{\sqrt{2}}$ c) $\dfrac{\sqrt{48}}{\sqrt{3}}$

b) $\dfrac{\sqrt{d^5}}{\sqrt{d^3}}$ d) $\dfrac{\sqrt{f^8}}{\sqrt{f^4}}$

Answers:
a) 5 c) 4
b) d d) f^2

Q: What does the reverse radical quotient rule say?

$$\sqrt{\dfrac{a}{c}} = \ ?$$

A: The reverse radical quotient rule says more or less what you'd expect it to say, namely this:

$$\sqrt{\dfrac{a}{c}} = \dfrac{\sqrt{a}}{\sqrt{c}}$$

Like the reverse radical product rule, the reverse radical quotient rule involves **splitting the square**, only here you take your axe and swing at the radical sideways. To the right are examples showing how you'd use the reverse radical quotient rule.

Examples

$$\sqrt{\dfrac{m}{v}} = \dfrac{\sqrt{m}}{\sqrt{v}} \qquad \sqrt{\dfrac{m}{3}} = \dfrac{\sqrt{m}}{\sqrt{3}}$$

$$\sqrt{\dfrac{3}{m}} = \dfrac{\sqrt{3}}{\sqrt{m}} \qquad \sqrt{\dfrac{25}{3}} = \dfrac{\sqrt{25}}{\sqrt{3}}$$

Silly example

$$\sqrt{\dfrac{peach}{pear}} = \dfrac{\sqrt{peach}}{\sqrt{pear}}$$

Now take out your axe and split these radicals using the reverse radical quotient rule:

a) $\sqrt{\dfrac{x}{y}}$ b) $\sqrt{\dfrac{2}{9}}$ c) $\sqrt{\dfrac{p}{7}}$ d) $\sqrt{\dfrac{elm}{oak}}$

Answers:
a) $\dfrac{\sqrt{x}}{\sqrt{y}}$ b) $\dfrac{\sqrt{2}}{\sqrt{9}}$ c) $\dfrac{\sqrt{p}}{\sqrt{7}}$ d) $\dfrac{\sqrt{elm}}{\sqrt{oak}}$

How do I use the reverse radical quotient rule in a problem?

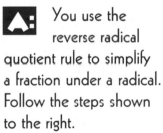

A: You use the reverse radical quotient rule to simplify a fraction under a radical. Follow the steps shown to the right.

Simplify:

A) $\sqrt{\dfrac{7}{25}}$,

B) $\sqrt{\dfrac{a}{c^2}}$

Steps

1st) See if either the numerator or the denominator contains a perfect square.

2nd) If it does, take out your axe and split that radical.

3rd) Simplify the square root of the perfect square.

Example A

$$\sqrt{\dfrac{7}{25}}$$

(**25** is a perfect square)

$$\sqrt{\dfrac{7}{25}}$$
$$= \dfrac{\sqrt{7}}{\sqrt{25}}$$
$$= \dfrac{\sqrt{7}}{5}$$

Example B

$$\sqrt{\dfrac{a}{c^2}}$$

(c^2 is a perfect square)

$$\sqrt{\dfrac{a}{c^2}}$$
$$= \dfrac{\sqrt{a}}{\sqrt{c^2}}$$
$$= \dfrac{\sqrt{a}}{c}$$

Simplify using the reverse radical quotient rule:

a) $\sqrt{\dfrac{v}{49}}$ c) $\sqrt{\dfrac{r^2}{s^2}}$

b) $\sqrt{\dfrac{11}{x^2}}$ d) $\sqrt{\dfrac{16}{49}}$

Answers:

a) $\dfrac{\sqrt{v}}{7}$ c) $\dfrac{r}{s}$

b) $\dfrac{\sqrt{11}}{x}$ d) $\dfrac{4}{7}$

 Now I have some sense
of how to work with radicals.
But what do I do when I have
a fraction, and both its numerator
and its denominator have one term
inside a radical and another term outside
a radical. In other words, how would
I simplify an expression like this:

$$\frac{6\sqrt{18}}{9\sqrt{2}}$$

The rule for doing this, called the **complex radical quotient rule**, works just like the complex radical product rule (**p. 132**), except that here you divide instead of multiply. You divide the terms **outside** the radical and keep that answer **outside the radical sign**; then you divide the terms **inside** the radical and keep that answer **inside the radical**. The general form for the solution looks like this:

$$\frac{a\sqrt{c}}{x\sqrt{n}} = \frac{a}{x}\sqrt{\frac{c}{n}}$$

To the right are examples showing how you use the complex radical quotient rule.

Examples

$$\frac{m\sqrt{v}}{r\sqrt{u}} = \frac{m}{r}\sqrt{\frac{v}{u}} \qquad \frac{3\sqrt{m}}{5\sqrt{r}} = \frac{3}{5}\sqrt{\frac{m}{r}}$$

$$\frac{m\sqrt{3}}{r\sqrt{5}} = \frac{m}{r}\sqrt{\frac{3}{5}} \qquad \frac{3\sqrt{6}}{5\sqrt{7}} = \frac{3}{5}\sqrt{\frac{6}{7}}$$

Simplify using the complex radical quotient rule:

a) $\dfrac{c\sqrt{e}}{n\sqrt{w}}$ c) $\dfrac{6\sqrt{y}}{8\sqrt{z}}$

b) $\dfrac{s\sqrt{12}}{x\sqrt{5}}$ d) $\dfrac{2\sqrt{8}}{3\sqrt{11}}$

Answers:

a) $\dfrac{c}{n}\sqrt{\dfrac{e}{w}}$ c) $\dfrac{3}{4}\sqrt{\dfrac{y}{z}}$

b) $\dfrac{s}{x}\sqrt{\dfrac{12}{5}}$ d) $\dfrac{2}{3}\sqrt{\dfrac{8}{11}}$

© Singing Turtle Press

138

Q: My teacher always asks me to "rationalize the denominator" of fractions. What does that mean? And how do I do it?

A: Rationalizing the denominator means playing around with the radical in the denominator to turn it into a whole number or a rational term. Just follow the steps to the right.

Rationalize the denominator of the fraction:

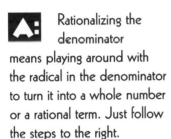

$$\frac{\sqrt{5}}{\sqrt{18}}$$

Steps

1st) If you can simplify the denominator, do so using the reverse radical product rule (**p. 129**).

2nd) Multiply numerator and denominator by the radical in the denominator.

3rd) Simplify numerator by using radical product rule (**p. 126**), if necessary. Simplify denominator by using definition of a square root (**p. 116**).

Example

$$\frac{\sqrt{5}}{\sqrt{18}} = \frac{\sqrt{5}}{3\sqrt{2}}$$

$$\frac{\sqrt{5}}{3\sqrt{2}} \cdot \frac{\sqrt{2}}{\sqrt{2}}$$

$$\frac{\sqrt{5}}{3\sqrt{2}} \cdot \frac{\sqrt{2}}{\sqrt{2}} = \frac{\sqrt{10}}{3 \cdot 2} = \frac{\sqrt{10}}{6}$$

In Step 1, you don't **always** have to simplify the denominator. It may already be in simplest radical form. For example, in $\frac{\sqrt{2}}{\sqrt{3}}$, the denominator, $\sqrt{3}$, already is in simplest radical form.

So here you would only need to multiply the numerator and denominator by $\sqrt{3}$.

Now try rationalizing the denominators of these fractions:

a) $\dfrac{\sqrt{2}}{\sqrt{3}}$ c) $\dfrac{\sqrt{3}}{\sqrt{8}}$

b) $\dfrac{5}{\sqrt{7}}$ d) $\dfrac{11}{\sqrt{27}}$

Answers:

a) $\dfrac{\sqrt{6}}{3}$ c) $\dfrac{\sqrt{6}}{4}$

b) $\dfrac{5\sqrt{7}}{7}$ d) $\dfrac{11\sqrt{3}}{9}$

Simplify these radical expressions:

a) $\sqrt{64}$

b) $\sqrt{11} \cdot \sqrt{11}$

c) $\left(\sqrt{5}\right)^2$

d) $-2\sqrt{3} + 9\sqrt{3}$

e) $-2\sqrt{3} - 9\sqrt{3}$

f) $8\sqrt{5} - -3\sqrt{5}$

g) $-2\sqrt{n} + 9\sqrt{n}$

h) $4\sqrt{7} + \left(-3\sqrt{7}\right)$

J) $\sqrt{2} \cdot \sqrt{3} \cdot \sqrt{5}$

k) $\sqrt{18} \cdot \sqrt{2}$

l) $\sqrt{75}$

m) $\sqrt{x^2}$

n) $3\sqrt{2} \cdot 4\sqrt{5}$

p) $\left(2\sqrt{7}\right)^2$

q) $\sqrt{\dfrac{11}{49}}$

r) $\dfrac{12\sqrt{5}}{16\sqrt{17}}$

s) $\dfrac{8}{\sqrt{5}}$

t) $\sqrt{a^4}$

Answer true or false:

u) $\sqrt{3} + \sqrt{2} = \sqrt{5}$

v) $\sqrt{3} + \sqrt{2} = 5$

w) $\sqrt{3} \cdot \sqrt{2} = \sqrt{6}$

x) $\sqrt{x} - \sqrt{y} = \sqrt{x - y}$

y) $\sqrt{c^2} = c$

z) $\sqrt{c^2} = c^2$

What is the perfect square of the following terms?

A) 9

B) y

C) 4x

D) $5x^2$

a) 8

b) 11

c) 5

d) $7\sqrt{3}$

e) $-11\sqrt{3}$

f) $11\sqrt{5}$

g) $7\sqrt{n}$

h) $\sqrt{7}$

j) $\sqrt{30}$

k) 6

l) $5\sqrt{3}$

m) x

n) $12\sqrt{10}$

p) 28

q) $\dfrac{\sqrt{11}}{7}$

r) $\dfrac{3}{4}\sqrt{\dfrac{5}{17}}$

s) $\dfrac{8\sqrt{5}}{5}$

t) a^2

u) false

v) false

w) true

x) false

y) true

z) false

A) 81

B) y^2

C) $16x^2$

D) $25x^4$

Factoring

When you factor, you're taking a mathematical expression and breaking it into its basic parts by finding factors, the terms that multiply together to give you the expression. And just taking apart a clock helps you understand what makes it tick, factoring an expression helps you see how it works and what it's made of. In short, you factor so you can learn what mathematical expressions are made of.

What is factoring?
And why should I learn
how to factor?

A: Have you ever been so curious to find out what something was made of that you just had to take it apart? Maybe it was a clock, a telephone, even an old car engine. All people get this urge from time to time — even mathematicians, only when they get the itch, they take apart mathematical expressions — by factoring.

When you factor, you're taking a mathematical expression and breaking it into its basic parts by finding **factors**, the terms that **multiply together** to give you the expression. And just as taking apart a clock helps you understand what makes it tick, factoring an expression helps you see how it works. In short, you factor so you can learn what mathematical expressions are made of.

Examples of various terms in their original and factored forms

	original form	$\rightarrow$	factored form
number:	21	$\rightarrow$	$7 \cdot 3$
monomial:	$4a^2$	$\rightarrow$	$2a \cdot 2a$
polynomial:	$6a + 12$	$\rightarrow$	$6 \cdot (a + 2)$

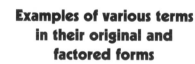

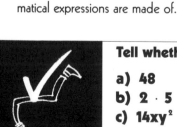

Tell whether these terms are in their original or factored forms:

a) 48

b) $2 \cdot 5$

c) $14xy^2$

d) $6y \cdot 6y$

e) $9 \cdot (x - 3)$

Answers:
a) original
b) factored
c) original
d) factored
e) factored

I hear that in order to factor, I first need to learn some concepts, namely: "monomial," "coefficient," "polynomial," "factor" and "greatest common factor."
Let me start at the beginning then: what is a monomial, and what is a coefficient?

 A **monomial** is a mathematical term with two parts:

1) the **coefficient**, which is made up of the number in front, along with its sign.

2) a **variable or a string of variables**, each of which is raised to an exponent.

Two typical monomials

$$-\,1/3\;x^5 \qquad\qquad 4\,a^2c^3$$

coefficient

variable raised to an exponent

coefficient

string of variables raised to exponents

Important point: the sign of the monomial is part of the coefficient's identity. In other words, **if the monomial is positive, the coefficient is positive; if the monomial is negative, the coefficient is negative.** As you see in the examples to the left, the monomial $4a^2c^3$ has a coefficient of $+\,4$; the monomial $-\,1/3\;x^5$ has a coefficient of $-\,1/3$. Keep in mind that when a monomial has no sign showing, like $4a^2c^3$, it actually has an **invisible positive sign**.

That is: $4a^2c^3$ really means $+\,4a^2c^3$.

 **Identify the coefficient in each of the following monomials:**

a) $7xyz$ d) $2/7\;uv^4$
b) $-\,4v^7$ e) $-\,9pq^2$
c) $.6m^5n$

Answers:
a) $+\,7$ d) $+\,2/7$
b) $-\,4$ e) $-\,9$
c) $+\,.6$

Q: My teacher says that even simple terms like "n" and "ac" are monomials. But how can this be when such terms seem to be missing both coefficients and exponents?

A: Aha, you just have to look harder.

Terms like **n** and **ac** actually have both coefficients and exponents; it's just that the coefficients and exponents are **invisible**.

Remember this: When no coefficients or exponents are showing, there's always an invisible **+ 1** lurking in the shadows.

In other words, the term **n** is actually $+1n^1$; its coefficient and exponent are both **+ 1**.

In the same way, the term **ac** is actually $+1a^1c^1$; its coefficient and its exponents are also **+ 1**.

Name the coefficient in each of these monomials:

a) x   d) $-p^2q^5$
b) − x   e) $x^5y^4z^3$
c) − pqr

Answers:
a) + 1   d) − 1
b) − 1   e) + 1
c) − 1

Q: **Can even a plain old number, like + 7 or − 2/5, be considered a monomial? And if so, why?**

 Yes, weird as it might seem, even a number — all by itself — may be considered a monomial. Here's why:

Remember from the **Exponents** section **(p. 94)** that a variable raised to the zero power is actually equal to **+ 1**. Since that's true, you could view a number like **+ 7** as the monomial: $+7a^0$, since a^0 just equals **1**. So again, there's something **invisible** that you need to think about. **Whenever you see a pure number term, imagine that there's an invisible variable to the zero power following that number.**

Since that invisible variable to the zero power is hiding in the shadows, **any number can quite fairly be thought of as a monomial**.

Q: O.K. Now I think I understand what a monomial is. But what in the world is a polynomial?

A: A **polynomial** is a train of two or more monomials hitched together to make one expression. We call it a **polynomial** because it contains **many** monomials ("poly" being the Greek word for "many").

Examples of various kinds of polynomials

Polynomial	**Binomial**	**Trinomial**
$9u^4 - 3u^3 + 5u^2 - 6u - 10$	$4a + 2$	$a^2 + 2a - 8$

Polynomial

$9u^4 - 3u^3 + 5u^2 - 6u - 10$

is a **polynomial**. Notice that it's made up of **five separate monomials**:

$$+ 9u^4, - 3u^3, + 5u^2,$$
$$- 6u \text{ and } - 10$$

Binomial

$4a + 2$

is a polynomial made up of **two monomials**:

$$+ 4a \text{ and } + 2$$

A polynomial with two monomials is called a **binomial**. ("bi" being Latin for "two").

Trinomial

$a^2 + 2a - 8$

is a polynomial made up of **three monomials**:

$$+ a^2, + 2a \text{ and } - 8$$

A polynomial with three monomials is called a **trinomial**. ("tri" being Latin for "three").

Are the following expressions monomials, binomials or trinomials?

a) $- 6a^2 - 8a + 4$ d) $- 4/5$

b) m^7

c) $9x - 7$ e) $- 3g^3 - 4g^2 - 11$

Answers:
a) trinomial d) monomial
b) monomial e) trinomial
c) binomial

146

Q: What is a factor?

A: If you view a mathematical term as one unit, **the factors of a term would be the pieces that make up that unit**. To grasp this idea, go back to the notion that factoring is like taking taking apart a clock. If a mathematical term is viewed as a fully-assembled clock, its **factors** are the individual gears that make the clock tick. And the operation of multiplication, in the sense that it connects the factors, would be the teeth that hold those gears together.

Examples of terms and the factors of which they are made

Term:	21	$4a^2$	$6a + 12$
Term's factors:	7 and 3	2a and 2a	6 and $(a + 2)$
Why?	$7 \cdot 3 = 21$	$2a \cdot 2a = 4a^2$	$6 \cdot (a + 2) = 6a + 12$

Q: How do I find all the factors of a number?

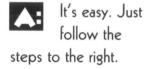 It's easy. Just follow the steps to the right.

Find all the factors of 12.

Steps

1st) List all the number pairs that multiply to give you the number.

2nd) Now list all the factors in order from least to greatest.

Example

$12 = 1 \cdot 12$

$12 = 2 \cdot 6$

$12 = 3 \cdot 4$

The factors of 12 are: 1, 2, 3, 4, 6 and 12

List all the factors of these numbers:

a) 8
b) 15
c) 24
d) 29
e) 50

Answers:
a) 1, 2, 4, 8
b) 1, 3, 5, 15
c) 1, 2, 3, 4, 6, 8, 12, 24
d) 1, 29
e) 1, 2, 5, 10, 25, 50

Q: How do I find all the factors of a monomial?

A: To find the factors of a monomial, first find the factors of the coefficient. Then find the factors of the variable string. Finally, combine the two lists of factors. Follow the steps shown to the right.

Find the factors of:

$$12ac^2$$

Steps

1st) List all pairs that multiply to give you the coefficient.

2nd) List all pairs that multiply to give you the variable string.

3rd) Combine the two lists of factors to get all the factors of the monomial.

Example

$12 = 1 \cdot 12$
$12 = 2 \cdot 6$
$12 = 3 \cdot 4$

$ac^2 = a \cdot c^2$
$ac^2 = ac \cdot c$
$ac^2 = ac^2 \cdot 1$

There are even more factors than are shown here — since one factor times another factor gives you yet a third factor. For example, since **2** and **a** are both factors, the term **2a** is still another factor. When you take these combination factors into account, the complete list of factors becomes so long it's hard to work with. To save space, we'll just write out the primary, or main, factors.

The factors of $12ac^2$ are:

$$1, 2, 3, 4, 6, 12, a, ac, c, c^2, ac^2$$

Now try listing the primary factors of these monomials:

a) $6x^2$
b) $2/3\ abc$
c) $10m^2n$
d) $11p^2q^2$

© Singing Turtle Press

149

Now I understand what a factor is, but what is a greatest common factor?

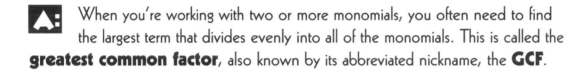

A: When you're working with two or more monomials, you often need to find the largest term that divides evenly into all of the monomials. This is called the **greatest common factor**, also known by its abbreviated nickname, the **GCF**.

Examples

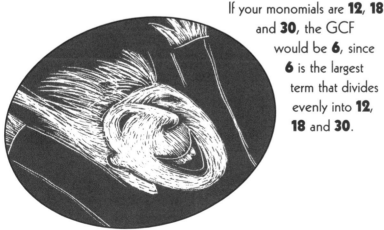

If your monomials are **12**, **18** and **30**, the GCF would be **6**, since **6** is the largest term that divides evenly into **12**, **18** and **30**.

If your monomials are **4a²** and **6a**, the GCF would be **2a**, since **2a** is the largest term that divides evenly into **4a²** and **6a**. Here's why: **2** is the largest factor of the coefficients: **4** and **6**; **a** is the largest factor of the variable terms: **a²** and **a**

A: Follow the steps shown to the right.

**Find the GCF for:
72, 90 and 108**

Steps

1st) Prime factorize each number, and list its factors in order.

2nd) Find the largest number common to each column.

3rd) Multiply these numbers to get the GCF.

Example

$72 = 2^3 \cdot 3^2$
$90 = 2^1 \cdot 3^2 \cdot 5^1$
$108 = 2^2 \cdot 3^3$

↓   ↓   ↓

2^1 3^2 **no number common**

↓   ↓

$2 \cdot 9 = 18$
18 is the GCF

Find the GCF for these sets of numbers:

a) 24, 40, 64
b) 36, 54, 72
c) 18, 54, 99
d) 48, 96, 120
e) 72, 108, 144

Answers:
a) 8
b) 18
c) 9
d) 24
e) 36

Now I see how to find the GCF for a group of numbers. But how would I find the GCF for a group of complicated monomials? In other words, how would I find the GCF for a group of monomials like this:

$$72ac^5, 90a^2c^4, 108ac^3d$$

 Follow the steps shown to the right.

Find the GCF for these monomials:

$72ac^5$

$90a^2c^4$

$108ac^3d$

Steps	**Example**
1st) Get GCF for coefficients (**p. 151**).	**GCF for 72, 90 and 108 is 18**
2nd) Arrange each variable string as a product of its factors.	$ac^5 = a^1 \cdot c^5$ $a^2c^4 = a^2 \cdot c^4$ $ac^3d = a^1 \cdot c^3 \cdot d^1$ $\downarrow \quad \downarrow \quad \downarrow$
3rd) Find the largest term common to each column. Multiply them together to get GCF of variable strings.	$a^1 \quad c^3 \quad$ **no common term** $a^1 \cdot c^3 = a^1c^3$ a^1c^3 **is GCF of variable strings**
4th) Multiply GCF of the coefficients with GCF of variable strings to get GCF of the monomials.	$18 \cdot a^1c^3 = 18ac^3$ $18ac^3$ **is the GCF**

Now try finding the GCF for these groups of monomials:

a) $2x, 4x, 8x$

b) $3ac, 6a^2, 9a$

c) $4pq^2, 8p^2q^2, 12pq$

d) $25m^3n^3, 15m^3n^2, 45m^2n^4$

e) $24a^2b^5, 48a^3b^4, 60a^4b^7$

f) $28x^5y^2z^4, 42x^2yz^3, 70x^4y^3z^6$

Answers:
a) $2x$ d) $5m^2n^2$
b) $3a$ e) $12a^2b^4$
c) $4pq$ f) $14x^2yz^3$

become a "mathemagician"

Q: Now I see how to get the GCF for a group of monomials. But ...
can this idea help me factor a polynomial?
What are the steps for factoring a polynomial?

A: Yes, once you know how to find the GCF for a bunch of monomials, you can use that skill to factor a polynomial. In fact, getting the GCF is the key to factoring many polynomials. Below you'll find the steps for doing this. **Factor this polynomial:** $6a^2 + 12a$

Steps	**Example**
1st) List the monomials that make up the polynomial, and find the GCF for them.	**Monomials are:** $+ 6a^2$ and $+ 12a$ **GCF of** $+ 6a^2$ and $+ 12a$ **is:** $6a$
2nd) Write down the GCF. To the right of it, make an empty set of parentheses.	$6a(\quad)$

Steps	**Example**
3rd) Ask: by what must you multiply the GCF to get the first monomial? Write down this answer as the first term inside parentheses.	$6a \cdot ? = 6a^2$ $6a \cdot a = 6a^2$ $\downarrow$ $6a(a \quad)$
4th) Repeat step three for all original monomials, writing each new answer after the previous one. When you're done, the polynomial is fully factored.	$6a \cdot ? = + 12a$ $6a \cdot (+ 2) = + 12a$ $\downarrow$ $6a(a + 2)$

Now try factoring these polynomials:

a) $15a^2 + 5a$
b) $8x^3 - 4x^2$
c) $12d^5 + 4d^3 + 2d$
d) $20ab^2 + 5a^2b - 10a^2b^2$

Answers:
a) $5a(3a + 1)$
b) $4x^2(2x - 1)$
c) $2d(6d^4 + 2d^2 + 1)$
d) $5ab(4b + a - 2ab)$

© Singing Turtle Press

Now I understand how to factor standard polynomials. But I also need to learn how to factor a special kind of polynomial called a quadratic trinomial. What exactly is this strange creature? And is there an easier method than trial-and-error for factoring one?

A: A quadratic trinomial is simply any trinomial in which the highest exponent is the number **2**.

<u>**Two examples of quadratic trinomials**</u>

$$a^2 - 2a - 8$$

$$x^2 + 7x + 10$$

Notice that as you read these quadratic trinomials from left to right, the exponents descend from **2** to **1** to **0** (all number terms having an invisible exponent of zero, as you saw on **p. 145**). That's because these quadratic trinomials are already in "descending order" (**p. 97**).

Must a polynomial be in descending to be a quadratic trinomial? No. For example, $-2a - 8 + a^2$ is not in descending order, but it's still a quadratic trinomial. But when factoring quadratics, it helps to use descending order. That's why you'll see descending order in this section. In general, quadratic trinomials factor into two parentheses, each of which holds a binomial.

For example, $a^2 - 2a - 8$ factors into the binomials: $(a + 2)(a - 4)$

And $x^2 + 7x + 10$ factors into these binomials: $(x + 2)(x + 5)$

Yes, there's a better technique than trial-and-error for factoring quadratics. You'll learn this technique in the next several pages.

Tell whether or not the following are quadratic trinomials:

a) $c^2 - 4c + 10$
b) $c^3 - 4c + 10$
c) $10 - 4c + c^2$
d) $q^7 - 4x^2 + 2x^2$
e) $p^5 - 4p^2 - 3$
f) $m^2 + m - 7$

Answers:
a) yes   d) no
b) no   e) no
c) yes   f) yes

First of all, what do I do with the variable when I factor a quadratic trinomial?

A: It's simple. For most of the quadratics you'll work with in Algebra I, the coefficient of the term to the second power is **+1**. Whenever this is true, you just take the variable — whatever it is — and plunk it down as the first term in each of the two parentheses.

Examples

For: $a^2 + 6a + 8$,
the variable is **a**.
Take **a** and place it first in each parenthesis in this way:

$$(a \quad)(a \quad)$$

For: $x^2 - 2x - 8$,
the variable is **x**.
Take **x** and place it first in each parenthesis, like this:

$$(x \quad)(x \quad)$$

Begin factoring these trinomials by writing two parentheses, with the variable positioned correctly:

a) $c^2 + 4c + 3$
b) $m^2 - 7m + 21$
c) $q^2 - 10q - 11$

Answers:
a) (c)(c)
b) (m)(m)
c) (b)(b)

155

O.K. That was pretty simple. But I understand that to factor a quadratic, I need to find all the pairs of factors for a given number. How do I do this?

A: It's true. In one step in the process of factoring quadratics, you need to find all the pairs of factors for a number. **When doing this, keep in mind that the pairs of factors for a positive number are different than the pairs of factors for a negative number.** At right you'll find examples showing this idea.

Pairs for a positive number

If you need to find all the pairs of factors for the number $+ 10$, you would find these four pairs:

$$(+ \, 1, + \, 10), (+ \, 2, + \, 5),$$

$$(- \, 1, - \, 10), (- \, 2, - \, 5)$$

Notice that in each pair, the numbers are either both positive or both negative. That's because only a positive times a positive or a negative times a negative will give you a positive number (**p. 49**).

Pairs for a negative number

If you need to find all the pairs of factors for the number $- 10$, you would find these four pairs:

$$(+ \, 1, - \, 10), (+ \, 2, - \, 5),$$

$$(- \, 1, + \, 10), (- \, 2, + \, 5)$$

Notice that in each pair, one number is positive, the other negative. That's because only a positive times a negative will give you a negative number (**p. 49**).

Show the pairs of factors for these numbers:

a) $+ 8$
b) $- 8$
c) $+ 20$
d) $- 20$

Answers:

a) $(+ 1, + 8), (+ 2, + 4), (- 1, - 8), (- 2, - 4)$
b) $(+ 1, - 8), (+ 2, - 4), (- 1, + 8), (- 2, + 4)$
c) $(+ 1, + 20), (+ 2, + 10), (+ 4, + 5), (- 1, - 20), (- 2, - 10), (- 4, - 5)$
d) $(+ 1, - 20), (+ 2, - 10), (+ 4, - 5), (- 1, + 20), (- 2, + 10), (- 4, + 5)$

Q: Now I see how to find all the pairs of factors for a number. But I hear that when factoring quadratics, I also need to figure out which pair, out of all the pairs, adds up to a certain number. How do I do this?

A: It's easy. You just need to use the rules for combining positive and negative numbers, specifically the same-sign rule (**pp. 36-38**) and the mixed-sign rule (**pp. 39-41**). The steps are shown below.

Finding a pair of factors that add up to a certain number

When factors add to a positive number

Let's say that in the middle of factoring a quadratic, you need to find a pair of factors for $+ \mathbf{10}$ that add up to $+ \mathbf{7}$.
You'd first ask: what are all the pairs of factors for $+ \mathbf{10}$? From the last page (**p. 156**), you can see that they are:

$$\left(+\,\mathbf{1,}\,+\,\mathbf{10}\right),\left(+\,\mathbf{2,}\,+\,\mathbf{5}\right),\left(-\,\mathbf{1,}\,-\,\mathbf{10}\right),\left(-\,\mathbf{2,}\,-\,\mathbf{5}\right)$$

Then you look at all those pairs to see which pair adds up to $+ \mathbf{7}$. Obviously the only pair of factors that add up to $+ \mathbf{7}$ is the pair: $\left(+\,\mathbf{2,}\,+\,\mathbf{5}\right)$, since $+\,\mathbf{2}\,+\,\mathbf{5}\,=\,+\,\mathbf{7}$

When factors add to a negative number

In another problem, you might need to find a pair of factors for $- \mathbf{10}$ that add up to $- \mathbf{3}$. Again, you'd first ask: what are all the pairs of factors for $- \mathbf{10}$? From the previous page, you know that they are:

$$\left(+\,\mathbf{1,}\,-\,\mathbf{10}\right),\left(+\,\mathbf{2,}\,-\,\mathbf{5}\right),\left(-\,\mathbf{1,}\,+\,\mathbf{10}\right),\left(-\,\mathbf{2,}\,+\,\mathbf{5}\right)$$

Looking at those pairs, you see that the only pair that adds up to $- \mathbf{3}$ is the pair: $\left(+\,\mathbf{2,}\,-\,\mathbf{5}\right)$, since $+\,\mathbf{2}\,-\,\mathbf{5}\,=\,-\,\mathbf{3}$

Try these mini-problems:

a) **What pair of factors for** $+ \mathbf{12}$ **add up to** $+ \mathbf{8}$?
b) **What pair of factors for** $- \mathbf{12}$ **add up to** $- \mathbf{1}$?
c) **What pair of factors for** $+ \mathbf{15}$ **add up to** $+ \mathbf{8}$?
d) **What pair of factors for** $+ \mathbf{15}$ **add up to** $- \mathbf{8}$?

Answers:
a) $\left(+\,\mathbf{2,}\,+\,\mathbf{6}\right)$
b) $\left(+\,\mathbf{3,}\,-\,\mathbf{4}\right)$
c) $\left(+\,\mathbf{3,}\,+\,\mathbf{5}\right)$
d) $\left(-\,\mathbf{3,}\,-\,\mathbf{5}\right)$

That wasn't too hard. But I still need to know how to factor a trinomial. How do I put these ideas together so I can actually factor one?

You follow the same basic steps when factoring any quadratic trinomial. In the next four pages you'll see these steps repeated for the four types of quadratic trinomials. Let's start by factoring the simplest kind of trinomial, one in which all three terms are positive. **Factor: $a^2 + 6a + 8$**

Steps	**Example**
1st) Using the first tip **(p. 155)**, you already have the parentheses and the variable.	$a^2 + 6a + 8$ $(a \quad)(a \quad)$
2nd) Ask: what's the coefficient of the middle term? What's the value of the last term?	Middle term's coefficient is: $+ 6$ Last term is: $+ 8$

Steps	**Example**
3rd) Then ask: what are the pairs of factors for the last term? Is there a pair of factors which add up to the coefficient of the middle term?	Since last term is positive, its factors are both positive or both negative **(p. 49)**. Pairs of factors of $+ 8$ are: $(+1, +8), (+2, +4), (-1, -8), (-2, -4)$ Only pair adding to $+6$ is: $(+2, +4)$
4th) Now just drop those factors (sign and number together) into the two parentheses.	$\begin{matrix} +2 & +4 \\ \downarrow & \downarrow \end{matrix}$ $(a + 2)(a + 4)$

Now try factoring these trinomials:

a) $x^2 + 7x + 6$
b) $v^2 + 15v + 50$
c) $a^2 + 20a + 100$
d) $m^2 + 5m + 4$

Answers:
a) $(x + 6)(x + 1)$
b) $(v + 10)(v + 5)$
c) $(a + 10)(a + 10)$
d) $(m + 4)(m + 1)$

Q: Now I see how to factor a trinomial in which all the terms are positive. But what about a trinomial in which the middle term is negative. Is there any difference in how I'd handle this problem?

A: Nope, you use the same technique. Follow the steps below.

Factor: $a^2 - 6a + 8$

Steps	**Example**
1st) Again, using the tip (**p. 155**), you have the parentheses and the variable.	$a^2 - 6a + 8$ $(a \quad)(a \quad)$
2nd) Ask: what's the coefficient of the middle term? What's the value of the last term?	Coefficient of middle term is: -6 Last term is: $+8$

Steps	**Example**
3rd) Ask: what are the pairs of factors for the last term? Is there a pair of factors which add up to the coefficient of the middle term?	Since last term is positive, its factors are both positive or both negative (**p. 49**). Pairs of factors for $+8$ are: $(+1, +8), (+2, +4), (-1, -8), (-2, -4)$ Only pair adding to -6 is: $(-2, -4)$
4th) Just drop those factors (sign and number together) into the two parentheses.	$\begin{array}{cc} -2 & -4 \\ \downarrow & \downarrow \end{array}$ $(a - 2)(a - 4)$

Now try factoring these trinomials:

a) $a^2 - 10a + 16$

b) $q^2 - 20q + 100$

c) $w^2 - 14w + 40$

d) $m^2 - 16m + 60$

Answers:

a) $(a - 8)(a - 2)$

b) $(q - 10)(q - 10)$

c) $(w - 4)(w - 10)$

d) $(m - 6)(m - 10)$

**Now I get the basic idea.
But what about trinomials
in which the first two terms are
positive and the last term is negative.
How do I factor a trinomial like this:**

$$a^2 + 2a - 8$$

A: You use the same, basic technique, but there's one difference when the last term is negative —
as it is here and on the next page. You must combine a positive and a negative number to get the
coefficient of the middle term. Follow the steps below. **Factor: $a^2 + 2a - 8$**

Steps	**Example**	**Steps**	**Example**

1st) Using the first tip (**p. 155**), write the parentheses with the variable.

$a^2 + 2a - 8$

$(a \quad)(a \quad)$

2nd) Ask: what's the coefficient of the middle term? What's the value of the last term?

Coefficient of middle term is: $+2$

Last term is: -8

3rd) Then ask: what are the pairs of factors for the last term? Is there a pair of factors which add up to the coefficient of the middle term?

4th) Now just drop those factors (sign and number together) into the two parentheses.

Since last term is negative, one of its factors is positive, the other negative (**p. 49**). Pairs of factors for -8 are:

$(+1, -8), (+2, -4), (-1, +8), (-2, +4)$

Only pair adding to $+2$ is: $(-2, +4)$

$$\begin{array}{cc} -2 & +4 \\ \downarrow & \downarrow \end{array}$$
$$(a - 2)(a + 4)$$

Now try factoring these trinomials:

a) $n^2 + 3n - 10$
b) $t^2 + 7t - 18$
c) $w^2 + 4w - 45$
d) $u^2 + u - 2$

Answers:
a) $(n + 5)(n - 2)$
b) $(t + 9)(t - 2)$
c) $(w + 9)(w - 5)$
d) $(u - 1)(u + 2)$

Q: Finally, what about the case in which the trinomial has a positive term followed by two negative terms. How do I factor a trinomial like this:

$$a^2 - 2a - 8$$

A: Follow the steps below. **Factor: $a^2 - 2a - 8$**

<u>Steps</u>	<u>Example</u>	<u>Steps</u>	<u>Example</u>
1st) Using the first tip (**p. 155**), make the parentheses and write in the variable.	$a^2 - 2a - 8$ $(a \quad)(a \quad)$	**3rd)** Then ask: what are the pairs of factors for the last term? Is there a pair of factors which add up to the coefficient of the middle term?	Since last term is negative, one of its factors will be positive, the other negative (**p. 49**). Pairs of factors for -8 are: $(+1, -8), (+2, -4), (-1, +8), (-2, +4)$ Only pair adding to -2 is: $(+2, -4)$
2nd) Ask: what's the coefficient of the middle term? What's the value of the last term?	Coefficient of middle term is: -2 Last term is: -8	**4th)** Drop those factors (sign and number together) into the two parentheses.	$\begin{array}{cc} +2 & -4 \\ \downarrow & \downarrow \end{array}$ $(a + 2)(a - 4)$

Now try factoring these trinomials:

a) $x^2 - 4x - 21$
b) $r^2 - 7r - 18$
c) $w^2 - 5w - 14$
d) $m^2 - 11m - 60$

Answers:
a) $(x - 7)(x + 3)$
b) $(r + 2)(r - 9)$
c) $(w - 7)(w + 2)$
d) $(m + 4)(m - 15)$

O.K., now I know how to factor quadratic trinomials. But how do I know that my answer is right? In other words, how can I be sure that the answer I got by factoring has the same value as the trinomial I started with?

 Good question. The answer lies in doing the **opposite of factoring — multiplying**. If you multiply the two binomials together, you should get back the trinomial you started with. The only question is: how in the world do you multiply two binomials together? The answer is to use a process called **F.O.I.L.,** which stands for:

Firsts, Outers, Inners, Lasts

On the next page you'll learn how to **F.O.I.L.** Right now, let's just identify what we mean by:

Firsts, Outers, Inners, Lasts.

Take an ordinary pair of binomials multiplying themselves:

$(a + 4)(a - 2)$. Notice that each parenthesis holds two monomials.

For example, the first parenthesis holds the monomials: $+ a$ and $+ 4$.

The second parenthesis holds: $+ a$ and $- 2$.

You can see this below, for each monomial is individually boxed. Each letter in **F.O.I.L.** stands for **a combination of two monomials**. The diagram below shows this.

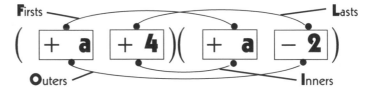

For: $(+ a - 3)(+ a + 5)$, **what would be the ...**

a) **Firsts?**
b) **Outers?**
c) **Inners?**
d) **Lasts?**

Answers:
a) $+ a$ and $+ a$
b) $+ a$ and $+ 5$
c) $- 3$ and $+ a$
d) $- 3$ and $+ 5$

Q: Now I see what is meant by Firsts, Outers, Inners and Lasts. But how do I actually multiply two binomials together using F.O.I.L.?

A: It's really quite simple. **You do four rounds of multiplication, then you combine your answers.**

Follow the steps to the right.

F.O.I.L.:

$$(a + 4)(a - 2)$$

Steps	**Example**
1st) Multiply the **F**irsts.	$(+a) \cdot (+a) = +a^2$
2nd) Multiply the **O**uters.	$(+a) \cdot (-2) = -2a$
3rd) Multiply the **I**nners.	$(+4) \cdot (+a) = +4a$
4th) Multiply the **L**asts.	$(+4) \cdot (-2) = -8$
5th) String all four answers together.	$+a^2 - 2a + 4a - 8$
6th) Combine answers from second and third steps using same or mixed-sign rule (**pp. 36-41**).	$= +a^2 + 2a - 8$

Now try F.O.I.L.ing these binomials:

a) $(a + 3)(a + 5)$
b) $(v + 3)(v - 6)$
c) $(n - 2)(n - 5)$
d) $(k - 7)(k + 9)$

Answers:
a) $a^2 + 8a + 15$
b) $v^2 - 3v - 18$
c) $n^2 - 7n + 10$
d) $k^2 + 2k - 63$

Q: Great. Now I know how to factor basic quadratics. But I've heard there's another kind of quadratic expression that I need to factor, called the "difference of two squares." What is this?

A: A **difference of two squares quadratic** looks like a quadratic trinomial that magically got turned into a binomial by having its middle term zapped out. Here's an example: $a^2 - 16$

To join the **"difference of two squares" club**, a polynomial must pass three separate tests:

1) It must be a binomial, meaning it has exactly two terms.

2) Each of those two terms must be a perfect square (**p. 123**).

3) One term must be positive, the other negative. To the right are some examples.

Examples

$$+ a^2 - 25$$

$$- x^2 + 49$$

$$4w^2 - 36$$

$$- 9u^2 + 64x^2$$

$$100x^2y^2 - 144b^2$$

Some people have a mini panic-attack when trying to decide whether a term like $100x^2y^2$ is a perfect square. But if you glance back at the definition of a perfect square (**p. 123**), it's not hard to tell. This definition says any term that can be viewed as some term times itself must be a perfect square. If you look at $100x^2y^2$, you notice that it can be viewed as

$$(10xy) \cdot (10xy)$$

This is all you need to decide that $100x^2y^2$ is a perfect square.

Do these expressions qualify for joining the "difference of two squares" club?

a) $y^2 - 81$

b) $- x^2 - 9$

c) $- 25a^2b^2 + 16$

d) $r^2 + 9r - 16$

Answers:
a) yes
b) no
c) yes
d) no

try our zany lesson plans

Q: Now I know what a difference of two squares quadratic looks like. But how do I factor a difference of two squares quadratic?

 A: Just follow the steps below. **Factor: $a^2 - 25$**

Steps	**Example**	**Steps**	**Example**

1st) Once you're sure you have a difference of two squares quadratic, set up two parentheses: one with a positive sign, the other with a negative sign.

$a^2 - 25$

$$(\quad + \quad)(\quad - \quad)$$

2nd) Find the square root of each term using definition of a square root (p. 116).

$$\sqrt{a^2} \qquad \sqrt{25}$$
$$= a \qquad = 5$$

3rd) Place the square root of the first term first in each parenthesis.

$$\begin{array}{cc} a & a \\ \downarrow & \downarrow \end{array}$$
$$(a + \quad)(a - \quad)$$

4th) Place the square root of the second term second in each parenthesis. That's it!

$$\begin{array}{cc} 5 & 5 \\ \downarrow & \downarrow \end{array}$$
$$(a + 5)(a - 5)$$

Now try factoring these expressions:

a) $t^2 - 9$
b) $16a^2 - 25$
c) $4m^2 - 36$
d) $121y^2 - 49x^2y^2z^2$

Answers:
a) $(t + 3)(t - 3)$
b) $(4a + 5)(4a - 5)$
c) $(2m + 6)(2m - 6)$
d) $(11y + 7xyz)(11y - 7xyz)$

Name the coefficient for these monomials:

a) $-7x^2yz^4$

b) $.9a^2b$

c) $-x$

d) y^2z^5

Find the GCF's for these groups of terms:

e) 30, 45 and 120

f) 36, 48 and 84

g) $10a^4b^3c$, $6a^3b^5c^2$, $12a^6b^2c$

h) $21r^2s$, $63rs^2t$, $77r^3s^4$

Factor these polynomials:

j) $12a^2b^4 - 6ab^3 + 2a^2b^5$

k) $9x^5y^4 - 18x^2y^7$

l) $15xyz + 20x^2y^2z^2$

m) $24tu^5 - 36t^5u^2 + 12tu$

Factor these trinomials:

n) $y^2 - 9y + 20$

p) $x^2 + 3x - 28$

q) $a^2 + 13a + 42$

r) $v^2 - 6v - 16$

F.O.I.L.:

s) $(m + 3)(m - 5)$

t) $(q - 6)(q - 9)$

u) $(w - 4)(w + 1)$

v) $(t + 10)(t + 10)$

Factor the difference of two squares:

w) $b^2 - 49$

x) $9x^2 - 81$

y) $16r^2s^2 - 121v^2$

z) $-64a^2b^2 + 100x^2$

A:

a) -7

b) $+.9$

c) -1

d) $+1$

j) $2ab^3\left(6ab - 3 + ab^2\right)$

k) $9x^2y^4\left(x^3 - 2y^3\right)$

l) $5xyz\left(3 + 4xyz\right)$

m) $12tu\left(2u^4 - 3t^4u + 1\right)$

s) $m^2 - 2m - 15$

t) $q^2 - 15q + 54$

u) $w^2 - 3w - 4$

v) $t^2 + 20t + 100$

e) 15

f) 12

g) $2a^3b^2c$

h) $7rs$

n) $\left(y - 4\right)\left(y - 5\right)$

p) $\left(x + 7\right)\left(x - 4\right)$

q) $\left(a + 6\right)\left(a + 7\right)$

r) $\left(v - 8\right)\left(v + 2\right)$

w) $\left(b + 7\right)\left(b - 7\right)$

x) $\left(3x + 9\right)\left(3x - 9\right)$

y) $\left(4rs + 11v\right)\left(4rs - 11v\right)$

z) $\left(10x + 8ab\right)\left(10x - 8ab\right)$

In fact there is. It's called the **celling rule,** and her... says: **You may cancel when you have identical factors on opposite sides of the fraction bar.** If you don't have this situation, you can **never** cancel, no matter how tempted you are to whip out your pencil and start wiping out terms. Knowing this rule will save you headaches, so please do yourself a favor, **memorize** it. In fact there is. It's called the **cancelling rule,** and here's what it says: **You may cancel only when you have identical factors on opposite sides of the fraction bar.** If you don't have this situation, you can **never** cancel, no matter how tempted you are to whip out your pencil and start wiping out terms.

Q: What is cancelling? And why should I learn how to cancel?

A: **Ever felt the need to tidy up your room? If so, you should be able to understand the need for cancelling, for cancelling is the art of tidying up mathematical expressions.**

To grasp the idea, imagine that one day, as you enter your bedroom, it's so filthy that you're knee-deep in trash. Despite yourself, you shout: "I can't take it any more!" So you grab a wastebasket and furiously start tossing out junk. Eventually you find that beneath all the trash you still have a pretty nice room.

In math, you don't have sloppy rooms to tidy, but you do have messy mathematical expressions. And instead of using a garbage pail, you need only grab your pencil, for with it you can cross out and toss out mathematical garbage. After you get rid of mathematical clutter, you'll be left with a simple and beautiful mathematical expression.

Like cleaning up your room, cancelling may be less than fun to do, but once you've done it, you feel so much better!

Well, cancelling sounds fine, but I'd like to see an example of the process so I can better understand it.

 Sure. Cancelling involves finding factors that stand over themselves in fractions, then crossing them out. After cancelling factors, you reduce their value to **1/1** or just plain **1**. Below are two examples.

Examples of the process of cancelling

You see the term: **3a/3**. "Hmmm," you say, "I bet I could tidy that up." Knowing that **3/3 = 1/1**, you strike out the **3**'s like this: **3̸a/3̸**, and rewrite the fraction as: **1a/1**. But you can do even better than that, for you know the numerator, **1a**, equals **a**. So you rewrite **1a/1** as:

a/1. Finally, you know that **a/1** simply means **a**. Congratulations! You just reduced the messy fraction

3a/3 to the tidier term: **a**

Use a similar approach to reduce a fraction with a variable in the denominator, a fraction like: **3/3a**. First cancel the **3**'s, to get:

3̸/3̸a = 1/1a. Again, since **1a = a**, you say: **1/1a = 1/a** That's it. You're done! **3/3a** reduces to **1/a**.

> Of course, once you become a cancelling whiz, you won't need to go through these steps in such slow, agonizing detail. With one swift stroke of the pencil, you'll reduce **3a/3** to **a** or **3/3a** to **1/a**.

Cancel and reduce these fractions:

a) **5x/5**

b) **5/5x**

c) **7tu/7**

d) **7/7tu**

Answers:
a) x
b) 1/x
c) tu
d) 1/tu

What is reducing? And how does reducing differ from cancelling?

Reducing and cancelling are like two sides of the same coin in the sense that they're two aspects of the same process.

Still it helps to distinguish the terms since they have slightly different meanings.

Cancelling

Strictly speaking, **cancelling** means **spotting identical factors on opposite sides of the fraction bar, then grabbing your pencil and crossing them out**. Since getting rid of junk feels good, cancelling gives you that same good feeling of getting rid of stuff you no longer need.

Reducing

Reducing means **shrinking** something, boiling it down to a more manageable size. So what do you reduce? You **reduce** the terms you've cancelled by changing their value to the more manageable form of **1/1** or **1**. By doing that, you also **reduce** the entire term to a more manageable form.

Illustration of the use of these terms

Look at the first example on the last page, **3a/3**. You **cancel** the **3**'s when you spot them and cross them out.

Then you **reduce** **3/3** to the more manageable form of **1/1**. By doing all of this, you **reduce** the entire term, **3a/3**, to the simpler term: **a**

 **Now that I have my cancelling vocabulary straight, is there any rule that tells me when I can and cannot cancel terms?**

In fact there is. It's called the **cancelling rule**, and here's what it says: **You may cancel only when you have identical factors on opposite sides of the fraction bar.**

If you don't have this situation, you can **never** cancel, no matter how tempted you are to whip out your pencil and start wiping out terms. Knowing this rule will save you headaches, so please do yourself a favor: **memorize** it.

How the cancelling rule works in real life

In the previous example of **3a/3**, you may cancel the **3**'s only because they are **identical factors on opposite sides of the fraction bar**.

In other words —

Fraction is: **3a/3**
Factors of numerator are: **1, 3** and **a**
Factors of denominator are: **1** and **3**

The factors that are **identical** in both the numerator and denominator are these: **1** and **3**. Cancelling **1**'s never does anything to reduce a fraction's value (try it and see), so don't bother with the **1**'s. But you can and should cancel the two **3**'s.

Tell what term(s) you can cancel in the following fractions:

a) $\dfrac{xy}{x}$ b) $\dfrac{4bc}{4b}$ c) $\dfrac{zy(p+q)}{z(v+w)}$ d) $\dfrac{xy(p+q)}{vw(p+q)}$

Answers:
a) x   c) z
b) 4 and b   d) (p + q) (b + d)

When terms cancel, they just disappear, don't they? And since that's true, I never have to worry about them again, right?

No, not so fast!

Cancelled terms never "disappear"; they reduce to **1/1** or **1**. This matters because cancelled terms will sometimes pop their heads up and appear in your answer. So ... no, you can't just forget about cancelled terms. Here's the rule:

Cancelled terms **fade away** when they're linked to other terms by **multiplication or division**. But they **appear** — and affect your answer — when they're linked by **addition or subtraction**. To the right are examples.

cancelled terms fade away

$$\frac{ac}{a}$$
$$= \frac{\cancel{a}c}{\cancel{a}}$$
$$= c$$

The **a**'s, which cancel, **fade away** from your answer. That's because they're linked to the other term, **c** , by **multiplication and division.**

cancelled terms appear in answer

$$\frac{a}{a} + \frac{c}{a}$$
$$= \frac{\cancel{a}}{\cancel{a}} + \frac{c}{a}$$
$$= 1 + \frac{c}{a}$$

But here the cancelled **a**'s turn into **1** and **appear** in your answer. That's because they're linked to another term by **addition.**

Cancel and give the simplified form:

a) $\dfrac{xy}{x}$ c) $8 - \dfrac{a}{a}$

b) $\dfrac{x}{y} + \dfrac{x}{x}$ d) $\dfrac{4cd}{cd}$

Answers:
a) y   c) 7
b) $\dfrac{x}{y} + 1$ d) 4

 **What are the general steps to follow when I reduce a fraction by cancelling?**

 Memorize the three steps shown below.

1st) <u>**FACTOR**</u> **the numerator and denominator completely.**

2nd) <u>**CANCEL**</u> **whatever factors you can by using the general principles of cancelling.**

3rd) <u>**REDUCE**</u> **the fraction by changing cancelled terms to 1's.**

We'll refer to these steps by using just the words: **Factor**, **Cancel** and **Reduce**, which we'll further abbreviate as: **F.C.R.**

On the next pages are examples showing how to use the **F.C.R.** steps for a variety of different problem types.

Q: How would I reduce fractions in which I can factor either the numerator or the denominator, fractions like these:

$$\frac{a + ac}{a} \quad \text{and} \quad \frac{a}{a + ac}$$

A: You factor whatever you can factor. Just follow the **F.C.R.** steps, as shown to the right.

Reduce the fractions:

A) $\dfrac{a + ac}{a}$,

B) $\dfrac{a}{a + ac}$

Steps	**Example A**	**Example B**
1st) Factor.	$\dfrac{a + ac}{a}$	$\dfrac{a}{a + ac}$
	$= \dfrac{a(1 + c)}{a}$	$= \dfrac{a}{a(1 + c)}$
2nd) Cancel.	$= \dfrac{\cancel{a}(1 + c)}{\cancel{a}}$	$= \dfrac{\cancel{a}}{\cancel{a}(1 + c)}$
3rd) Reduce.	$= 1 + c$	$= \dfrac{1}{1 + c}$

Try simplifying these fractions using the F.C.R. steps:

a) $\dfrac{x + xy}{x}$ c) $\dfrac{mn + mp}{m}$

b) $\dfrac{d}{d + de}$ d) $\dfrac{t}{tu - tv}$

Answers:

a) $1 + y$ c) $n + p$

b) $\dfrac{1}{1 + e}$ d) $\dfrac{1}{u - v}$

Q: How would I reduce a fraction in which I can factor both the numerator and the denominator, a fraction like this:

$$\frac{acm + acn}{acu + acv}$$

A: You use the same **F.C.R.** steps, only here you need to factor both the numerator and the denominator. Follow the steps to the right.

Reduce the fraction:

$$\frac{acm + acn}{acu + acv}$$

Steps

1st) **F**actor.

2nd) **C**ancel.

3rd) **R**educe.

Example

$$\frac{acm + acn}{acu + acv}$$

$$= \frac{ac(m + n)}{ac(u + v)}$$

$$= \frac{\cancel{ac}(m + n)}{\cancel{ac}(u + v)}$$

$$= \frac{m + n}{u + v}$$

Now try reducing these fractions:

a) $\dfrac{xy + xz}{xp + xq}$

b) $\dfrac{ced + cev}{cew - cez}$

c) $\dfrac{wxy - wyz}{awy - wyb}$

d) $\dfrac{qx + qw - qr}{qv + qy}$

Answers:

a) $\dfrac{y + z}{p + z}$

b) $\dfrac{d + v}{w - z}$

c) $\dfrac{x - z}{a - b}$

d) $\dfrac{x + w - r}{v + y}$

How would I reduce a fraction that has terms raised to exponents, a fraction like this:

$$\frac{acm + acn}{a^2cu + a^2cv}$$

A: You still follow the F.C.R. steps. Follow the example shown to the right.

Reduce the fraction:

$$\frac{acm + acn}{a^2cu + a^2cv}$$

Steps	**Example**
	$\dfrac{acm + acn}{a^2cu + a^2cv}$
1st) **F**actor.	$= \dfrac{ac(m + n)}{a^2c(u + v)}$
2nd) **C**ancel.	$= \dfrac{\cancel{a}\cancel{c}(m + n)}{a^{\cancel{2}}\cancel{c}(u + v)}$
3rd) **R**educe.	$= \dfrac{m + n}{a(u + v)}$

To understand the cancelling step here, think of $\dfrac{a}{a^2}$ as $\dfrac{a}{a \cdot a}$. When you cancel terms here, the single **a** in the numerator cancels with only one of the **a**'s in the denominator, like this: $\dfrac{\cancel{a}}{a \cdot \cancel{a}}$. This tells you why the final answer still has an **a** in the denominator.

Try reducing these fractions:

a) $\dfrac{xy + xz}{x^2w + x^2a}$

b) $\dfrac{ab + ac}{a^2d - a^2w}$

c) $\dfrac{m^2n^3p + m^2n^2q}{m^2n^2}$

d) $\dfrac{x^3y^2 - x^2y^4}{x^2y^2}$

Answers:

a) $\dfrac{y + z}{xw + xa}$

b) $\dfrac{b + c}{ad - aw}$

c) $np + b$

d) $x - y^2$

I understand the three previous examples. But sometimes I get confused about what I can and cannot cancel. For example, in the problem:

$$\frac{a}{a + c},$$

it seems like I should be able to cancel the a in the numerator with the a in the denominator. But my teacher says I can't. Why can't I cancel those two a's?

Excellent question. In $\dfrac{a}{a + c}$, **a** is a factor of the numerator, but for you to cancel the two **a**'s, **a** also would need to be a factor of the denominator (**p. 171**). So the question is: why <u>isn't</u> **a** a factor of the denominator? To answer this, let's remember what it means to be a factor.

Refresher course: what's a factor?

The definition of a factor (**pp. 142-145**) says: **for a term to be a factor of some expression, you need to be able to multiply that term by something to get the expression.**

For example, **3** is a factor of **21** because **3 · something = 21**, namely: **3 · 7 = 21**. And **6a** is a factor of **6a² + 12a** because

6a · something = 6a² + 12a, namely:

$$6a \cdot (a + 2) = 6a^2 + 12a$$

Going back to the question ...

Now that that's clear, look again at the denominator of

$\dfrac{a}{a + c}$. For **a** to be a factor of the denominator,

a + c, you'd need to be able to multiply **a** by something to get **a + c**. Can you? You can search, but the answer is "no." That means that **a** is not a factor of **a + c**. And that means that the two **a**'s in the fraction don't cancel, for you can cancel only factors (**p. 171**).

Tell whether or not the variable a is a factor of the expression:

a) **5a**

b) **5 + a**

c) **a(b + c)**

d) **a + b + c**

e) **x(a − b)**

f) **a(a − b)**

g) **ab(a − b)**

h) **bc(b − a)**

Answers:

a) **is a factor**

b) **isn't a factor**

c) **is a factor**

d) **isn't a factor**

e) **isn't a factor**

f) **is a factor**

g) **is a factor**

h) **isn't a factor**

Q: I'm beginning to see that when a term is linked to other terms only by addition or subtraction, it's not a factor. But when it's linked by multiplication, it is a factor. What I'm wondering about now is something a little different.

In a fraction like: $\dfrac{a}{a + c}$, are there any factors at all for the denominator?

A: Another good question, for it brings up a crucial point. Even though neither **a** nor **c** is a factor of the denominator, still the whole expression: $(a + c)$ is a factor of the denominator.

Why? Well, can't you rewrite the denominator as: $1 \cdot (a + c)$?

Since you can, you can view the whole quantity: $(a + c)$ as a factor of the denominator.

Burn this into your mind: the **whole numerator** and the **whole denominator** are always considered **factors of themselves**. This idea is critical, for as you'll soon see, it allows you to do a special kind of cancelling.

> When you're talking about some quantity as a factor, teachers usually want you to stick that quantity inside parentheses. The parentheses show that the factor is the whole quantity, not the individual terms that make it up. For example, since **a + c** is a factor of the denominator in $\dfrac{1}{a + c}$, you'd write it as: $(a + c)$, and you'd read it as "the quantity **a + c**."

Name the factor(s) of the numerator and of the denominator for these fractions:

a) $\dfrac{a(b - c)}{b - c}$ b) $\dfrac{x - y + z}{x(y + z)}$

Answers:
a) factors of numerator: a and (b – c)
factor of denominator: (b – c)
b) factor of numerator: (x – y + z)
factors of denominator: x and (y + z)

178

Q: Well then ... if an entire numerator or an entire denominator may be viewed as a factor, does that mean I can cancel an entire numerator or denominator?

In other words, would I be able to cancel and reduce fractions like these:

$$\frac{a + c}{a + c}, \quad \frac{3(a + c)}{a + c} \quad \text{and} \quad \frac{a + c}{3(a + c)}$$

 A: Yes. Here's how. **Simplify:** A) $\dfrac{a + c}{a + c}$, B) $\dfrac{3(a + c)}{a + c}$, C) $\dfrac{a + c}{3(a + c)}$

Steps	Example A	Example B	Example C
1st) Spot numerators or denominators that are factors of themselves. Put them in parentheses to show that they're factors of themselves.	$\dfrac{a + c}{a + c}$ $= \dfrac{(a + c)}{(a + c)}$	$\dfrac{3(a + c)}{a + c}$ $= \dfrac{3(a + c)}{(a + c)}$	$\dfrac{a + c}{3(a + c)}$ $= \dfrac{(a + c)}{3(a + c)}$
2nd) Cancel.	$= \dfrac{\cancel{(a + c)}}{\cancel{(a + c)}}$	$= \dfrac{3\cancel{(a + c)}}{\cancel{(a + c)}}$	$= \dfrac{\cancel{(a + c)}}{3\cancel{(a + c)}}$
3rd) Reduce.	$= 1$	$= 3$	$= \dfrac{1}{3}$

Try reducing these fractions:

a) $\dfrac{x + y}{x + y}$

b) $\dfrac{x - y}{4(x - y)}$

c) $\dfrac{7(p + q - z)}{p + q - z}$

d) $\dfrac{6(m - n)}{8(m - n)}$

Answers:
a) 1   c) 7
b) $\frac{1}{4}$ d) $\frac{3}{4}$

Q: I understand that I can't reduce a fraction like: $\dfrac{a}{a+c}$

But what about the flip of that, a fraction like: $\dfrac{a+c}{a}$

Can I reduce this kind of fraction?

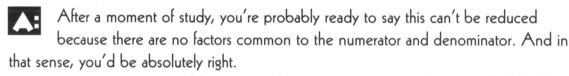

A: After a moment of study, you're probably ready to say this can't be reduced because there are no factors common to the numerator and denominator. And in that sense, you'd be absolutely right.

However you're now plunging into a "grey area" of algebra.

While many teachers would accept $\dfrac{a+c}{a}$ as an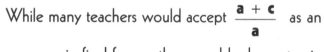

answer in final form, others would ask you to simplify it by using a trick.

To understand this trick, you first need to learn a rule called the **split-the-numerator rule**. The next several pages will teach you how this rule works.

Q: What does the split-the-numerator rule say?

$$\frac{a + b - c + d}{x} = \,?$$

 The split-the-numerator rule says this:

$$\frac{a + b - c + d}{x} = \frac{a}{x} + \frac{b}{x} - \frac{c}{x} + \frac{d}{x}$$

Or, in English: When a fraction's numerator has two or more terms linked by " + " or " − " signs, you can rewrite the fraction by:

a) splitting the numerator into a series of numerators, each of which stands over the denominator, and

b) hitching the fractions together by placing " + " or " − " signs at the appropriate spots between them.

Examples of the split-the-numerator rule

$$\frac{m + p - q}{r} = \frac{m}{r} + \frac{p}{r} - \frac{q}{r}$$

$$\frac{x^2 - 2y + z}{3q} = \frac{x^2}{3q} - \frac{2y}{3q} + \frac{z}{3q}$$

Silly example

$$\frac{ape - cow}{cat} = \frac{ape}{cat} - \frac{cow}{cat}$$

Rewrite using the split-the-numerator rule:

a) $\dfrac{c + e}{v}$

b) $\dfrac{q^2 - 9q}{11}$

c) $\dfrac{3 - x^3 + y^2}{b^3}$

d) $\dfrac{7p + g + m}{4h}$

Answers:

a) $\dfrac{e}{v} + \dfrac{c}{v}$

b) $\dfrac{q}{11} - \dfrac{9q^2}{11}$

c) $\dfrac{y^2}{b^3} - \dfrac{x^3}{b^3} + \dfrac{3}{b^3}$

d) $\dfrac{7p}{4h} + \dfrac{g}{4h} + \dfrac{m}{4h}$

Q: Can I also use the split-the-numerator rule when I have a complex denominator? In other words, can I use the rule for fractions like these:

$$\frac{2a - b}{a + b} \qquad \text{and} \qquad \frac{2a - b}{x(a + b)}$$

A: **Yes, you can use the split-the-numerator rule no matter how complex your denominator might be.** What you need to decide, though, is whether using the rule makes your answer look more simple or more complicated. Teachers differ on this point. Check with your teacher to learn his/her preference.

Examples of the split-the-numerator rule

$$\frac{2a - b}{a + b} = \frac{2a}{a + b} - \frac{b}{a + b}$$

$$\frac{2a + b}{x(a + b)} = \frac{2a}{x(a + b)} + \frac{b}{x(a + b)}$$

Silly Example

$$\frac{ape - cow}{cat + dog} = \frac{ape}{cat + dog} - \frac{cow}{cat + dog}$$

Split the numerators of these fractions:

a) $\dfrac{a + b}{c - d}$ c) $\dfrac{x^2 - 9}{x + y}$

b) $\dfrac{a - b}{c - d}$ d) $\dfrac{x^2 + 9}{x + y}$

Answers:

a) $\dfrac{a}{c - d} + \dfrac{b}{c - d}$ c) $\dfrac{x^2}{x + y} - \dfrac{9}{x + y}$

b) $\dfrac{a}{c - d} - \dfrac{b}{c - d}$ d) $\dfrac{x^2}{x + y} + \dfrac{9}{x + y}$

Q: Now I understand the split-the-numerator rule, but how does it help me simplify the fraction I saw a few pages back, this fraction:

$$\frac{a + c}{a}$$

A: If you use the split-the-numerator rule on this fraction, the **a**'s will cancel nicely. Follow the steps to the right.

Simplify:

$$\frac{a + c}{a}$$

Steps

1st) Use the split-the-numerator rule (**p. 181**).

2nd) Cancel.

3rd) Reduce.

Example

$$\frac{a + c}{a}$$

$$= \frac{a}{a} + \frac{c}{a}$$

$$= \frac{\cancel{a}}{\cancel{a}} + \frac{c}{a}$$

$$= 1 + \frac{c}{a}$$

Try simplifying these fractions with the split-the-numerator rule:

a) $\dfrac{x + y}{x}$ c) $\dfrac{a^2 + b}{a^2}$

b) $\dfrac{y - x}{x}$ d) $\dfrac{a^2 + b}{a}$

Answers:
a) $1 + \dfrac{y}{x}$ c) $1 + \dfrac{b}{a^2}$

b) $\dfrac{y}{x} - 1$ d) $a + \dfrac{b}{a}$

try our "challenge" problem

Now I understand the split-the-numerator rule, and I see how to use it. But what guarantee do I have that it's true?

Good question. And fortunately, the answer is quite simple, for it stems from a basic fraction rule you learned back in elementary school.

As you recall, when adding fractions with the same denominator, you just add the numerators and keep the denominator.

For example: $\dfrac{2}{7} + \dfrac{4}{7} = \dfrac{2+4}{7}$. Adding numerators, this answer will be: $\dfrac{6}{7}$

What's important is that thanks to the symmetric property (**p. 10**), you can flip the first statement around, to get:

$$\dfrac{2+4}{7} = \dfrac{2}{7} + \dfrac{4}{7}$$

But if you just ponder this last statement for a moment, you'll see that it uses the same idea as the split-the-numerator rule. In other words, the split-the-numerator rule is simply the algebraic version of a rule you already learned — way back in elementary school.

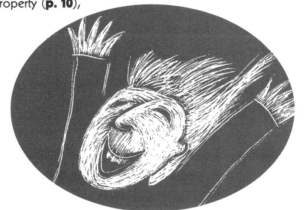

Q:

Cancel and reduce:

a) $\dfrac{7e}{7}$

b) $\dfrac{11}{11y}$

c) $\dfrac{pq}{p}$

d) $\dfrac{x}{y} + \dfrac{x}{x}$

e) $\dfrac{m}{mn - mr}$

f) $\dfrac{xy + xv}{xw + xz}$

g) $\dfrac{abc + abd}{ab^2e + ab^2f}$

Name the factors in the numerator and denominator:

h) $\dfrac{x + y}{a + b}$

j) $\dfrac{x(x + y)}{a + b}$

k) $\dfrac{x^2 - 5}{7(x^2 - 5)}$

Cancel and reduce:

l) $\dfrac{m + n}{m + n}$

m) $\dfrac{6(u - v)}{u - v}$

n) $\dfrac{p - q}{8(p - q)}$

Split the numerator and rewrite:

p) $\dfrac{x + y - z}{a}$

q) $\dfrac{x - y}{a - b}$

r) $\dfrac{a^2 - 3}{b^2 + 4}$

Split the numerator and reduce:

s) $\dfrac{p + q}{p}$

t) $\dfrac{q - p}{p}$

u) $\dfrac{b^2 + c}{b}$

A:

a) e

b) $\dfrac{1}{y}$

c) q

d) $\dfrac{x}{y} + 1$

e) $\dfrac{1}{n - r}$

f) $\dfrac{y + v}{w + z}$

g) $\dfrac{c + d}{be + bf}$

h) numerator: $(x + y)$
   denominator: $(a + b)$

j) numerator: x and $(x + y)$
   denominator: $(a + b)$

k) numerator: $(x^2 - 5)$
   denominator: 7 and $(x^2 - 5)$

l) 1

m) 6

n) $\dfrac{1}{8}$

p) $\dfrac{x}{a} + \dfrac{y}{a} - \dfrac{z}{a}$

q) $\dfrac{x}{a - b} - \dfrac{y}{a - b}$

r) $\dfrac{a^2}{b^2 + 4} - \dfrac{3}{b^2 + 4}$

s) $1 + \dfrac{q}{p}$

t) $\dfrac{q}{p} - 1$

u) $b + \dfrac{c}{b}$

...ake any triangle whatso...
length of one leg a; the
hypotenuse c. To grasp this theorem,
imagine that you have a choice about
mowing some lawns. Pretend that each
square in the diagram represents a big
lawn with overgrown grass. Your
choice is to either mow both lawns
a^2 and b^2... or just mow lawn...
you understand the Pythagorean theorem,
you... it makes no difference; the two
choices are the same. To grasp this theorem, imagine that you have a choice

$$a^2 + b^2 = c^2$$

What am I actually doing when I'm solving an equation with one variable?

A: When you solve an equation, you're discovering the identity of the variable; you're finding out the value it must have to make the equation true. Here's another way to view this. You, the student, are like a detective hired to figure out who committed a crime. The variable is like the unknown person who committed the crime. And the equation is like the collection of clues you start out with that can help you figure out who the criminal is.

As you solve an equation, you work through the clues in the equation, trying to figure out the variable's identity. Once you've solved the equation, you say something like: "Oh, **x = 11**." That's like the scene at the end of a movie in which the detective declares: "Ah, now I know ... It was Victoria deVille who committed the crime."

by visiting www.AlgebraWizard.com

Is there some kind of law that tells what I may and may not do while solving an equation with one variable?

A: Yes, just as real-life detectives are bound by the law when they go sleuthing, you, the student, are bound by laws when you solve equations. The most important law of all is this: **Whatever you do to one side of the equation, you must immediately do the same thing to the other side of the equation.** Here's what the law means to you, the math-sleuth:

If you **add** something to one side of the equation, you must immediately **add** it to the other side,

If you **subtract** something from one side of the equation, you must immediately **subtract** it from the other side.

If you **multiply or divide** one side of the equation by a number or a term, you must immediately **multiply or divide** the other side by that same number or term.

If you **square** one side of the equation, you must immediately **square** the other side.

If you **take the square root** of one side of the equation, you must immediately **take the square root** of the other side.

**Hmmm ... I'm starting to get it.
But is there a model to help me understand
why I always have to do the same
thing to both sides of the equation?**

 Yes, think of an equation as like a scale.

As you know, all scales have two pans — one on the right, one on the left, and a balance point, called the fulcrum, directly between those pans. An equation is like a scale because it also has two pans and a balance point. The left side of the equation is the left pan; the right side is the right pan. And the equal sign is the fulcrum because it's the point around which the equation balances.

Common sense tells you that if you have exactly three pennies in both pans of a scale, the scale will balance. And if you were to add two pennies to the left pan, you'd need to add two pennies to the right pan to keep the scale in balance. In the same way, whatever you do to one side of an equation, you must immediately do the same thing to the other side to keep the equation in balance.

And why must you keep an equation in balance? Well, if you don't, it would no longer be an equation, and in that case you'd have no rules to allow you to discover the variable's identity.

What does an equation with one variable look like? And what are the names of its parts?

Below you'll see a fairly typical example of an equation in one variable. You'll use this equation as a model. By learning how to solve it, you'll learn how to solve all equations like it. Here are its parts:

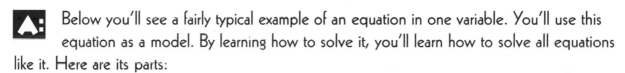

$$2(a + 3) + 4a - 9 = 8 + 3a - 4(a - 6)$$

left side   equal sign   right side

The **variable** is the letter **a**. Any term with a number multiplying or dividing the variable (such as **+ 4a** or **+ 3a**) is called a **variable term**. And any term that is simply a number (such as **+ 8** or **− 8**) is called a **number term**.

Identify the parts of this equation: $3x + 7 = 12 - 4x$

a) $3x + 7$
b) $+ 12$
c) $- 4x$
d) $12 - 4x$
e) x

Answers:
a) **left side**
b) **number term**
c) **variable term**
d) **right side**
e) **variable**

Q: What phases will I go through when I solve an equation with one variable?

 You'll find the three phases described below.

1st) <u>SIMPLIFY</u> each side of the equation. In this phase, you boil down each side so that it ends up having, at most, a number term and a variable term. This is the phase in which you "narrow the field" for figuring out who the "criminal" variable is. The order of operations (**p. 57**) will be your trusty assistant during this phase of the investigation.

2nd) <u>ISOLATE</u> a single variable on one side of the equation; isolate a single number term on the other side of the equation. This is the phase in which you get the dastardly variable all by itself so you can figure out who it is.

3rd) <u>SOLVE</u> for the variable. Solving means closing out the case by revealing the identity of the guilty variable.

We'll refer to these phases by the code words: **Simplify**, **Isolate** and **Solve**, which we'll further abbreviate as: **S.I.S.** In the next few pages, you'll learn how to become a pro at each of these phases. Then you'll learn how to put them all together solve a case, that is, an equation. By the way, these are called **phases** rather than **steps** because each phase can involve many steps.

How do I proceed during the first phase of solving equations — simplifying?

A: **Simplifying** means boiling down each side of the equation to a simpler form. To do this, use your trusty order of operations (**p. 57**). Here's how you simplify the model equation.

Simplify both sides of: $2(a + 3) + 4a - 9 = 8 + 3a - 4(a - 6)$

<u>Steps</u>	<u>Example</u>
1st) Multiply using the distributive property (**pp. 15-16**).	$2(a + 3) + 4a - 9 = 8 + 3a - 4(a - 6)$ $2a + 6 + 4a - 9 = 8 + 3a - 4a + 24$
2nd) Group like terms (**p. 42**).	$+ 2a + 4a \quad + 6 - 9 = + 3a - 4a \quad + 8 + 24$
3rd) Use same-sign rule (**pp. 36-38**).	$+ 6a \quad + 6 - 9 = + 3a - 4a \quad + 32$
4th) Use mixed-sign rule (**pp. 39-41**).	$+ 6a \quad - 3 \quad = - a \quad + 32$

Work through the simplifying phase for these equations:

a) $5(x - 3) + 10 = 2(x + 9) - 8$

b) $- 3(y + 7) - 3 = -(8 + y) + 6y$

c) $19 + 2(2c - 3) = 6 - 3(2c + 1)$

d) $- 6(- p + 2) + 3 - 4p = 11 - (8 + p) - p$

Answers:

a) $5x - 5 = 2x + 10$

b) $- 3y - 24 = - 8 + 5y$

c) $4c + 13 = - 6c + 3$

d) $2p - 9 = 3 - 2p$

Q: The first part of the investigation is complete. On to the isolating phase. When I'm working toward getting the "guilty" variable isolated and all alone, is there a rule that tells how I dispose of annoying terms that are in the way?

A: Yes, the rule is called the **opposites rule**. Here's what it says: **To get rid of a term from either side of the equation, you just do the opposite operation.**

In other words, to get rid of a term that is ...

… connected to its side by **addition**,
    subtract it from both sides.
… connected by **subtraction**,
    add it to both sides.
… connected by **multiplication**,
    divide both sides by it.
… connected by **division**,
    multiply both sides by it.
… inside a **square root** sign,
    square both sides.
… **squared**,
    take the **square root** of both sides.

Q: This rule make some sense, but I'd understand it better if I could see examples of its use. Suppose I have a variable, c, which I need to isolate. How would I use the opposites rule to get rid of those irritating terms that are in the way, so that I can get **c** all by itself — and nail it to the wall?!

A: Study the four mini-examples below:

$$c + 3 = 5$$

$$\begin{array}{r} c + 3 = 5 \\ -3 \quad -3 \\ \hline c = 2 \end{array}$$

3 is connected by **addition**. To get rid of it, **subtract 3** from both sides.

$$c - 3 = 5$$

$$\begin{array}{r} c - 3 = 5 \\ +3 \quad +3 \\ \hline c = 8 \end{array}$$

3 is connected by **subtraction**. To get rid of it, **add 3** to both sides.

$$3 \cdot c = 12$$

$$\frac{\cancel{3} \cdot c}{\cancel{3}} = \frac{12}{3}$$

$$c = 4$$

3 is connected by **multiplication**. To get rid of it, **divide** both sides by **3**, and reduce.

$$\frac{c}{3} = 4$$

$$\cancel{3} \cdot \left(\frac{c}{\cancel{3}} \right) = 3 \cdot (4)$$

$$c = 12$$

3 is connected by **division**. To get rid of it, **multiply** both sides by **3**, and simplify.

Solve these mini-equations for the variable c:

a) $c + 11 = 17$

b) $c - 9 = 23$

c) $5 \cdot c = 105$

d) $c/7 = 6$

e) $c^2 = 49$

f) $c^2 = 100$

g) $\sqrt{c} = 6$

h) $\sqrt{c} = 7 - 4$

Answers:

a) $c = 6$

b) $c = 32$

c) $c = 21$

d) $c = 42$

e) $c = 7$

f) $c = 10$

g) $c = 36$

h) $c = 9$

 I want to say I understand the last page, but a couple of points still confuse me. For example, in the first two mini-examples, what actually happened to the terms I "got rid of" by adding or subtracting? What really happened to those 3's?

Also, how do I get rid of terms when I have even more terms, as in a problem like this:

$$4a + 6 = 8 - 2a$$

 Let's take these questions one at a time.

What happened to those 3's?

In the first mini-example you started with:

$$c + 3 = 5$$

Then you subtracted **3** on both sides, like this:

$$
\begin{array}{r}
c + 3 = 5 \\
-3 \quad -3 \\
\hline
c = 2
\end{array}
$$

What happened to the **3**'s on the left side? They turned into **0** because:

$$+ 3 - 3 = 0$$

Since **0** has **no value** to speak of, the left side ends up with **no number term**, but you still have to bring down the **c** since it's part of the left side. So the left side simply becomes the term: **c**. Over on the right side, you're left with **2** since **5 − 3 = 2**

How to get rid of more terms

Suppose you're trying to solve this equation:

$$4a + 6 = 8 - 2a$$

To isolate the variable, you want to get rid of the **− 2a** on the right side, so you add it to both sides. That step looks like this:

$$
\begin{array}{r}
4a + 6 = 8 - 2a \\
+ 2a \qquad \quad + 2a \\
\hline
6a + 6 = 8
\end{array}
$$

Notice how the **a** terms disappear on the right side because **− 2a + 2a = 0**, and **0** is not worth writing down. But you still have the **8** on the right side, and you must write that down.

Good. Now I understand how to get rid of terms. But how do I work through the second phase of the investigation — isolating?

Isolating means working toward getting a **single variable term on one side** and a **single number term on the other side**. After simplifying, the model equation had become:

$$+\, 6a - 3 = -\, a + 32$$

To the right are the steps showing how to **isolate**.

Steps

1st) Do the same operation to both sides to **isolate the variable term**. (In this case the variable term, **7a**, ends up on the left side.)

2nd) Do the same operation to both sides to **isolate the number term**. (Here the number term, **35**, ends up on the right side.)

Example

$$
\begin{array}{rl}
+\,6a - 3 &= -\,a + 32 \\
+\,a & \quad +\,a \\
\hline
7a - 3 &= +\,32
\end{array}
$$

$$
\begin{array}{rl}
7a - 3 &= +\,32 \\
+\,3 & \quad +\,3 \\
\hline
7a &= \quad 35
\end{array}
$$

In both **step 1** and **step 2** you had a choice. **Example:** in **step 1**, instead of getting rid of − **a** by adding **a** to both sides, you could have gotten rid of + **6a** by subtracting **6a** from both sides. How to decide which to do? **Always get rid of the term with the lesser coefficient.** + **6a** has a + **6 coefficient**, − **a** has a − **1** coefficient. You get rid of the − **a** because its coefficient is smaller. Following this tip keeps terms positive, making life easier.

Work through the isolating phase for these equations:

a) $5x - 5 = 2x + 10$
b) $-\,3y - 24 = -\,8 + 5y$
c) $4c + 13 = -\,6c + 3$
d) $2p - 9 = 3 - 2p$

Answers:
a) $3x = 15$
b) $-\,16 = 8y$
c) $10c = -\,10$
d) $4p = 12$

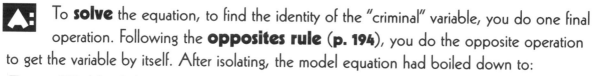

Q: So far so good. But what's involved in the third and final phase of solving equations — solving?

A: To **solve** the equation, to find the identity of the "criminal" variable, you do one final operation. Following the **opposites rule (p. 194)**, you do the opposite operation to get the variable by itself. After isolating, the model equation had boiled down to:

7a = 35. Here's how you now **solve** the equation.

<u>**Steps**</u>

1st) Do the opposite operation to **get the variable all by itself**.
(Here **7** is multiplying **a**, so you just divide both sides by **7**, then cancel the **7**'s.)

2nd) Work out the operation and behold your answer. You've cracked the case by figuring out the variable's identity.

<u>**Example**</u>

$$7a = 35$$
$$\frac{\cancel{7}a}{\cancel{7}} = \frac{35}{7}$$

$$a = 5$$

Work through the solving phase for these equations:

a) 3x = 15
b) − 16 = 8y
c) 10c = − 10
d) 4p = 12

Answers:
a) x = 5
b) y = − 2
c) c = − 1
d) p = 3

198

Q: I think I'm starting to understand the phases. But it would help me to see the whole process — all three phases — displayed on one page. What would that look like?

© Singing Turtle Press

A: To the right you'll get the **big picture** for how you solved the model equation using the **S.I.S.** phases. And then you can test your skill by doing the QuikChek.

Phases	Example
	$2(a + 3) + 4a - 9 = 8 + 3a - 4(a - 6)$
1st) **S**implify.	$\Downarrow$
	$6a - 3 = -a + 32$
2nd) **I**solate.	$6a - 3 = -a + 32$
	$\Downarrow$
	$7a = 35$
3rd) **S**olve.	$7a = 35$
	$\Downarrow$
	$a = 5$

Work through the S.I.S. phases to solve these equations:

a) $4(x + 2) = 8(4 - 2)$

b) $5(d - 3) - 2d = 2(d + 1) + 4$

c) $-3(p - 7) + p - 9 = 8(p - 1) - 4p - 4$

d) $11 - 3(w + 2) = 7 - (4w + 5)$

Answers:
a) $x = 2$
b) $d = 21$
c) $p = 4$
d) $w = -3$

Now I see how to solve an equation like the model equation. But how do I solve an equation in which the variable, instead of being multiplied by a number, is divided by a number? In other words, how would I solve an equation like this:

$$c/4 + 5 = 11 - 4$$

A: You solve it the same way you solved the model equation. The only difference is that in the **solving** phase, instead of dividing both sides by a number, you multiply both sides by a number. Follow the **S.I.S.** phases shown at right.

Solve:

$$c/4 + 5 = 11 - 4$$

Phases	Example
1st) Simplify.	$c/4 + 5 = 11 - 4$ $c/4 + 5 = 7$
2nd) Isolate.	$c/4 + 5 = 7$ $\underline{-5 \quad -5}$ $c/4 = 2$
3rd) Solve.	$c/4 = 2$ $\cancel{4} \cdot (c/\cancel{4}) = 4 \cdot (2)$ $c = 8$

Try solving these equations:

a) $w/3 - 4 = 2 \cdot 5$
b) $6 + x/2 = 8(3 - 1)$
c) $-9 + y/5 = 6$
d) $7(4 - 2) = z/6 + 5$

Answers:
a) w = 42
b) x = 20
c) y = 75
d) z = 54

So far, so good. But how do I solve an equation in which the variable term is squared? For example, how would I solve an equation like this:

$$4a^2 - 3a^2 - 2 = 7 \cdot 2$$

Isn't this much harder than what I've been doing?

 Not necessarily. As long as you're not dealing with a quadratic trinomial (**p. 154**), you just work through the steps as shown in the previous pages. The only new step is that in the **solving** phase you need to take the square root of both sides. Follow the steps to the right.

Solve:

$$4a^2 - 3a^2 - 2 = 7 \cdot 2$$

Phases	**Example**
1st) Simplify.	$4a^2 - 3a^2 - 2 = 7 \cdot 2$ $a^2 - 2 = 14$
2nd) Isolate.	$a^2 - 2 = 14$ $\underline{+2 \quad +2}$ $a^2 = 16$
3rd) Solve.	$a^2 = 16$ $\sqrt{a^2} = \sqrt{16}$ $a = 4$

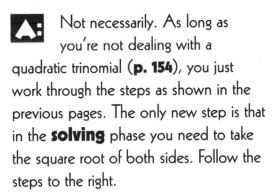

Solve these equations:

a) $8a^2 + 6 - 7a^2 = 24 + 7$
b) $4b^2 - 2b^2 + 10 = 108$
c) $6q^2 + 3 = 7q^2 - 6$
d) $600 = 2 \cdot (3t^2)$

Answers:
a) $a = 5$
b) $b = 7$
c) $q = 3$
d) $t = 10$

Now I have some sense of how to solve basic equations with one variable. But I also need to learn how to solve equations in which the variable is inside absolute value fenceposts. How would I solve a simple absolute value equation, like this:

$$|a| = 7$$

A: If you remind yourself that absolute value just means distance from zero (**p. 78**), this equation tells you that **a** stands for all numbers exactly **7** units away from zero. It's easy to see that there are only **two** numbers **7** units from zero: **7** and -7. So that means that in this equation, **a = 7** or **a** $= -7$. That's all there is to it. Amazing, huh?

And in general, to solve — or begin solving — any absolute value equation, you just split the single equation into two cases: one positive, the other negative. It helps to show the split this way:

$$|a| = 7$$
means
$$a = 7 \qquad \text{or} \qquad a = -7$$

You use this same approach no matter how complex the equation. For example, the equation:

$$|2a + 6| = 10$$
means
$$2a + 6 = 10 \qquad \text{or} \qquad 2a + 6 = -10$$

Do this split-up to begin solving absolute value equations.

Solve — or begin solving — these absolute value equations:

a) $|a| = 9$

b) $|w| = 13$

c) $|5z - 12| = 8$

d) $|9 - 4q| = 11$

Answers:

a) $a = 9$ or $a = -9$

b) $w = 13$ or $w = -13$

c) $5z - 12 = 8$ or $5z - 12 = -8$

d) $9 - 4q = 11$ or $9 - 4q = -11$

O.K., that wasn't as bad as I had feared. But what else do I need to do to finish solving an absolute value equation that splits into two cases? In other words, how would I finish solving an equation like this:

$$|2a + 6| = 10$$

A: To finish solving a complex absolute value equation like this, you need to solve each of the two cases. **Your answer will include the answers from both cases.** Follow the steps shown to the right.

Solve:

$$|2a + 6| = 10$$

Steps

1st) Split the equation into two cases.

2nd) Solve each case for the variable.

3rd) Use both answers.

Example

$$|2a + 6| = 10$$

Case 1		Case 2
$2a + 6 = 10$	**or**	$2a + 6 = -10$

Case 1:
$$2a + 6 = 10$$
$$\underline{\quad -6 \quad -6}$$
$$2a = 4$$
$$\frac{2a}{2} = \frac{4}{2}$$
$$a = 2$$

Case 2:
$$2a + 6 = -10$$
$$\underline{\quad -6 \quad -6}$$
$$2a = -16$$
$$\frac{2a}{2} = \frac{-16}{2}$$
$$a = -8$$

or

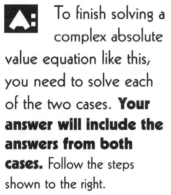

Now try solving these absolute value equations:

a) $|2x - 3| = 11$

b) $|3c + 1| = 10$

c) $|5y - 6| = 9$

d) $|10 - 3d| = 7$

Answers:

a) x = 7 or x = −4

b) c = 3 or x = −11/3

c) y = 3 or y = −3/5

d) d = 1 or d = 17/3

Hmmm .... what about quadratic trinomials. I know how to factor them, but is there any way to solve an equation in which I have a quadratic trinomial set equal to zero? In other words, can I solve an equation like this:

$$x^2 + 2x - 8 = 0$$

 Yes, yes, yes. But to understand how, first you need to consider what this quadratic trinomial, $x^2 + 2x - 8$, factors into. That helps you see what the problem means.

What does this problem mean?

As you learned in the **Factoring** section (**p. 154**), this quadratic trinomial factors into:

$(x + 4)(x - 2)$ And that means the

equation, $x^2 + 2x - 8 = 0$, is identical

to the equation: $(x + 4)(x - 2) = 0$

As you saw earlier (**p. 188**), solving an equation means figuring out what the variable needs to be to make the equation true. So to solve this equation, you just need to figure out what **x** needs to equal so that:

$(x + 4)$ **times** $(x - 2)$ **equals 0.**

Great, but how do I do that?

First, think about any equation in which two quantities, multiplied together, give you **0**. You can think about this

by looking at a general equation, like: $(a) \cdot (b) = 0$

Studying it, ask when it would be true. The only time it's true is if either **a** or **b** equals **0**, or if both **a** and **b** equal **0**.

Going back to the quadratic equation, that means the only way that $(x + 4)(x - 2)$ can equal **0** is if either $(x + 4)$ or $(x - 2)$ equals **0**, or if both equal **0**. You'll use this idea on the next page to solve this equation.

Q: Now I understand the theory for solving a quadratic equation. But how do I put it into practice? How would I actually solve an equation like this:

$$x^2 + 2x - 8 = 0$$

A: Follow the steps to the right.

Solve:

$x^2 + 2x - 8 = 0$

Steps

1st) Factor the trinomial.

2nd) Using the idea from **p. 204**, break the equation into two cases.

3rd) Solve each case.

4th) Take the answer from both cases as the complete answer.

Example

$x^2 + 2x - 8 = 0$

$(x + 4)(x - 2) = 0$

$x + 4 = 0$ or $x - 2 = 0$

$x + 4 = 0$	$x - 2 = 0$
$-4 \quad -4$	$+2 \quad +2$
$x = -4$	$x = +2$

$x = -4$ or $x = +2$

Solve these equations:

a) $x^2 + 10x + 16 = 0$
b) $a^2 - 15a + 56 = 0$
c) $0 = t^2 - 4t - 12$
d) $0 = v^2 + v - 20$

Answers:
a) $x = -8$ or $x = -2$
b) $a = 7$ or $a = 8$
c) $t = 6$ or $t = -2$
d) $v = 4$ or $v = -5$

 **O.K., by now I've learned how to solve basic equations, absolute value equations and quadratic equations. There's one other kind of equation I need to learn how to solve — equations using something called the Pythagorean theorem. First of all, what is the Pythagorean theorem? And why should I bother learning it?**

A: As far as people who study this sort of thing can tell, the **Pythagorean theorem** was discoverd around 4,000 years ago by the ancient people living in Babylonia (modern-day Iraq), and it was originally used to help people lay out property lines.

To make sure that hot-tempered Gungunum didn't wind up in a fistfight with his neighbor Ishbi over where Gungunum's wheat field ended and Ishbi's barley field began, Babylonian mathematicians got down to work. After a while, someone figured out how to get the exact length of one side of a right triangle, given any two of the other sides, and that new level of accuracy in measurement put an end to most of the fights.

This discovery came to be known as the **Pythagorean theorem** because a greek mathematician named **Pythagoras** got the credit for proving it. So helpful was the **Pythagorean theorem** that the ancients quickly put it to use not only for laying out property lines, but also for navigation, astronomy and other pursuits. And it's still used today by homebuilders, surveyors, scientists and more.

What new terms do I need to learn to understand the Pythagorean theorem?

A: You need to learn a number of **geometric** terms, because the Pythagorean theorem is a geometric theorem. Below you'll find these concepts along with a diagram.

Definitions

- A **right triangle** is a triangle with **one right angle**.
- A **right angle** is an angle with a measurement of **90 degrees**. You can remember a right angle as the angle formed by the sides in the capital letter **L**.
- The **legs** are the two sides that form the right angle.
- The **hypotenuse** (pronounced: "high-pot-i-noose") is the side directly across from the right angle. In other words, it's the **side that's not part of the right angle**.

An average right triangle and its parts

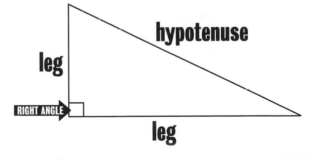

hypotenuse

leg

RIGHT ANGLE

leg

Identify the parts of this right triangle:

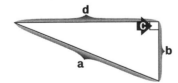

d

c

b

a

Answers:
a) **hypotenuse**
b) **leg**
c) **right angle**
d) **leg**

discussion, questions, feedback

O.K. Now I know the names for the parts of a right triangle. So I think I'm ready for the Pythagorean theorem. What does it say?

A: The world-famous, time-tested Pythagorean theorem says this ... drumroll, please. **Take any right triangle whatsoever. Name the length of one leg a; the other leg, b; the hypotenuse, c. No matter what this right triangle may look like, it will always be true that:**

$$a^2 + b^2 = c^2$$

What the Pythagorean theorem actually means

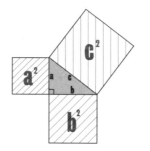

Square on side a plus square on side b equals square on side c.

Remember!
From geometry, the area of a square is the length of a side of that square times itself. That's why the square built on side **a** has area a^2; the square on side **b** has area b^2; the square on side **c** has area c^2.

To grasp this theorem, imagine that you have a choice about mowing some lawns. Pretend that each square in the diagram represents a big lawn with overgrown grass. Your choice is this: either mow lawns a^2 and b^2 — or just mow lawn c^2. If you understand the Pythagorean theorem, you'd say it makes no difference; the two choices are the same, since $a^2 + b^2 = c^2$

Q: Now I grasp the basic concept of the Pythagorean theorem, but how would I use it? For example, if I'm given the lengths of both legs in a right triangle, could I use the Pythagorean theorem to find the length of that triangle's hypotenuse?

A: Yes, to do so, just follow the steps to the right.

Given: a right triangle's legs have lengths 5 inches and 12 inches. **Find:** length of hypotenuse.

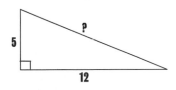

5, 12, ?

Steps

1st) Determine values for **a**, **b** and **c**. Then plug them into the formula:

$$a^2 + b^2 = c^2$$

2nd) Using the definition of an exponent (**p. 86**), get the values of the terms on the equation's left side, then add those numbers together.

3rd) Take the square root of both sides to find **c**. The value of **c** is the length of the hypotenuse. You may need a calculator if your answer isn't a natural number (**p. 23**).

Example

$$a = 5, \ b = 12, \ c = c$$
$$5^2 + 12^2 = c^2$$

$$25 + 144 = c^2$$
$$169 = c^2$$

$$\sqrt{169} = \sqrt{c^2}$$
$$13 = c$$

Find the hypotenuse, rounding answers to the tenths place, if necessary:

a) legs have lengths 3 cm. and 4 cm.
b) legs have lengths 8 miles and 15 miles
c) legs have lengths 24 meters and 32 meters
d) legs have lengths 13 feet and 31 feet
e) legs have lengths 10 lightyears and 17 lightyears

Answers:
a) hypotenuse = 5 cm.
b) hypotenuse = 17 miles
c) hypotenuse = 40 meters
d) hypotenuse ≅ 33.6 feet
e) hypotenuse ≅ 19.7 lightyears

Now I know how to find the length of the hypotenuse if I'm given the lengths of the two legs. But what about the other situation? Can I find the length of the second leg if I'm given the length of the hypotenuse and the length of one leg?

 Yes, you can do that too. Follow the steps to the right.

Given: a right triangle. One leg is 9 inches; hypotenuse is 15 inches. Find length of second leg.

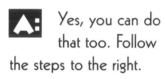

15

9

?

Steps

1st) Determine values for **a**, **b** and **c**. Then plug them into the formula:

$$a^2 + b^2 = c^2$$

2nd) Work out the exponents using definition of an exponent (**p. 86**). Then subtract the number term on the left from both sides to isolate the variable.

3rd) Take the square root of both sides. The value of the variable is the length of the second leg.

Example

$$a = a, \ b = 9, \ c = 15$$

$$a^2 + 9^2 = 15^2$$

$$a^2 + 81 = 225$$

$$\begin{array}{r} a^2 + 81 = 225 \\ -\ 81 \quad -\ 81 \\ \hline a^2 = \ 144 \end{array}$$

$$\sqrt{a^2} = \sqrt{144}$$

$$a = 12$$

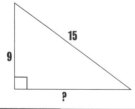

Find length of second leg, rounding answers to the tenths place, if necessary:

a) leg = 12 inches; hypotenuse = 13 inches
b) leg = 20 miles; hypotenuse = 33 miles
c) leg = 6.7 lightyears; hypotenuse = 10.1 lightyears
d) hypotenuse = 43.7 meters; leg = 30 meters
e) hypotenuse = 12 feet; leg = 10 feet

Answers:
a) leg = 5 inches
b) leg ≈ 26.2 miles
c) leg ≈ 7.6 lightyears
d) leg ≈ 31.8 meters
e) leg ≈ 6.6 feet

Solve these equations:

a) $4z + 8 = 2z - 6$

b) $3(x - 7) + 9 = 11 - 2(4 + x)$

c) $\dfrac{q}{8} + 5 = 2 \cdot 4$

d) $-f + 4f + 2(3 - f) = 6f - (f - 1)$

e) $|g| = 10$

f) $|w + 6| = 8$

g) $|3m - 9| = 15$

h) $|2q - 3| = 27$

j) $d^2 + 3d - 54 = 0$

k) $n^2 - 12n + 32 = 0$

l) $v^2 + 11v + 30 = 0$

m) $t^2 - 10t - 11 = 0$

Find length of the hypotenuse:

n) legs are 12 cm. and 16 cm.

p) legs are 10 inches and 24 inches

q) legs are 7 feet and 9 feet

r) legs are 13 meters and 20 meters

Find length of second leg:

s) leg = 6 cm.;
   hypotenuse = 10 cm.

t) leg = 3 mm.;
   hypotenuse = 11 mm.

u) leg = 25 inches;
   hypotenuse = 36 inches

v) leg = 100 miles;
   hypotenuse = 300 miles

a) $z = -7$

b) $x = 3$

c) $q = 24$

d) $f = 5/4$

e) $g = 10$ or $g = -10$

f) $w = 2$ or $w = -14$

g) $m = 8$ or $m = -2$

h) $q = 15$ or $q = -12$

j) $d = 6$ or $d = -9$

k) $n = 4$ or $n = 8$

l) $v = -5$ or $v = -6$

m) $t = 11$ or $t = -1$

n) hypotenuse = 20 cm.

p) hypotenuse = 26 inches

q) hypotenuse $\cong$ 11.4 feet

r) hypotenuse $\cong$ 23.9 meters

s) second leg = 8 cm.

t) second leg $\cong$ 10.6 mm.

u) second leg $\cong$ 25.9 inches

v) second leg $\cong$ 282.8 miles

Coordinate Plane

special points and y-intercepts. What exactly are these? And why are they called intercepts in the first place? To see why these lines are called intercepts, think about intercept- ed passes in a foot-

Why should I learn how to graph on the coordinate plane?

© Singing Turtle Press

A: For one thing, it's fun. For once in algebra, you actually get to **see** something. In other words, instead of spacing out as you look at an abstract equation, like $y = \frac{3}{5}x + 11$, you actually **see** what this equation looks like as a line. The same holds true for points and numbers. Instead of just staring at an abstract pair of numbers like $(7, -2)$, you **see** the point that these numbers refer to.

But there are even more important reasons to learn how to graph. First of all, **graphs have a wide range of uses in the real world**. Since graphs allow you to compare one quantity with another quantity, they're used to to show all sorts of relationships. Here are a few examples …

An **oceanographer** might use a graph to show how the number of dolphins in our seas has changed over the last 100 years. Or, a **sportswriter** could use a graph to chart how a player's batting average has gone up and down from season to season. And graphs are used in the sciences: **astronomy, physics, chemistry, virtually any science you can think of**. You might wonder how all these relationships can be shown on the standard **x-y graph** you study in algebra. Don't be deceived by those bland-looking letters **x** and **y**. They're flexible; they can stand for whatever you need them to stand for.

In any case, let's start exploring the fascinating and versatile world of graphs …

214

What are the main elements of the coordinate plane?

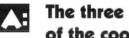 **The three main elements of the coordinate plane are:**

a) the **x-axis**, a straight line running left and right.

b) the **y-axis**, a straight line running up and down.

c) the **origin**, the point where the x- and y-axes cross.

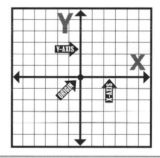

Note: Some people wonder: "How large is a point?" Asked another way: if you make a dot on a sheet of graph paper, is the dot you've made the same size as the point it stands for? The answer is no, for a point has **no size whatsoever**; it's just a location. In the same way, **a line has no breadth**; it is pure extension. That means that if you were a tightrope walker, you wouldn't want to walk on an algebraic line, for it has no thickness to hold you up.

Identify the elements of this coordinate plane:

Answers:
a) the y-axis
b) the origin
c) the x-axis

I hear people talking about weird things called "coordinates." What are coordinates, and what do people mean by the coordinates of a point?

A: You hear about coordinates on sci-fi t.v., as when the captain of the Enterprise reveals his coordinates so he may get "beamed up" to the ship. Essentially, **coordinates are directional tools that tell someone how to find something**. Just as directions help you locate a person's house, algebraic coordinates help you locate a point on a plane. In the coordinate plane, each point has exactly **two coordinates: an x-coordinate and a y-coordinate**.

Typical point, represented by its coordinates

$$(2, -4)$$

x-coordinate   y-coordinate

Note: the **x-coordinate** is always written first, the **y-coordinate** always second. You can remember this by the fact that **x** comes before **y** in the alphabet.

What are the x- and y-coordinates of these points?

a) $(3, 5)$

b) $(-1, 4)$

c) $(-5, -2)$

d) $(6, -12)$

Answers:

a) x-coordinate is 3; y-coordinate is 5

b) x-coordinate is − 1; y-coordinate is 4

c) x-coordinate is − 5; y-coordinate is − 2

d) x-coordinate is 6; y-coordinate is − 12

Now I have a sense of what coordinates are, but how do I actually use them? In other words, let's say I know the coordinates of some point. How do I use them to find out where that point is located on the coordinate plane?

 Good question. Fortunately the process is simple (and fun!). Just follow the steps below. **Locate the point with coordinates** $(3, -4)$

Steps

1st) Starting with your pencil point at the origin, look at the **x-coordinate**. If it's **positive**, move that many spaces to the **right**. If it's **negative**, move that many spaces to the **left**. (In this example, since the **x-coordinate** is $+3$, you move **3** spaces to the **right**.)

2nd) With your pencil point at this new location, glance at the **y-coordinate**. If it's **positive**, move that many space **up**. If it's **negative**, move that many spaces **down**. (In this example, since the **y-coordinate** is -4, you go **4** spaces **down**.)

3rd) The place where your pencil point lands after the second step is the point represented by those coordinates. In this problem, you've located the point: $(3, -4)$

Example

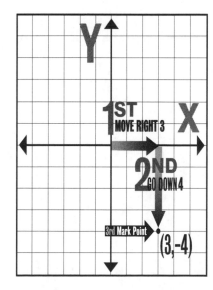

 (© Singing Turtle Press)

217

Q: Graph these points on the coordinate plane:

a) $(2, 7)$

b) $(-3, 6)$

c) $(-5, -2)$

d) $(7, -4)$

e) $(-7, 7)$

f) $(2, -6)$

g) $(4, 4)$

h) $(-2, -2)$

j) $(-6, -5)$

k) $(-5, 1)$

l) $(1, 1)$

m) $(3, -2)$

A: Below are the points on the coordinate plane:

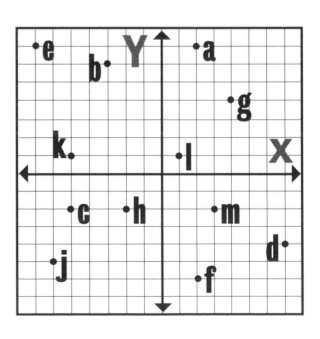

Now I understand how to use coordinates. But I've noticed that many formulas use weird-looking coordinates, symbols like x_1 and y_2. How do I make sense of coordinates like these?

It's true that formulas use strange-looking coordinates, but with a little practice, you'll get the idea. Formulas use what are called **subscripts**, little numbers placed at the right foot of the big number. To the right you'll see how to decode these funny-looking symbols.

How to crack the subscript code

Imagine that some formula — for example, the slope formula — asks you to think about two points in general. To do this, just call the points **Point 1** and **Point 2**, which you can abbreviate as P_1 and P_2. To name the coordinates of these points, just use the clever system below.

- the x-coordinate of P_1 is called x_1
- the y-coordinate of P_1 is called y_1
- the x-coordinate of P_2 is called x_2
- the y-coordinate of P_2 is called y_2

What would the following coordinates represent?

a) x_2

b) y_1

c) x_1

d) y_2

Answers:

a) x-coordinate of P_2

b) y-coordinate of P_1

c) x-coordinate of P_1

d) y-coordinate of P_2

Q: What is the slope of a line?

A: One nice thing about **slope** is that it's a concept you already know about from everyday life.

People talk about the slope of hills; golf commentators discuss the gentle slope of putting greens. So experience tells you that slope has to do with steepness. In math, slope has a specific, technical meaning: **it means the steepness of lines on the coordinate plane**.

From life, you also have a sense of what **steepness** means. For example, after climbing two hills, you should be able to say which one was steeper (at least your leg muscles will tell you the next day). But math, exact science that it is, allows you to measure steepness with perfect, numerical precision. In the next few pages you'll learn how.

In algebra, the symbol for **slope** is the letter **m**. Here are some other interesting things to know about slope:

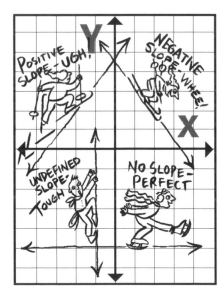

- **A horizontal line, having no steepness, has a slope of 0.**
- **A vertical line, having absolute steepness, has a slope that's undefined.**
- **Lines that rise from left to right have a positive slope.**
- **Lines that fall from left to right have a negative slope.**

What is the formula for the slope of a line?

 **The formula for the slope of a line, a formula you'll want to memorize, is this:**

$$m = \frac{y_2 - y_1}{x_2 - x_1},$$

where (x_1, y_1) and (x_2, y_2) are the coordinates of any two points on the line.

How to begin using this formula

Suppose you want to find the slope of the line that runs through the points $(-3, 6)$ and $(10, -4)$. To do this, you first need to find your four coordinates: x_1, y_1, x_2, y_2

To do that, name one of the points P_1. Name the other point P_2. It makes no difference which one you name which. So for kicks, you flip a coin and decide that P_1 is $(-3, 6)$ and P_2 is $(10, -4)$.

Since P_1 is $(-3, 6)$, that means $x_1 = -3$, and $y_1 = 6$.

Since P_2 is $(10, -4)$, that means $x_2 = 10$, and $y_2 = -4$.

State the values for x_1, y_1, x_2, y_2:

a) P_1 is $(5, 6)$

b) P_2 is $(-7, 11)$

c) P_1 is $(-2, -5)$; P_2 is $(8, -13)$

d) P_1 is $(11, 8)$; P_2 is $(-7, -4)$

Answers:

a) $x_1 = 5$; $y_1 = 6$

b) $x_2 = -7$; $y_2 = 11$

c) $x_1 = -2$; $y_1 = -5$; $x_2 = 8$; $y_2 = -13$

d) $x_1 = 11$; $y_1 = 8$; $x_2 = -7$; $y_2 = -4$

Q: O.K., stating the coordinates is simple enough. But how do I use them to get the slope? In other words, if I know the coordinates of two points, how would I actually find the slope of the line passing through those points?

 A: Follow the steps below. **Find slope of line through** $(2, -5)$ **and** $(-7, 4)$.

Steps	**Example**
1st) Call one of the points P_1; call the other point P_2. Then write out values for x_1, y_1, x_2, y_2.	let P_1 be $(2, -5)$; let P_2 be $(-7, 4)$ then $x_1 = 2$; $y_1 = -5$; $x_2 = -7$; $y_2 = 4$
2nd) Write the slope formula.	$m = \dfrac{y_2 - y_1}{x_2 - x_1}$
3rd) Plug values into the formula, then calculate the slope.	$m = \dfrac{4 - (-5)}{-7 - 2} = \dfrac{9}{-9} = -1$

Find the slope of the lines passing through these points:
a) $(4, 3)$ and $(9, 6)$
b) $(8, -2)$ and $(6, 5)$
c) $(-10, 5)$ and $(15, -20)$
d) $(-3, -6)$ and $(8, 7)$

Answers:
a) $m = \dfrac{3}{5}$
b) $m = -\dfrac{7}{2}$
c) $m = -1$
d) $m = \dfrac{13}{11}$

 **Now I see how to get the slope when I'm given two points. But one thing keeps bothering me ... How do I know that this formula makes sense? In other words, what's my guarantee that this formula truly measures steepness?**

 Good question. And if you just study the formula, along with some examples, the answer should pop out at you.

Looking at the slope formula, $m = \dfrac{y_2 - y_1}{x_2 - x_1}$, you can see that the **numerator** describes change along the **y-axis**, while the **denominator** describes change along the **x-axis**. In other words, the **numerator tells how much higher one point is than the other (vertical drop)**; the **denominator tells how much further to the right one point is than the other (horizontal distance)**.

Looking at the examples to the right, you can see that the line with slope of **5/3** is steeper than the line with slope of **1/3**. The reason should now be of clear. From the lower left point to either of the two other points, you move **3** spaces to the right, meaning there is a horizontal distance of **3**. But on the line with slope of **5/3**, the **vertical drop is 5**, while on the line with slope of **1/3**, **the vertical drop is just 1**.

Slope is just vertical drop divided by horizontal distance. So a large vertical drop with a small horizontal distance gives you a steep line; while a small vertical drop with a large horizontal distance gives you a less steep line.

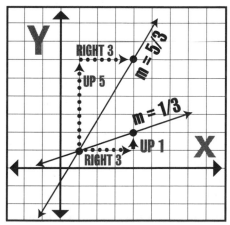

223

Suppose I know one point a line passes through, and I also know the slope of that line. Can I somehow use this information to graph the line?

 Most definitely. First let's do this for the case in which the slope is positive.
Graph the line with slope of 3/4 passing through $(-1, -2)$.

Steps

Note: If slope is **positive**, its **numerator** tells how many spaces you move **up**; **denominator** tells how many spaces you move **right**.

1st) Mark the starting point. In this example, the starting point is $(-1, -2)$.

2nd) Look at slope's numerator and go **up** that value. (In this example, you go up **3** since numerator is **3**.)

3rd) Look at slope's denominator and move **right** that value. (Here you move right **4** since denominator is **4**.) Mark point at which you arrive.

4th) Draw the line between the two points.

Example

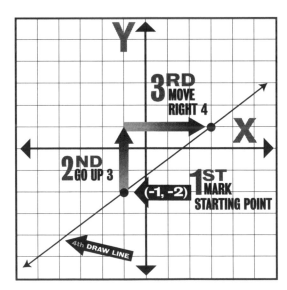

Graph these lines on the coordinate plane:

a) the line through (– **2,** – **3**) with slope of **4/5**.

b) the line through (– **4, 1**) with slope of **1/3**.

c) the line through (**1, 2**) with slope of **3/2**.

d) the line through (**3,** – **2**) with slope of **5/1**.

A: Below are the lines graphed on the coordinate plane:

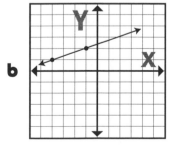

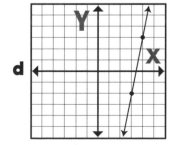

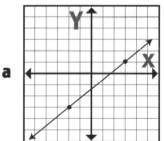

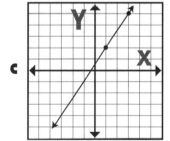

Now I see how to graph the line when the slope is positive. But how do I do this when the slope is negative?

 You follow a similar technique. Follow the steps below.
Graph the line with slope of $-7/5$ passing through the point $(-2, 3)$.

Steps

Note: If slope is **negative,** its **numerator** tells how many spaces you move **down**; its **denominator** still tells how many spaces you move **right**.

1st) Mark the starting point. In this example, the starting point is $(-2, 3)$.

2nd) Look at slope's numerator and go **down** that value. (In this example, you go down **7** since numerator is **7**.)

3rd) Look at slope's denominator and move **right** that value. (Here you move right **5** since denominator is **5**.) Mark point at which you arrive.

4th) Draw the line between the two points.

Example

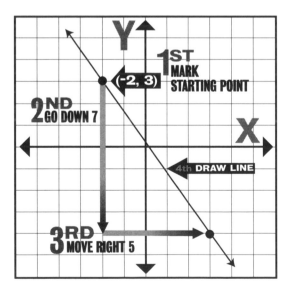

Graph these lines on the coordinate plane:

a) the line through (– **4, 2**) with slope of – **5/7** .

b) the line through (– **2, – 2**) with slope of – **1/6**.

c) the line through (– **4, – 1**) with slope of – **1/3**.

d) the line through (– **2, 4**) with slope of – **7/4**.

A: Below are the lines graphed on the coordinate plane:

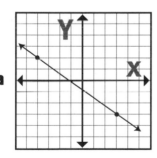

a

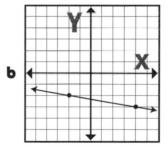

b

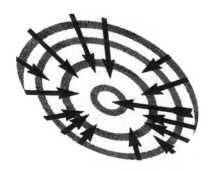

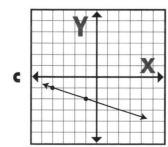

c

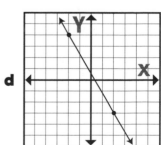

d

Q:

I hear about special points called x-intercepts and y-intercepts. What exactly are these? How do I indicate these points? And why in the world are they called "intercepts" in the first place?

A: The **x-intercept** is the **point where a line crosses the x-axis**; the **y-intercept**, that **point where a line crosses the y-axis**. For example, if a line crosses the x-axis at the point $(-2, 0)$, you'd say the **x-intercept** is $(-2, 0)$, or, in a shorthand way of talking, you can say the x-intercept is -2, since the line crosses the x-axis at -2. In the same way, if a line crosses the y-axis at $(0, 3)$, the **y-intercept** is $(0, 3)$, or just $+3$.

To see why these points are called **intercepts**, think about intercepted passes in football. Turning on your **imagination**, try to see the **x-axis** as the flight of a forward pass. Then go a step further. Imagine that a line crossing the **x-axis** is **the path of a defensive player running to intercept the pass**. The point where his/her path crosses the ball's flight is where the **intercept** is made, so it's the **x-intercept**. In the same way, if you view the **y-axis** as a forward pass, the point where a line crosses it is the **y-intercept**.

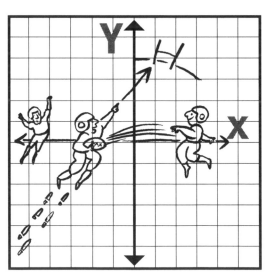

Q: Name the x- and y-intercepts for each of these four lines:

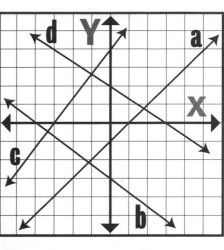

A: The x- and y-intercepts are named below:

a) x-intercept is 1; y-intercept is −1.

b) x-intercept is −4; y-intercept is −3.

c) x-intercept is −3; y-intercept is 4.

d) x-intercept is 3; y-intercept is 2.

Q: What is the slope-intercept formula for a line?

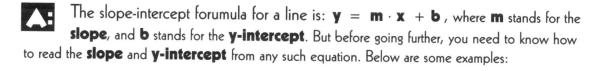

A: The slope-intercept forumula for a line is: $y = m \cdot x + b$, where **m** stands for the **slope**, and **b** stands for the **y-intercept**. But before going further, you need to know how to read the **slope** and **y-intercept** from any such equation. Below are some examples:

Suppose the formula for a line is: $y = 3x + 7$ Since **3** stands where **m** goes in the formula, the **slope** of this line is **3**. Since **7** stands where **b** goes in the formula, the **y-intercept** of this line is **7**.

Now look at this formula:
$$y = -2/3\ x + 5$$
Since $-2/3$ stands in **m**'s place, the slope of this line is $-2/3$. Since **5** stands in **b**'s place, the **y-intercept** of this line is **5**. Starting to make sense?

Finally look at this formula:
$$y = 8x - 2$$
Obviously the slope is **8**. But how about the **y-intercept**? To avoid confusion, rewrite this equation as: $y = 8x + (-2)$

Now you see that -2 stands in **b**'s place. This tells you that the **y-intercept** of this line is -2.

Name the slopes and y-intercepts of the following lines:

a) $y = 8x + 4$

b) $y = \dfrac{2}{5}x + 9$

c) $y = 3x - 6$

d) $y = -\dfrac{3}{4}x - 11$

Answers:
a) $m = 8$; $b = 4$
b) $m = \dfrac{2}{5}$; $b = 9$
c) $m = 3$; $b = -6$
d) $m = -\dfrac{3}{4}$; $b = -11$

Q: O.K. Now I know how to find the slope and y-intercept from an equation. But how can this help me? For example, can I use this information to graph a line written in slope-intercept form?

A: Yes, you can. **Graph this line:** $y = 4/3x - 2$

| **Steps** | **Example** |

1st) Note **y-intercept** and mark it. In this example, the y-intercept is **−2**.

2nd) Note the **slope**. Then using the slope and the technique on **p. 224**, find a second point on the line. Mark this point.

3rd) Draw the line between the two points. That's all there is to it. You've successfully graphed the line represented by the original equation.

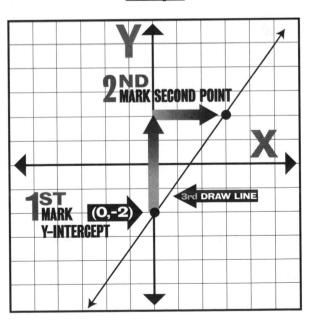

Graph these lines on the coordinate plane:

a) $y = 2x + 1$

b) $y = 4/3\,x - 2$

c) $y = -2/3x + 2$

d) $y = -3/2\,x - 1$

Below you'll see these lines graphed on the coordinate plane:

a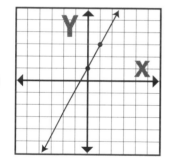

c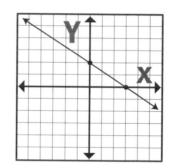

b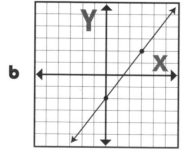

d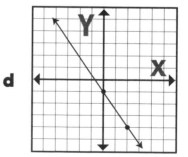

Suppose I know both the slope of a line and the coordinates of one point on the line. Can I use this information to find the equation of the line?

 Yes, just follow the steps below. **Find the equation in slope-intercept form of a line with slope of 2/3 that passes through $(-4, 1)$.**

Steps

1st) Write the slope-intercept formula. Then plug in value of slope for **m**. Also plug in **x-coordinate** for **x**, and **y-coordinate** for **y**.

2nd) Solve equation for **b**, the **y-intercept**.

3rd) Plug values of **m** and **b** into $y = m \cdot x + b$ That's the equation of the line.

Example

$$y = m \cdot x + b$$
$$\downarrow \quad \downarrow \quad \downarrow$$
$$+1 = 2/3 \cdot (-4) + b$$
$$+1 = -8/3 \quad + b$$
$$\underline{+8/3 \quad +8/3}$$
$$11/3 = b$$
$$y = \frac{2}{3}x + \frac{11}{3}$$

Diagram

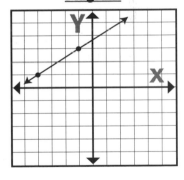

Write the equations of lines through these points and with these slopes:

a) through $(-3, 4)$ with m = 5

b) through $(6, -1)$ with m = 3/4

c) through $(-2, -7)$ with m = $-1/3$

d) through $(-4, 8)$ with m = $-6/7$

Answers:
a) $y = 5x + 19$
b) $y = 3/4 \, x - 11/2$
c) $y = -1/3 \, x - 23/3$
d) $y = -6/7 \, x + 32/7$

Suppose I know the coordinates of two points that a line passes through. How can I find the equation of the line that goes through these points?

 Follow the steps below. **Find equation of line through** $(1, 3)$ **and** $(-2, -3)$.

Steps	**Example**	**Diagram**

1st) Use the coordinates to find the slope, using the technique shown on **p. 222**.

$$m = \frac{-3 - 3}{-2 - 1} = 2$$

2nd) Choose either of your two points. (It makes no difference which point you use.) Plug in coordinates of that point and value of slope. Solve for **b**.

Choose point: $(1, 3)$

$$\begin{array}{ccc} y & = & m \cdot x + b \\ \downarrow & & \downarrow \quad \downarrow \\ 3 & = & 2 \cdot 1 + b \\ 3 & = & 2 + b \end{array}$$

3rd) Plug values for **m** and **b** into slope-intercept formula.

$$1 = b$$
$$y = 2x + 1$$

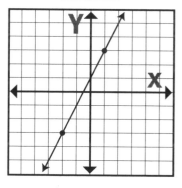

Now try finding the equations of lines through these points:

a) $(1, 5)$ and $(2, 8)$
b) $(5, -2)$ and $(10, 2)$
c) $(3, 6)$ and $(-9, 10)$
d) $(7, -6)$ and $(-14, 0)$

Sometimes my teacher or textbook shows me an equation that's not written in slope-intercept form. Then I'm asked to put it into slope-intercept form. How do I do this? In other words, how would I put an equation like this into slope-intercept form:

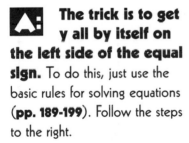

$$4x - 2y = 10$$

A: **The trick is to get y all by itself on the left side of the equal sign.** To do this, just use the basic rules for solving equations (**pp. 189-199**). Follow the steps to the right.

Rewrite the equation:

$$4x - 2y = 10$$

in slope-intercept form.

Steps

1st) Get rid of any terms on same side as y by adding or subtracting the same thing to both sides.

2nd) Divide both sides of equation by the coefficient in front of y.

3rd) Simplify the right side using the split-the-numerator rule (**pp. 181-183**). Equation is now in slope-intercept form.

Example

$$\begin{array}{rrr} 4x & - 2y & = & 10 \\ - 4x & & & - 4x \\ \hline & - 2y & = & - 4x + 10 \end{array}$$

$$\frac{- 2y}{- 2} = \frac{- 4x + 10}{- 2}$$

$$y = -4x/-2 + 10/-2$$

$$y = 2x - 5$$

Now try writing these equations in slope-intercept form:

a) $-6x + 2y = 8$
b) $15x + 3y = 27$
c) $8y + 2x = -24$
d) $-2x + 9y = -99$
e) $7y + 3x = -35$

Answers:

a) $y = 3x + 4$
b) $y = -5x + 9$
c) $y = -\frac{1}{4}x - 3$
d) $y = \frac{2}{9}x - 11$
e) $y = -\frac{3}{7}x - 5$

© Singing Turtle Press

235

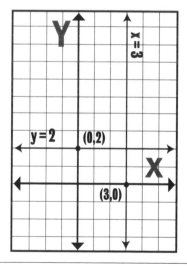

Now I understand the slope-intercept formula better, and I see that I can use it for lines with a measurable slope. But what about horizontal lines, which have a slope of zero, and vertical lines, which have a slope that's undefined. What do the equations of these lines look like?

Equations of **vertical** and **horizontal** lines are simple.

Vertical line equations look like: **x = some number**
Example: equation of vertical line through (**3, 0**) is: **x = 3**
Why? Because **x = 3** means all points whose x-coordinate is **3**. This set includes points like (**3, 1**) and (**3, −1**), etc.

Horizontal line equations look like: **y = some number**
Example: equation of horizontal line through (**0, 2**) is: **y = 2**
For **y = 2** means all points whose y-coordinate is **2**. This set includes points like: (**1, 2**) and (−**1, 2**), etc.

Now try finding the equations of these lines:

a) vertical line through (− 3, 0)
b) vertical line through (4, − 1)
c) horizontal line through (0, − 5)
d) horizontal line through (− 2, 7)

Answers:
a) x = − 3
b) x = 4
c) y = − 5
d) y = 7

your questions answered ...

What does it mean to solve two equations in two variables?

First, let's think about what's makes equations in two variables special.

If you're observant, you've probably noticed that unlike the equations you worked with earlier (which use only one variable, such as x), equations in this section use two variables: x and y. That's because these are special equations, equations representing lines. There are two names for such equations. They're called equations in two variables (for obvious reasons); they're also called linear equations, since they stand for lines.

Now, to see what it means to solve two equations, think of each equation as a line. Common sense says that if two lines intersect, they intersect in one point, right? So solving two linear equations means finding that one point where the two lines meet.

This is a little like the story of Cinderella and the glass slipper. Just as only one pair of slippers in the whole kingdom fit Cinderella's feet, only one point, out of all points on the coordinate plane, lies on both lines. Your mission, in solving two linear equations is to find that one, magic point.

O.K., now I have some idea of what it means to solve two equations with two variables. And I've heard that there's a nice method for doing this called substitution. But how do I do this?

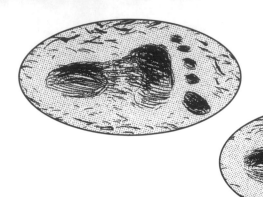

 The **substitution method** asks you to substitute a quantity from one equation into the other equation. From a more creative (and gross) viewpoint, it's like taking a hypodermic needle, sucking up one equation, and injecting it into the other equation. At right you'll see the first two steps in this five-step process:

Solve:
$$x + y = 3$$
$$y - 3x = -1$$

Steps

1st) Choose whichever equation looks simpler to work with. Using rules for working with equations (**pp. 189-199**), move terms around so that one variable is isolated You can choose to isolate x or y; either will work fine. (In this example, you isolate x.)

2nd) Write down the other equation. Then inject the value for the variable found in 1st step into this equation.

Example

Choose: x + y = 3

$$\begin{array}{r} x + y = 3 \\ -y \quad -y \\ \hline x = 3 - y \end{array}$$

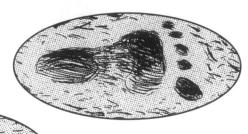

$$y - 3 \quad x \quad = -1$$
$$\downarrow$$
$$y - 3(3 - y) = -1$$

Solve top equation in each pair of equations for x. Then inject that value for x into the bottom equation. Show the result.

a) x − y = −5
   y + 3x = −3

b) x + 3y = −2
   2x − y = 3

Answers:

a) y + 3(y − 5) = −3

b) 2(−3y − 2) − y = 3

238

I see how to substitute the value of one variable into the second equation. But how do I complete the process of solving two equations?

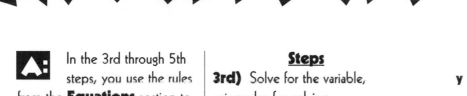

A: In the 3rd through 5th steps, you use the rules from the **Equations** section to solve for the variable. When you left off on the last page, you had this equation:

$$y - 3(3 - y) = -1$$

Steps

3rd) Solve for the variable, using rules for solving equations (**pp. 189-199**).

4th) Choose either of the original equations (it makes no difference which). Inject value for variable you found in 3rd step. Solve for the other variable.

5th) To get answer, write down both the x and y values as an ordered pair.

Example

$$y - 3(3 - y) = -1$$
$$\downarrow$$
$$y = 2$$

$$x + y = 3$$
$$\downarrow$$
$$x + 2 = 3$$
$$x = 1$$

solution: $(1, 2)$

Picking up where you left off on the previous QuikChek, finish solving the pairs of equations. Refer back to equations on last page's QuikChek.

a) $y + 3(y - 5) = -3$

b) $2(-3y - 2) - y = 3$

Answers:

a) solution: $(-2, 3)$

b) solution: $(1, -1)$

Q: Now I know how to solve two equations in two variables. But it would be nice to see what this actually means on a graph?

Can I see what the problem I just solved would look like on a graph

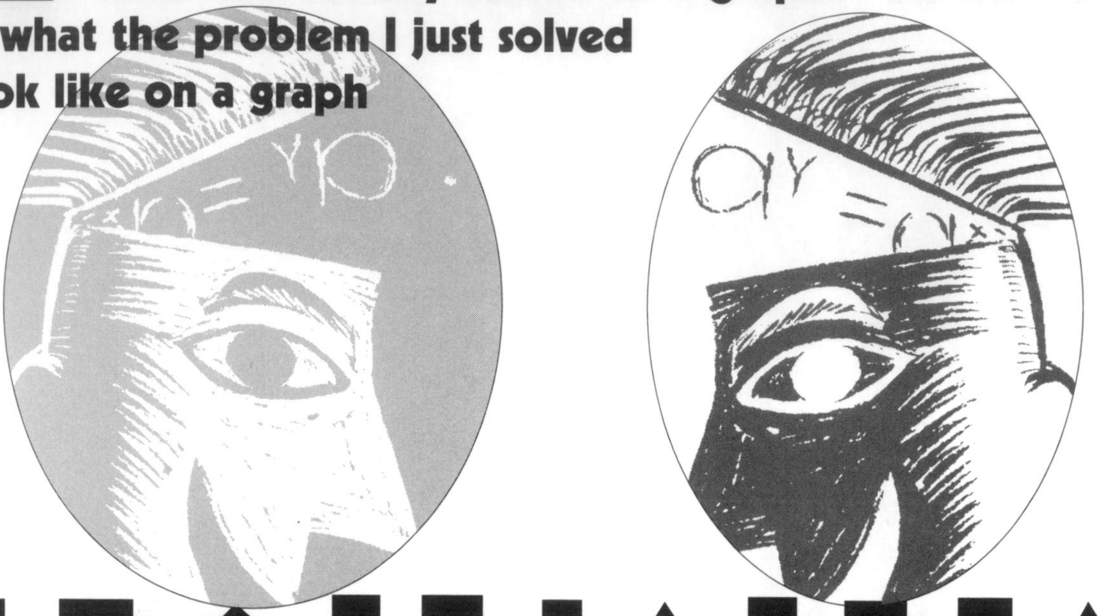

A: Yes. As you learned above, solving two equations in two variables means finding that one point on the coordinate plane where the two lines intersect. In the example you solved, the equations were:

$$x + y = 3$$

and

$$y - 3x = -1$$

To the right you'll see a graph showing these lines and the point at which they meet, which, as you saw on **p. 239**, is the point: **(1, 2)**

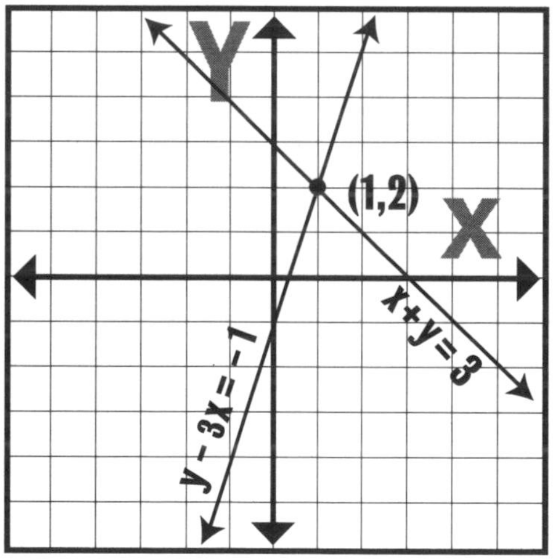

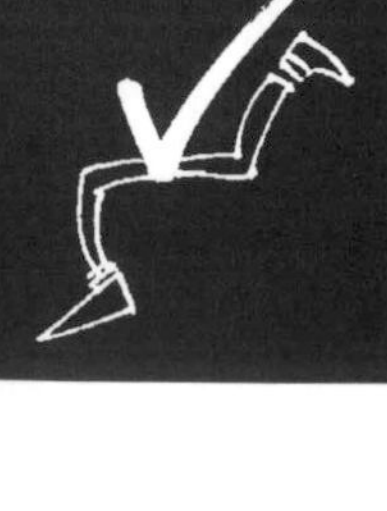

For practice, try solving these pairs of equations from start to finish:

a) $x + y = 1$
$x - y = -5$

b) $x + 2y = 6$
$x - 2y = -2$

c) $2x - y = -6$
$x - 4y = 4$

Answers:
a) $(-2, 3)$
b) $(2, 2)$
c) $(-4, -2)$

I've heard that there's a special formula for finding the distance between any two points on a plane. What is this formula?

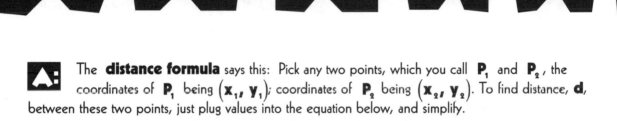

A: The **distance formula** says this: Pick any two points, which you call P_1 and P_2, the coordinates of P_1 being (x_1, y_1); coordinates of P_2 being (x_2, y_2). To find distance, **d**, between these two points, just plug values into the equation below, and simplify.

$$d = \sqrt{\left(x_2 - x_1\right)^2 + \left(y_2 - y_1\right)^2}$$

How this formula works ... or: The Pythagorean theorem comes back

The distance formula comes from the Pythagorean theorem. Here's how: Looking at the diagram to the right, you see that with any two points, P_1 and P_2, you can make a right triangle, one of whose legs runs vertically, the other running horizontally. The length of the horizontal leg is $x_2 - x_1$; the length of the vertical leg is $y_2 - y_1$.

Using the Pythagorean theorem,

$$d^2 = \left(x_2 - x_1\right)^2 + \left(y_2 - y_1\right)^2$$

And if you just take the square root of both sides, you get this:

$$d = \sqrt{\left(x_2 - x_1\right)^2 + \left(y_2 - y_1\right)^2}$$

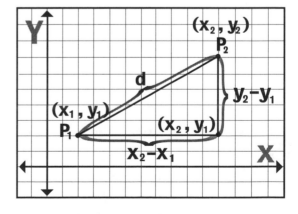

And that, it turns out, is the distance formula. So you see: **All Math Ties Together!!!**

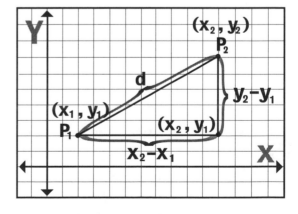

Now I have some sense of why the distance formula is true. But how do I use it?

 Just follow the steps to the right.

Find the distance between these two points:

$$\left(4, -6\right)$$

and

$$\left(-1, 5\right)$$

Steps

1st) Name one of the points P_1; name the other point P_2. Then write out values for x_1, y_1, x_2, y_2

2nd) Write the distance formula.

3rd) Plug values into formula. Then simplify to find the distance.

Example

let $\left(4, -6\right)$ be P_1;

let $\left(-1, 5\right)$ be P_2.

Then: $\begin{aligned} x_1 &= 4; y_1 = -6 \\ x_2 &= -1; y_2 = 5 \end{aligned}$

$d = \sqrt{\left(x_2 - x_1\right)^2 + \left(y_2 - y_1\right)^2}$

$d = \sqrt{\left(-1 - 4\right)^2 + \left(5 - -6\right)^2}$

$d = \sqrt{\left(-5\right)^2 + \left(11\right)^2}$

$d = \sqrt{25 + 121}$

$d = \sqrt{146}$

Now try finding the distance between each pair of points:

a) $\left(1, 2\right)$ and $\left(4, 6\right)$

b) $\left(-1, 6\right)$ and $\left(-6, -6\right)$

c) $\left(3, -2\right)$ and $\left(6, 5\right)$

d) $\left(-5, 2\right)$ and $\left(3, -3\right)$

Answers:
a) 5
b) 13
c) $\sqrt{58}$
d) $\sqrt{89}$

© Singing Turtle Press

Find slope of the line through these points:

a) $(6, 3)$ and $(8, 7)$

b) $(-4, 11)$ and $(5, -6)$

State slope and y-intercept:

c) $y = 6x + 12$

d) $y = -\dfrac{3}{11} - 5$

Find slope-intercept equation:

e) through $(2, 4)$; $m = 5$

f) through $(-3, -7)$; $m = -2/3$

Find slope-intercept equation of line through these points:

g) $(-3, 1)$ and $(6, 4)$

h) $(-4, -3)$ and $(-8, 0)$

i) $(6, 5)$ and $(4, -5)$

Rewrite these equations in slope-intercept form:

k) $4x - y = 2$

l) $2x + 9y = -3$

Find equations of these horizontal and vertical lines:

m) horizontal, through $(3, 5)$

n) vertical, through $(3, 5)$

Solve the two equations:

p) $x + 2y = 2$
   $2x - y = 9$

q) $x + 3y = 6$
   $x - y = -6$

Find the distance between the two points:

r) $(8, 4)$ and $(-4, -1)$

s) $(3, -5)$ and $(7, 2)$

a) 2

b) $-17/9$

c) $m = 6$; $b = 12$

d) $m = -3/11$; $b = -5$

e) $y = 5x - 6$

f) $y = -2/3 x - 9$

g) $y = 1/3 x + 2$

h) $y = -3/4 x - 6$

i) $y = 5x - 25$

k) $y = 4x - 2$

l) $y = -2/9 x - 1/3$

m) $y = 5$

n) $x = 3$

p) $(4, -1)$

q) $(-3, 3)$

r) 13

s) $\sqrt{65}$

Graph these points:

a) $(2, 1)$

b) $(-3, 4)$

c) $(3, -2)$

d) $(-4, -4)$

Graph the lines with these slopes that pass through these points:

e) $m = 3$; through $(-2, 1)$

f) $m = 1/2$; through $(1, 2)$

g) $m = -2$; through $(-1, -3)$

h) $m = -3/4$; through $(0, 1)$

Graph the lines represented by these equations:

j) $y = 3x + 1$

k) $y = -2x - 2$

l) $y = 2/3 x - 3$

m) $y = -1/3 x + 2$

A:

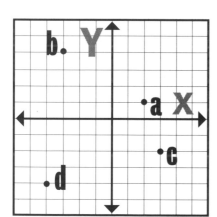

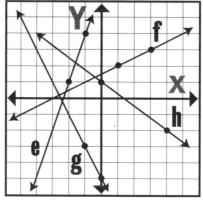

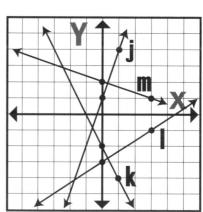

Word Problems

Imagine that you're away by a helicopter dropped into the b of Kinnikanu. After parachuting down, you'd probably appreciate having a mini-dictionary so you could ask the locals survival questions like, "Hey, where can I grab a burger and fries around here?" The same holds for the algebra wilderness. You need a mini-

Word problems ... ?
Aaaagggghhh!!! Panic attack!
Obviously I could use a step-by-step
approach so I don't freak out every
time I see a word problem. Is there any sort of
step-by-step technique that can help me?

Yes, help is at hand. Just learn the five basic steps for word problems, described below:

1st) Figure out which Quantity you're trying to find. This is easy. Just read the sentence that ends with a question mark (almost always the last one) and **notice what the problem asks you to find.** It could be anything: the speed of a train, the percent of kids with green eyes, the age of a girl named Kelly, a number of guinea pigs, etc.

2nd) Assign a Variable to stand for this quantity. It helps to choose a letter that's the same as the first letter of the quantity. For example, choose **s** for **speed**, **k** for **Kelly**, **g** for **guinea pigs**, etc. You also may need to express other quantities in terms of the variable. For example, if **k** is **Kelly's** age, and Sandra is two years older than Kelly, let **k + 2** stand for **Sandra's** age.

3rd) Write one or two equations to Translate from **English** to **"Mathlish,"** from **words** to **mathematical symbols**. This step sets you up to solve the problem.

4th) Solve for the variable. Use your equation-solving skills to **find the variable's value.**

5th) Once you get the variable's value, **tell the Meaning of the answer**. For example, if after solving the equation, you find that **g = 12**, go ahead and write: "The number of guinea pigs is 12." Writing this sentence connects your answer to the meaning of the problem.

Quantity-Variable-Translate-Solve-Meaning ...
Recall the order with this delightful thought:
Quick Vicky Trapped Several Mice.

Q: What exactly is "Mathlish"? And is there a guide to help me translate from English to "Mathlish"?

A: Imagine that you're whisked away by helicopter and air-dropped into the backcountry of Kinnikanu. After parachuting down, you'd probably appreciate having a **mini-dictionary** so you could ask the locals survival questions like, "Hey, where can I grab a burger and fries around here?" The same holds for the **Algebra Wilderness**. You need a mini-dictionary so you can translate from **English** to **"Mathlish,"** that strange, seemingly foreign language that math is written in. Here's the mini-dictionary you need:

English	Mathlish
is/was/will be/equals/the result is	$=$
of	$\times$ **or** $\cdot$
a number	**n**
the opposite of a number	**− n**
three consecutive integers	**n, n + 1, n + 2**
three consecutive odd or even integers	**n, n + 2, n + 4**
sum/more than/ increased by/and	$+$
difference/less than/decreased by	$-$
product/times/multiplied by	$\times$ **or** $\cdot$
quotient/over/divided by	$\div$ **or fraction symbol:** $/$
what number/what fraction	**n**
what percent	**n/100**
quantity	( )

THE OPPOSITE OF A NUMBER

MATHLISH TRANSLATION SERVICE

-n

ENGLISH   MATHLISH

Great, but how do I actually use this mini-dictionary to translate simple algebraic phrases from English to Mathlish?

It's quite simple. First think through what the statement means, then change it from **English** to **Mathlish**. You'll grasp this best by studying examples, so here are a few:

English	Mathlish
five more than a number	n + 5
five less than a number	n − 5
five times a number	5n
a number divided by five	n/5
two less than five times a number	5n − 2
seven more than twice a number	2n + 7

English	Mathlish
four more than the opposite of a number	− n + 4
nine times the opposite of a number	9 · (− n) or − 9n
three times the quantity of a number and seven	3(n + 7)
four times the quantity of twice a number decreased by eight	4(2n − 8)
two consecutive integers	n + n + 1

Now try translating these phrases from English to Mathlish:
a) six less than a number
b) nine times a number
c) three times the opposite of a number
d) six times the quantity of three less than four times a number

Answers:
a) n − 6
b) 9n
c) − 3n
d) 6(4n − 3)

visit **www.AlgebraWizard.com**

Q: One little question...
When I translate a quantity like
"four less than a number," it makes
no difference whether I write **n − 4**
or **4 − n**, for these two phrases mean the
same thing. Right?

A: Uh ... sorry, but no. This is a
common misunderstanding, so you'd
do well to learn the truth now.

n − 4 means "**4** less than **n**," but **4 − n** means "**n** less than **4**."
Still not convinced that these are different?
Just consider the values of these phrases if **n** equals **9**.

If **n = 9**, then ...

n − 4		4 − n
= 9 − 4	**but**	= 4 − 9
= 5		= −5

Moral of the story: **n − 4** is **not the same** as **4 − n**.

Tip: to avoid this confusion,
**always write the variable
first**. For example,
♦ Instead of writing **five
more than a number** as
5 + n, write it as
n + 5.
♦ Instead of writing **five less
than a number** as
5 − n (which is wrong),
write it as **n − 5**.

Try writing these phrases using algebraic symbols:

a) **four more than a number**
b) **four less than a number**
c) **one hundred less than a number**
d) **one hundred more than a number**

Answers:
a) n + 4
b) n − 4
c) n − 100
d) n + 100

Now I see how to set up phrases in word problems, but how do I translate whole sentences from English to Mathlish?

First notice the word or phrase that translates as an **equal sign**. As you saw on **p. 247**, this includes words or phrases like: **is, was, will be, equals, the result is**, etc. Then notice the phrases on either side of the equal sign. Translate those into **Mathlish**. See the examples below:

| A number | multiplied by | two | **is** | eight more than the number. |

$$n \qquad \times \qquad 2 \qquad = \qquad n + 8$$

| The opposite of a number divided by four | **equals** | ten less than the number. |

$$\frac{-n}{4} \qquad\qquad = \qquad n \; - \; 10$$

| What percent | of | forty | **is** | thirty-five? |

$$\frac{n}{100} \; \cdot \; 40 \; = \; 35$$

| The sum of three consecutive integers | **is** | thirty. |

$$n + n+1 + n+2 \qquad = \qquad 30$$

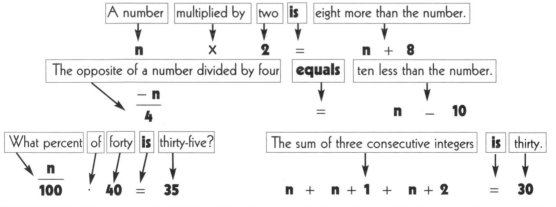

Now try translating these English statements into Mathlish:

a) Ten more than a number equals the number multiplied by two.
b) What percent of fifty is forty?
c) The sum of two consecutive integers is 21.
d) Nine more than the opposite of a number equals twice the number.

Answers:
a) $n + 10 = 2n$
b) $n/100 \cdot 50 = 40$
c) $n + n + 1 = 21$
d) $-n + 9 = 2n$

Q: How do I actually go through the steps for solving a word problem in which I'm asked to find a number?

A: Let's learn by solving this problem: **Nine more than the opposite of a number is three less than twice the number. What is the number?** Here are the "Quick Vicky" steps:

Steps	Example	Steps	Example
1st) Note the **Q**uantity you're looking for.	**You're looking for the number.**	**4th) S**olve for the variable.	$-n + 9 = 2n - 3$
			$-n + 9 = 2n - 3$
			$\underline{+n \qquad\quad +n}$
2nd) Let a **V**ariable stand for it.	**let n = the number**		$+9 = 3n - 3$
			$\underline{+3 \qquad\quad +3}$
3rd) Translate from English to Mathlish.	**Nine more than the opposite of n is three less than twice n.**		$+12 = 3n$
			$4 = n$
	$-n + 9 = 2n - 3$	**5th)** Tell the **M**eaning of your answer.	**The number is 4.**

Now try solving for the variable in these word probems:

a) **Seven less than four times a number equal three times the number.**
b) **One less than four times a number is four more than three times the number.**
c) **Two more than a number divided by five is fourteen less than the number.**
d) **Three times the quantity of a number increased by two equals one more than twice the number.**

Answers:
a) n = 7
b) n = 5
c) n = 20
d) n = −5

How do I go through the steps for a word problem in which I'm asked to find a percent?

A: You'll find out by solving this problem from beginning to end: **What percent of 80 is 72?**
Here are the steps:

Steps	**Example**	**Steps**	**Example**
1st) Note the **Q**uantity you're looking for.	**You're looking for the percent.**	**4th)** **S**olve for the variable.	$n/100 \cdot 80 = 72$
			$(100) \cdot n/100 \cdot 80 = 72 \cdot (100)$
2nd) Let a **V**ariable stand for it.	**let n = the percent**		$80n = 7200$
			$\dfrac{80n}{80} = \dfrac{7200}{80}$
3rd) **Tr**anslate from English to Mathlish.	**What percent of 80 is 72?**		$n = 90$
	$n/100 \cdot 80 = 72$	**5th)** Tell the **M**eaning of your answer.	**72 is 90% of 80.**

Now try solving these percent word problems:

a) **What percent of 40 is 16?**
b) **What percent of 65 is 80?**
c) **27 is what percent of 36?**
d) **120 is what percent of 100?**

Answers:
a) 16 is 40% of 40.
b) 80 is 123% of 65.
c) 27 is 75% of 36.
d) 120 is 120% of 100.

Q: So far so good... but there's one kind of percent problem that throws me for a loop — problems about a percent of increase. How do I overcome my confusion here?

A: Just remember that **the increase is added to the original amount**. Keep this in mind, and you'll do fine.

For example, look at this problem:

What is the result when 40 is increased by 150%?

Many students correctly let **n = the result**, but then make a wrong turn by setting the problem up like this:

$$n = 40 \cdot \frac{150}{100}$$

Wrong — for the wording means you increase **40** by **150** percent of **40**. So you first write down **40**, then **add the increase to it**, like this:

$$n = 40 + 40 \cdot \frac{150}{100}$$

And here's how you finish this problem:

$$n = 40 + 60$$
$$n = 100$$

The result is 100.

Try these percent increase problems:

a) **What's the result when 25 is increased by 20%?**
b) **What's the result when 60 is increased by 30%?**
c) **140 gets increased by 40%. What's the result?**
d) **500 gets increased by 35%. What's the result?**

Answers:
a) result is 30
b) result is 78
c) result is 196
d) result is 675

Q: What are the steps for doing problems about consecutive integers?

A: Consecutive integer problems work like the problems you've just looked at. Just remember that if the problem asks for **consecutive integers**, you use: **n, n + 1, n + 2, etc.** And if it asks for **consecutive even or odd integers**, you use: **n, n + 2, n + 4, etc.** Let's try this problem as an example:
Three consecutive integers add up to 63. What are they?

<u>Steps</u>	<u>Example</u>	<u>Steps</u>	<u>Example</u>
1st) Note the **Q**uantity you're looking for.	**You're looking for the three consecutive integers.**	**4th) S**olve for the variable.	$3n + 3 = 63$ $\underline{\quad -3 \quad -3\quad}$ $3n = 60$
2nd) Let a **V**ariable stand for the quantities.	**let n = the first integer** **n + 1 = the second integer** **n + 2 = the third integer**		$n = 20$
3rd) Translate from English to Mathlish.	**Three consecutive integers add up to 63.** **n + n+1 + n+2 = 63**	**5th)** Tell the **M**eaning of your answer.	**first integer is 20** **second integer is 21** **third integer is 22**

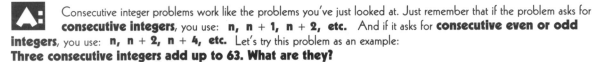

Now try working out these consecutive integer problems:
a) **Two consecutive integers add up to 35. What are they?**
b) **Three consecutive integers add up to 36. What are they?**
c) **Two consecutive even integers add up to 26. What are they?**
d) **Three consecutive odd integers add up to 33. What are they?**
e) **Four consecutive integers add up to 106. What are they?**

Answers:
a) 17, 18
b) 11, 12, 13
c) 12, 14
d) 9, 11, 13
e) 25, 26, 27, 28

Q: What are some tips for doing age problems?

A: The trick lies in the set-up. First, you need to know how to **express people's ages in relation to one another**. Then you need to know how to **change timeframes**. Let's look at each skill individually.

Expressing ages in relation to each other

To show people's ages in relation to each other, just take account of the age difference between them. Example: suppose you're solving some problem for **Joe's age**. Naturally you begin by letting **j = Joe's age**. If the problem says Fred is **2** years younger than Joe, you'd say:

j − 2 = Fred's age. Why? Because Fred is **2** years **younger** than Joe. [i.e.: if Joe were **10**, Fred would be **10 − 2**, or **8**.] On the other hand, if the problem says Fred is **6** years **older** than Joe, you'd still let **j = Joe's age**, but now you'd say: **j + 6 = Fred's age**, since Fred is **6** years **older** than Joe.

Changing timeframes

Age problems often ask you to consider a timeframe other than the present. For example, a problem might ask you to think about people's ages **3** years from now. To do this, simply add **3** to the ages of the people. For example, suppose you already had:

j = Joe's age, and **j + 6 = Fred's age**. If the problem discussed Joe and Fred **3** years from now, Joe's age at that time in the future would be **j + 3**, and Fred's age at that future time would be would be $(j + 6) + 3$ — or **j + 9**.

Express ages in relation to each other, or in relation to the timeframe:

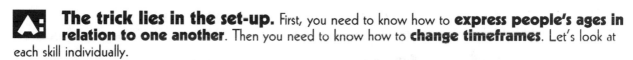

a) Jake's 3 years older than Sally. Solve for Sally's age.
b) Ted's 5 years younger than Bob. Solve for Bob's age.
c) Jenny's age now is k + 3. What's her age 5 years from now?
d) Mark's age now is z − 4. What's his age 7 years from now?

Answers:
a) s = Sally's age; s + 3 = Jake's age
b) b = Bob's age; b − 5 = Ted's age
c) k + 8 = Jenny's age 5 years from now
d) z + 3 = Mark's age 7 years from now

Now I have some sense of how to set up an age problem. But how do I perform the steps in an age problem?

A: Let's solve this problem: **Fred is ten years older than Joe. In 5 years, Fred will be twice Joe's age. How old is Joe now?** Here are the "Quick Vicky" steps:

<u>Steps</u>	<u>Example</u>	<u>Steps</u>	<u>Example</u>
1st) Note the **Q**uantity you're looking for.	**You're looking for Joe's age now.**	**4th) S**olve for the variable.	

4th) example:
$$j + 15 = 2j + 10$$
$$\underline{-\,j \qquad\qquad -\,j}$$
$$+\,15 = j + 10$$
$$\underline{+\,15 = j + 10}$$
$$\underline{-\,10 \qquad -\,10}$$
$$+\,5 = j$$

2nd) Let a **V**ariable stand for it.

let j = Joe's age now
Since Fred is ten years older than Joe,
j + 10 = Fred's age now

3rd) Translate from English to Mathlish.

In five years, Fred will be twice Joe's age.

$$(j + 10) + 5 = 2 \cdot (j + 5)$$

5th) Tell the **M**eaning of your answer.

Joe is 5 years old now.

Solve these age problems:

a) **Bill is six years older than Tom. In three years Bill will be twice Tom's age. How old is Tom now?**

b) **Mira is five years older than Tanya. In three years, twice Mira's age will be triple Tanya's age. How old is Mira now?**

 **What's the general formula for solving problems involving rate, time and distance?**

The general formula for problems involving rate, time and distance is this:

rate · time = distance

You want to have this so well memorized that you mumble it in your sleep. And there are two related formulas, which it also helps to memorize. They are:

rate = distance/time
&
time = distance/rate

In using these formulas, you'll frequently see the quantities abbreviated. That is, **r** stands for rate; **t** stands for time; and **d** stands for distance. So the main formula often will be written: **r · t = d**

In case you're wondering, this formula just tells you a common-sense truth: If you multiply the speed at which you're travelling by the length of time you travel, you get the distance you travel.

For example, if you're travelling in a car at **40 miles per hour**, and you drive steadily at that speed for **1 hour**, you'll have travelled **40 miles**, since **40 · 1 = 40**. If you travel at the same speed but travel for **3** hours, you'll have travelled **120 miles** since: **40 · 3 = 120**

Can you figure out how to get the two related formulas from the first formula?

Try it as a challenge problem.

Q: How do I use the formulas for rate, time and distance to solve simple rate-time-distance word problems?

A: **In simple problems, you know two of the three quantities, and you must find the third quantity.** Here are the steps to follow:

Steps	Example A	Example B	Example C
1st) Original problem.	r = 35 mph t = 2 hours find: d	d = 12 miles t = 3 hours find: r	r = 55 mph d = 165 miles find: t
2nd) Write the equation with the quantity you need isolated.	r · t = d	r = d/t	t = d/r
3rd) Plug values into the equation.	35 · 2 = d	r = 12/3	t = 165/55
4th) Solve and tell what the answer means.	70 miles = d	r = 4 mph	t = 3 hours

Solve for the third quantity:

a) r = 25 mph; t = 5 hours; d = ?
b) d = 450 miles; r = 10 mph; t = ?
c) t = 11 hours; d = 275 miles; r = ?

Answers:
a) d = 125 miles
b) t = 45 hours
c) r = 25 mph

That wasn't too hard, but when these problems get more complicated, I get all confused. Is there any way to just look at a rate-time-distance problem and get some idea of what to do?

Yes, this involves two steps: first, identifying the type of rate-time-distance problem you have; then writing the correct **master equation** so you can solve the problem. Here's a chart that describes the two types of rate-time-distance problems, and also shows the **master equation** for each type.

	distance$_1$ = distance$_2$ type problems	distance$_1$ + distance$_2$ = distance$_{total}$ type problems
Meaning:	Two distances are equal.	One distance plus another distance equals a total distance.
Examples:	**a)** Kevin climbs up a trail, then climbs down the same trail. **b)** Samantha walks from home to school. Later, her sister Madeline also walks from home to school.	**a)** Two trains leave from the same station, one heading east, the other heading west. **b)** Two cars start a certain distance apart, then travel toward each other and meet.
Interpretation:	One distance is the same as the other distance.	The distance traveled by one person or vehicle plus the distance traveled by the other person or vehicle equals a total distance.
Master Equation:	$d_1 = d_2$	$d_1 + d_2 = d_{total}$

Q: O.K., but now I'd like to see how I'd actually work through each type of problem. How about if we start with a problem of the type: $d_1 = d_2$ What are the steps for setting up and solving this kind of problem?

A: Let's solve this problem: **Cheryl takes six hours to climb up a trail walking two miles per hour. Going down the trail, she walks four miles per hour. How long does it take her to walk down the trail?** First, note that this is a $d_1 = d_2$ problem since distance up equals distance down. Here are the **first three steps** in this problem:

Steps

1st) Note **Q**uantity you're looking for.

2nd) Let a **V**ariable stand for it.

3rd) **Tr**anslate by setting up equations for d_1 and d_2, using the formula: $r \cdot t = d$

Example

looking for Cheryl's time coming down the trail

let t = Cheryl's time coming down trail

distance up the trail: (d_1)

r	$\times$	t	$=$	d_1
2 mph	$\times$	6 hours	$=$	d_1
2	$\times$	6	$=$	d_1

distance down the trail: (d_2)

r	$\times$	t	$=$	d_2
4 mph	$\times$	t hours	$=$	d_2
		4t	$=$	d_2

Given the information, set up equations for d_1 and d_2

a) Juan takes 8 hours to climb up a trail walking 3 miles per hour. Going down the trail, he walks 6 miles per hour. How long does it take Juan to walk down the trail? [First, just set up equations for d_1, the distance up, and for d_s, the distance down.]

Answers:
a) $3 \times 8 = d_1$
$6 \times t = d_2$

become a "mathemagician"

O.K. Now I see how to start solving a problem like this. But how do I finish solving it?

When you left off, you had found these equations:

$$2 \times 6 = d_1$$

and

$$4t = d_2$$

To finish solving this problem, follow these **four steps**:

Steps	**Example**
4th) Write the master equation.	$d_1 = d_2$
5th) Plug in the values for d_1 and d_2 that you got from your two equations.	$2 \times 6 = 4t$
6th) Solve for the variable.	$12 = 4t$
	$\dfrac{12}{4} = \dfrac{4t}{4}$
	$3 = t$
7th) Say what the answer **M**eans.	Cheryl's time coming down the trail is 3 hours.

Finish the QuikChek problem by solving for t:

a) When you left off, you had found:

$$3 \times 8 = d_1$$
$$6 \times t = d_2$$

Now solve for t, Juan's time coming down.

Answer:
a) t = 4
It took Juan
four hours
to come down.

What about problems of the type:

$$d_1 + d_2 = d_{total}$$

How would I do a problem like this?

 Let's try this problem: **Two trains leave a station at the same time. One heads west at 60 mph; the other heads east at 80 mph. How far apart will they be after 5 hours?** First note that this is a $d_1 + d_2 = d_{total}$ problem since the distances traveled by the two trains, added together, equal the **total** distance they'll be apart. Here are the first **three steps** in solving this problem:

Steps

1st) Note **Q**uantity you're looking for.

2nd) Let a **V**ariable stand for it.

3rd) **Tr**anslate by setting up equations for d_1 and d_2, using the formula: $r \cdot t = d$

Example

looking for total distance trains will be apart

let d_{total} = this total distance

distance of westbound train (d_1)

r	$\times$	t	= d_1
60 mph	$\times$	5 hours	= d_1
		300	= d_1

distance of eastbound train: (d_2)

r	$\times$	t	= d_2
80 mph	$\times$	5 hours	= d_2
		400	= d_2

Given the information, set up and solve equations for d_1 and d_2:

a) Two airplanes leave the same airport at the same time. One heads north at 500 mph; the other heads south at 700 mph. How far apart will they be after 4 hours? [First, just set up and solve equations for d_1, the distance of the northbound plane, and for d_2, the distance of the southbound plane.]

Q: Again I see how to start solving the word problem. But how do I finish solving it?

A: When you left off you had found these equations:

$$d_1 = 300$$
$$d_2 = 400$$

Now just follow these **four simple steps** to solve the problem.

Steps	**Example**
4th) Write the master equation.	$d_1 + d_2 = d_{total}$
5th) Plug in the values for d_1 and d_2 that you got from your two equations.	$300 + 400 = d_{total}$
6th) Solve for the variable.	$700 = d_{total}$
7th) Say what the answer **M**eans.	After 5 hours, the trains will be 700 miles apart.

Finish the QuikChek problem by solving for d_{total}:

a) When you left off, you had found that:

$$d_1 = 2,000$$
and
$$d_2 = 2,800$$

Answer:

a) $d_{total} = 4,800$

After 4 hours, the planes will be 4,800 miles apart.

263

Translate these phrases from English to Mathlish:
a) seven less than a number
b) five more than the opposite of a number
c) three times the quantity of a number increased by six

Translate these problems from English to Mathlish:
d) Six more than the opposite of a number is twelve less than twice the number.
e) What percent of seventy is forty-five?
f) The sum of three consecutive even integers is forty-eight. What are the integers?

Solve for the number:
g) Five more than twice a number equals twenty-five less than four times the number.
h) Forty-three more than the opposite of a number is the same as seven more than five times the number.
j) Four times the quantity of a number increased by one is fourteen more than three times the number.

Solve these percent problems:
k) What percent of 50 is 15?
l) What percent of 84 is 118?
m) 125 is what percent of 150?

What is the result when ...
n) 40 is increased by 30%
p) 200 is increased by 75%
q) 825 is increased by 40%

What are the integers if ...
r) two consecutive integers add up to 99?
s) three consecutive odd integers add up to 87?
t) four consecutive even integers add up to 116?

a) $n - 7$
b) $-n + 5$
c) $3(n + 6)$

d) $-n + 6 = 2n - 12$
e) $\dfrac{n}{100} \cdot 70 = 45$
f) $n + n + 2 + n + 4 = 48$

g) $n = 15$
h) $n = 6$
j) $n = 10$

k) 30%
l) $\cong$ 140%
m) $\cong$ 83%

n) 52
p) 350
q) 1,155

r) 49, 50
s) 27, 29, 31
t) 26, 28, 30, 32

Age problems:

a) Gwynn is five years older than Mel. Ten years from now, five times Mel's age will be four times Gwynn's age. How old is Mel now?

b) Jed is six years older than Caroline. Four years from now, three times Caroline's age will equal twice Jed's age. How old is Caroline now?

Solve for rate, time or distance:

c) r = 55 mph
    t = 6 hours
    find: d

d) d = 120 miles
    t = 3 hours
    find: r

e) r = 65 mph
    d = 455 miles
    find: t

Solve these rate-time-distance problems:

f) Sandra takes six hours to bike from her house to her friend's house going ten miles per hour. Coming back it takes her only five hours. What is her speed coming back?

g) On Monday, it takes Kevin six hours to climb Mt. Whitney walking two miles per hour. On Tuesday he climbs Mt. Whitney again, but it takes him only four hours. What is his rate on Tuesday?

h) Sam and Pam walk away from a video arcade. Sam walks west at three miles per hour; Pam goes east at four miles per hour. If Sam and Pam stick to those rates, how far apart will they be after five hours?

j) Two trains start heading toward Amityville at the same time. One's coming down from the north at 100 mph; the other is steaming up from the south at 150 mph. If it takes them three hours to reach Amityville, how far apart were they when they started?

a) Mel is 10 years old now.
b) Caroline is 8 years old now.

f) speed coming back is 12 mph
g) rate on Tuesday is 3 mph

c) d = 330 miles
d) r = 40 mph
e) t = 7 hours

h) 35 miles apart after 5 hours
j) 750 miles apart when they started

learn amazing math tricks

Supplies

Glossary

Note: words highlighted in definitions are defined elsewhere in the glossary.

absolute value: the **distance** between a **number** and zero.
Absolute value is always positive because distance is always positive.

additive identity property: property that says when you add zero to any **number** or term,
you get back the number or term you started with.

associative property: property that says that in addition and multiplication, the way the terms are grouped makes no
difference. In other words, $a + \left(b + c\right) = \left(a + b\right) + c$ and $a \cdot \left(b \cdot c\right) = \left(a \cdot b\right) \cdot c$

base: the bottom number in an **exponential term**. Example: in the exponential term x^7,
the base is **x**, while the **exponent** is **7**.

binomial: a **polynomial** made up of two **monomials**.

cancelling: the act of tidying up mathematical expressions.

coefficient: the **number** that stands in front of the **variable** or **variable string** in a **monomial**.
A coefficient may be positive or negative. Example: in the monomial $5x^2y$, the coefficient is $+ 5$;
in the monomial $- 5x^2y$, the coefficient is $- 5$.

commutative property: property that says that in addition and multiplication, the order of the terms makes no difference.
In other words, $a + b$ is the same as $b + a$, and $a \cdot b$ as the same as $b \cdot a$.

consecutive integers: **integers** that are one apart from one another. Example: **4, 5** and **6** are consecutive integers.

coordinate: a number which, by acting as a directional tool, helps you locate a point on the **coordinate plane**.
Each point on the coordinate plane has both an **x-coordinate** and a **y-coordinate**.

coordinate plane: the x-y plane, used for graphing **points**, **lines**, and more.

denominator: the quantity below a fraction bar is the denominator. (Compare with **numerator**.)

descending order: a way of writing a **polynomial** so that its **exponents** decrease from left to right.

distance: the measure of the length of a **line** between two distinct **points**.

distributive property: a property that says this: If you have a parenthesis containing a bunch of terms linked by addition or subtraction signs,
any number or term that multiplies the parenthesis multiplies every term inside the parenthesis.
That is: $a\left(b + c\right) = a \cdot b + a \cdot c$ and $a\left(b - c\right) = a \cdot b - a \cdot c$

equation: any mathematical expression that has an equal sign and quantities on both the left and right sides of the equal sign.
An equation tells you that these two quantities are equal.

even numbers: the set of all numbers: $\left\{- \infty \ldots - 6, - 4, - 2, 0, 2, 4, 6 \ldots \infty\right\}$ (Compare with **odd numbers**.)

exponent: a little number or term that sits on the right shoulder of another number or term called the **base**.
The exponent tells you how many times the base is multiplying itself. For example: in the **exponential term** x^7,
the exponent **7** tells you that **x** is multiplying itself **7** times.

exponential term: the **base** and the **exponent**, viewed as a whole.

factor: one of two or more terms which, multiplied together, give you some **product**.
Examples: **3** and **5** are factors of **15** because $3 \cdot 5 = 15$; and **x** and x^3 are factors of x^4 because $x \cdot x^3 = x^4$.

factoring: the act of splitting a mathematical expression into its basic parts.

fraction: a term made up of a **numerator** and a **denominator**.
When you see a fraction, it means that the numerator is being divided by the denominator.

greatest common factor: the largest number or term that divides evenly into two or more numbers or terms.
For example: **5** is the greatest common factor for **15**, **30** and **65**; and x^2y is the greatest common factor for x^2y^3 and x^3y.

infinity: a way of expressing that which is the ultimate in largeness or smallness. **Positive infinity** means that which is large beyond our ability to count it; **negative infinity** means that which is small beyond our ability to count it.
The symbol for infinity is this: ∞

integers: the set of all **whole numbers** plus the negatives of the **natural numbers**: $\{-\infty \ldots -3, -2, -1, 0, 1, 2, 3 \ldots \infty\}$

intercept: the point where a line crosses the **x-axis** or the **y-axis**. The point where a line crosses the x-axis is the **x-intercept**; the point where it crosses the y-axis is the **y-intercept**.

irrational numbers: the set of all numbers that cannot be written as an integer divided by another integer.

like terms: terms that represent the same kinds of things.
For example, **4x** and **11x** are like terms; $7p^2q$ and $5p^2q$ are like terms.

line: straight extension with no thickness. There is one and only one line between any two distinct **points**.

linear equation: an **equation** that represents a line.
One type of linear equation is the **slope-intercept equation**: $y = m \cdot x + b$

mixed-sign rule: the rule for combining numbers with different signs.

monomial: a term made up of either: **a)** a **number**, or **b)** a **coefficient** along with a **variable** or a **variable string**.

Examples of monomials are: $3, -3, 5x, -5x, 7x^3z, -7x^3z$

multiplicative identity property: property that says when you multiply any **number** or term by **1**, you get back the number or term you started with.

natural numbers: the set of all counting numbers: $\{1, 2, 3, 4, 5 \ldots \infty\}$

negative exponent: an **exponent** that has a negative sign.

negative infinity: a mathematical way of referring to that which is small beyond our ability to count it.
The symbol for negative infinity is this: $-\infty$

neighbor-sign rule: the rule for dealing with two signs that are directly next to each other.
This rule tells you that the two signs merge to become one sign.

number: a symbol used to indicate how many of a certain quantity you're dealing with.

numerator: the quantity above a fraction bar is the numerator. (Compare with **denominator**.)

odd numbers: the set of all numbers: $\{-\infty \ldots -5, -3, -1, 1, 3, 5 \ldots \infty\}$ (Compare with **even numbers**.)

order of operations: the set of rules that tells you which operation to perform before which other operation.

origin: the point on a **coordinate plane** where the **x-axis** and **y-axis** meet.

percent: a way of indicating how much of a quantity you're dealing with. Percent means "out of one hundred," so when you state a percent, you're saying how many hundredths of something you have. Example: **12** percent means **12/100**.

perfect square: what you get when you square a number or a term.

point: a location on the **coordinate plane**. A point has no size.

polynomial: a string of two or more **monomials**.

product: what you get when you multiply numbers or terms together. Example: when you multiply **3** by **5**, the product is **15**.

quadratic trinomial: a trinomial in which the highest exponent is **2**.

radical: the root of a number. In Algebra I, the term radical means **square root**.

rational numbers: the set of numbers that can be written as an **integer** divided by another integer. There's one exception: any number divided by zero is not a rational number; it is undefined.

real numbers: Combine the **rational numbers** and the **irrational numbers**. When you put them together, you get the set of real numbers.

reciprocal: the flip of a fraction. For example: **4/3** is the reciprocal of **3/4**; and **5x/3y** is the reciprocal of **3y/5x**..

reflexive property: a property that says that anything is equal to itself. That is: $a = a$

same-sign rule: rule that tells you how to combine a group of numbers that are either all positive or all negative.

slope: the measure of the steepness of a **line** on the **coordinate plane**.

square root: Choose any number or term. Then find that special number or term which, when multiplied by itself, gives you the number or term you started with. For example, start with **9**. Since $3 \cdot 3 = 9$, **3** is the square root of **9**. Or start with $25x^2$. Since $5x \cdot 5x = 25x^2$, **5x** is the square root of $25x^2$.

squaring: the act of multiplying a number or term by itself. Example: if you square **7**, you get **49**.

symmetric property: property that says the left and right sides of an equation are interchangeable. In other words, if it's true that $a = b$, then it's also true that $b = a$.

transitive property: property by which you discover that two quantitites are equal because both of them are equal to a third quantity. Here's an example with **b** acting as the third quantity: If $a = b$ and $b = c$, then $a = c$.

trinomial: a string of three **monomials**.

variable: a letter that stands for a mystery quantity whose value you want to discover. In general algebraic rules and principles, variables stand for any **number** whatsoever.

variable string: two or more variables multiplied together. Examples of variable strings are: **xyz** and a^2bc^3

whole numbers: the set of all **natural numbers**, plus zero: $\{0, 1, 2, 3, 4, 5 \ldots \infty\}$

x-axis: the axis that runs horizontally (left and right) on the **coordinate plane**.

x-coordinate: the **coordinate** of a **point** that tells you how far that point stands to the left or right of the **origin**.

x-intercept: point where a line crosses the **x-axis**.

y-axis: the axis that runs vertically (up and down) on the **coordinate plane**.

y-coordinate: the **coordinate** of a **point** that tells you how far that point stands above or below the **origin**.

y-intercept: point where a line crosses the **y-axis**.

try our zany lesson plans

What are the NCTM Principles & Standards?
And how does the Algebra Survival Guide conform to them?

Responding to concerns about the quality of U.S. math education, the National Council of Teachers of Mathematics (NCTM) in 2000 laid out the Principles & Standards for School Mathematics. This document sets forth general guidelines on how math is best taught. Due to the quality of its ideas, the Principles & Standards is now widely used to develop math curricula and to improve math teaching techniques.

In an attempt to make the **Algebra Survival Guide** as up-to-date as possible, I have strived to make the **Guide** align as closely as possible with the Principles & Standards.

Interestingly, the Principles and Standards make a revolutionary recommendation that algebra become part of the curriculum from kindergarten through 12th grade. The Principles & Standards authors were not envisioning kindergartners solving quadratic equations. Rather the thinking is that students can begin to grasp some of the major conceptual underpinnings of algebra — for example the idea of patterns, or the notion of ratio — long before ninth grade, when algebra traditionally is taught.

Below I have excerpted in italics some of the major algebra competencies from the Principles & Standards, and I have indicated how the **Guide** helps students master these competencies.

Algebra Principles & Standards for Grades 3-5:

"All students should identify such properties as commutativity, associativity, and distributivity and use them to compute with whole numbers."
The **Algebra Survival Guide** teaches students the commutative, associative, and distributive properties in its Properties chapter. The **Guide** offers colorful metaphors to help students remember these concepts. What's more, the **Guide** shows students how to use the distributive property and takes pains to ensure that students avoid mistakes when using it.

"All students should represent the idea of a variable as an unknown quantity using a leter or a symbol."
The **Guide** helps children explore the concept of a variable in the Equations chapter. Here students learn that a variable stands for a mystery quantity whose value they are trying to discover. In the Exponents and Radicals chapters, students learn that in general algebraic rules, a variable also may stand for any quantity whatsoever.

Algebra Principles & Standards for Grades 6-8:

"All students should explore relationships between symbolic expressions and graphs of lines, paying particular attention to the meaning of intercept and slope."
In its Coordinate Plane chapter, the **Guide** helps students grasp the relationship between the equation of a line and the graph of a line. Students learn how to write equations of lines and how to graph them. This chapter also teaches students the meaning of slope and y-intercepts, and it offers metaphorical ways of understanding these concepts.

"All students should use symbolic algebra to represent situations and to solve problems, especially those that involve linear relationships."
The Coordinate Plane chapter teaches students how to solve a system of two linear equations.

"All students should recognize and generate equivalent forms for simple algebraic expressions ..."
In the chapters on Exponents, Radicals, Factoring and Cancelling, the **Guide** teaches students how to recognize and generate equivalent algebraic expressions.

Algebra Principles & Standards for Grades 9-12:

"All students should write equivalent forms of equations, inequalities, and systems of equations and solve them with fluency."
The **Algebra Survival Guide's** Coordinate Plane chapter teaches students how to derive equivalent forms of linear equations. It also teaches students how to solve a system of two linear equations.

"All students should use symbolic algebra to represent and explain mathematical relationships."
Through its discussion of the various rules of algebra, the **Guide** teaches students to explain mathematical relationships using logic.

How to order more copies of the Algebra Survival Guide

Phone orders: Call Singing Turtle Press' toll-free number: 1/888-308-MATH
Have your VISA or MasterCard ready, and be prepared to give the following information:
your name / complete mailing address / home phone number / number of copies you'd like
credit card type and number / name as it appears on credit card / expiration date

Fax orders: Fax us the same information at this number: 1/505-438-7742
For your convenience, you may just fill out the order form below and fax that to us.

Postal orders: Fill out the form below and send it to:
Orders / Singing Turtle Press
#770, 3530 Zafarano Drive #6
Santa Fe, NM 87507

**Satisfaction guaranteed: Books in new condition may be returned
to the publisher for a full refund — no questions asked.**

P R I C I N G   I N F O R M A T I O N

U.S. orders --

Price per book: $19.95
Shipping:
$7 for first book,
$3 for each additional book

Canadian orders in U.S. $ --

Price per book: $19.95
Shipping:
$8 for first book,
$4 for each additional book

Canadian orders in Canadian $ --

Price per book: $31.95
Shipping:
$10 for first book,
$5 for each additional book

Order Form

Your name: _____

Street address: _____
_____

City: _____

State/Province: _____ Zip Code: _____

Country: _____

Area code: _____ Phone number: _____

Please mark your payment option:
___ check or money order enclosed
(Make checks payable: SINGING TURTLE PRESS)

___ VISA ___ MasterCard

Card number: _____

Name as it appears on card: _____

Expiration date: ____ / ____

SIGNATURE: _____

1. Number of copies you'd like to order: .... _____

2. # of copies x price per book (see above) .... _____

3. Shipping fee (see above): .... _____

4. Sub-total: (add lines 2 and 3) .... _____

5. (Orders shipped to New Mexico addresses,
multiply amount on previous line by .064375
for gross receipts tax.) Show this amount here: .... _____

6. Grand total (line 4, or lines 4 + 5): .... _____

Optional, but helpful to us:
I am a ...

___ public/private school student
___ homeschooling student
___ parent of school student
___ parent of homeschooling
student

___ teacher
___ tutor
___ school administrator
___ other: _____
_____

HOW TO PLAY THE ALGEBRA WILDERNESS "BORED" GAME

Goal: To be the first player to reach **FINISH**.

How to throw: Use the Target page to figure out how many spaces to move on any turn. The player flips a coin and sees where it lands on the target. If it lands on heads, the throw is positive; if it lands on tails, the throw is negative. For example, if the coin lands heads up on the 2 ring, it counts as a $+2$. But if it lands tails up on the 2 ring, then it counts as a -2. If the coin lands on the **Pitfall** in the center, the player must go back to **START**. So beware!

Rules: Each player places a token on **START** (use dimes, buttons or other small trinkets). Then throw to see who goes first. Player with the highest throw goes first, $+3$ being the highest number, -3 being the lowest. Players move forward for positive numbers, backward for negative numbers. Note that if your first throw is negative, you wind up in **NegativeLand**. To escape, you must throw positive numbers. For example, if while on -2 you throw $+1$, you advance to -1; if while on -2 you throw $+2$, you return to **START**. But if while on -2 you throw -1, you wind up on -3, since negative numbers move you backward. One consoling thought: if you're on -3 and you throw a negative number, you can't move backwards further; you stay put, since **NegativeLand** ends at -3.

PositiveLand has three types of spaces: **Question spaces**, **Special spaces** and **Consequence spaces**. The Question spaces are either **QuikChek spaces** or **Target Practice spaces**. Suppose you land on a **QuikChek space**. On your next turn, an opposing player searches through the **Algebra Survival Guide**, finds a QuikChek problem from a section you've recently studied and asks you this question. If you answer incorrectly, you stay on that QuikChek space and wait for your next turn, when you'll try to answer a different QuikChek problem. If you answer correctly, you get to throw. And as a reward, you're guaranteed that your throw won't move you backwards. Here's how: whenever you answer a QuikChek or Target Practice correctly, you take the **absolute value** of the number you throw. That is, you'd move **forward 3 spaces** whether you throw a $+3$ or a -3, since the absolute value of both of these numbers is $+3$ **(see p. 78 for details)**. **Target Practice spaces** work the same way, except that you get asked a question from a Target Practice you've done. If you land on a **Special space**, something special happens. After landing on the x^2 **space**, you square the value of your throw. Example: if you throw -2, you get to move forward **4** spaces since $(-2)^2 = +4$ **(see p. 86 and p. 49 if this doesn't yet make sense)**. After landing on the **MuscleMan space**, MuscleMan flips the value of whatever number you throw, making positive throws negative and negative throws positive. Example: if after landing on MuscleMan you throw $+3$, you must go back **3** spaces since MuscleMan turns $+3$ into -3. That's because MuscleMan flips the sign of exponents **(see p. 101 for details)**.

Consequence spaces immediately move you forward or backward. For example, if you land on the Consequence space "Ask a brilliant question. Go ahead 4 spaces," you immediately move forward 4 spaces, coming to rest on a QuikChek space. Be aware that one **Consequence space** is perilous: the **Pitfall space**. Do your best to avoid this space, for when you land on it, you fall through the **Pitfall** and land back at **START** (Yikes!).

Decide Now! space: You may take either of two paths in this game. You can take the short, dangerous path across the **Pitfall**, or the longer, safer route along the top of the **A**. Choose your path when you reach the **Decide Now!** Target Practice space. If you overshoot this space, decide your path as you fly past this space. If you land on this space, you must wait till your next turn and answer a Target Practice correctly. Then you throw, and after throwing, you choose which path to take. Be aware that whichever path you take, you must go backwards along this same path if MuscleMan later shoves you backwards. That is, if you take the short path and manage to avoid the Pitfall, you could still fall down the Pitfall if MuscleMan later sends you backwards. Also, if by chance you land on the **Decide Now!** space more than once in a game, you are allowed to choose a different route the second time.

Good luck, and may the best player win!!!

Index

Cancelling

The F.C.R. steps to follow:

1st) Factor

2nd) Cancel

3rd) Reduce

Split-the-numerator rule

$$\frac{a - b + c}{x} = \frac{a}{x} - \frac{b}{x} + \frac{c}{x}$$

Equations

The three S.I.S. phases:

1st) Simplify

2nd) Isolate

3rd) Solve

The Pythagorean theorem:

$$a^2 + b^2 = c^2$$

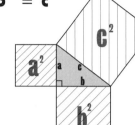

Coordinate Plane

Slope of a line:

$$m = \frac{y_2 - y_1}{x_2 - x_1}$$

Slope-intercept equation of a line:

$$y = m \cdot x + b$$

(where m = slope, and b = y-intercept)

Distance between two points:

$$d = \sqrt{\left(x_2 - x_1\right)^2 + \left(y_2 - y_1\right)^2}$$

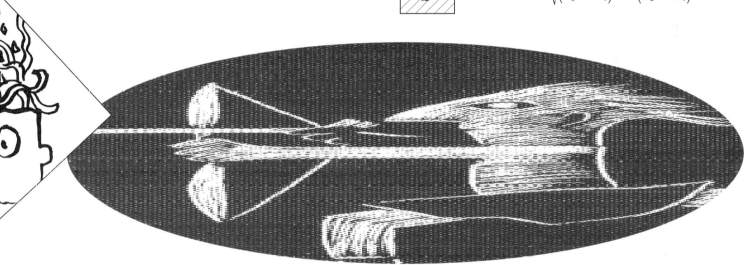

W o r d   P r o b l e m s

The five basic steps for solving word problems can be remembered by this phrase:

"Quick Vicky Trapped Several Mice."

Q -- See what **Q**uantity you need to find.

V -- Let a **V**ariable stand for that quantity.

Tr -- **Tr**anslate from English to Mathlish.

S -- **S**olve for the variable.

M -- Tell what the variable **M**eans.

Algebra Survival Guide
Emergency Fact Sheet

Exponents

Definition of exponent of one

$$a^1 = a$$

Same-base product rule

$$a^x \cdot a^n = a^{x+n}$$

Same-base quotient rule

$$\frac{a^x}{a^n} = a^{x-n}$$

Definition of zero exponent

$$a^0 = 1$$

Definition of negative exponent

$$a^{-x} = \frac{1}{a^x}$$

Negative exponent in denominator

$$\frac{1}{a^{-x}} = a^x$$

Exponent-to-exponent rule

$$\left(a^x\right)^n = a^{x \cdot n}$$

Exponent product rule

$$\left(a \cdot c\right)^x = a^x \cdot c^x$$

Exponent quotient rule

$$\left(\frac{a}{c}\right)^x = \frac{a^x}{c^x}$$

Radicals

Definition of a square root

$$\sqrt{a} \cdot \sqrt{a} = a$$

Other definitions of a square root

$$\left(\sqrt{a}\right)^2 = a$$

$$\sqrt{a^2} = a$$

Radical product rule

$$\sqrt{a} \cdot \sqrt{c} = \sqrt{a \cdot c}$$

Reverse radical product rule

$$\sqrt{a \cdot c} = \sqrt{a} \cdot \sqrt{c}$$

Complex radical product rule

$$a\sqrt{c} \cdot x\sqrt{n} = a \cdot x\sqrt{c \cdot n}$$

Radical product shortcut

$$\left(a\sqrt{c}\right)^2 = a^2 \cdot c$$

Radical quotient rule

$$\frac{\sqrt{a}}{\sqrt{c}} = \sqrt{\frac{a}{c}}$$

Reverse radical quotient rule

$$\sqrt{\frac{a}{c}} = \frac{\sqrt{a}}{\sqrt{c}}$$

Complex radical quotient rule

$$\frac{a\sqrt{c}}{x\sqrt{n}} = \frac{a}{x}\sqrt{\frac{c}{n}}$$

Properties

Reflexive property
$a = a$

Symmetric property
If $a = b$, then $b = a$.

Transitive property
If $a = b$, and $b = c$,
then $a = c$.

Commutative property
$a + b = b + a$
$a \cdot b = b \cdot a$

Associative property
$a + (b + c) = (a + b) + c$
$a \cdot (b \cdot c) = (a \cdot b) \cdot c$

Distributive property
$a(b + c) = a \cdot b + a \cdot c$
$a(b - c) = a \cdot b - a \cdot c$

Additive identity property
$a + 0 = a$

Multiplicative identity property
$a \cdot 1 = a$

Sets of Numbers

Natural numbers
$\{1,\ 2,\ 3,\ 4,\ 5 \ldots \infty\}$

Whole numbers
$\{0,\ 1,\ 2,\ 3,\ 4,\ 5 \ldots \infty\}$

Integers
$\{-\infty \ldots -2, -1,\ 0,\ 1,\ 2,\ \ldots \infty\}$

Rational numbers
All numbers that can be written as a fraction of integers.
Examples:
$5/7,\ -3/11,\ 72.6,\ -2,031$

Irrational numbers
All numbers that cannot be written as a fraction of integers.
Examples:
$\sqrt{2},\ \pi,\ -\sqrt{7},\ \sqrt[3]{11}$

Real numbers
The combination of all the rational and all the irrational numbers.
Examples:
$5,\ \sqrt{7},\ -1,\ -\sqrt{3},\ 7/11$
$0,\ 68.423,\ -486.7,\ 22/43$

Positive & Negative Numbers

Same-sign rule
$+a + c = +(a + c)$
$-a - c = -(a + c)$

Mixed-sign rule
Ignoring signs, see which number is larger. Take the sign of that number, then subtract the smaller number from the larger number.

Neighbor-sign rule

$a + (+c)$ $a - (+c)$
$= a + c$ $= a - c$

$a + (-c)$ $a - (-c)$
$= a - c$ $= a + c$

Multiplication rule

$(+) \cdot (+) = +$ $(-) \cdot (+) = -$

$(+) \cdot (-) = -$ $(-) \cdot (-) = +$

Division rule

$+/+ = +$ $-/+ = -$

$+/- = -$ $-/- = +$

Order of Operations

This sentence can help you remember the order of operations:

"Please Eat More Dessert -- Nate's
　　Great
　　　　Strawberry
　　　　　　Mousse."

P — Parentheses
E — Exponents
M — Multiplication
D — Division
N — Neighbor-sign rule
Gr — Grouping
S — Same-sign rule
M — Mixed-sign rule